D0520091

Cookie Kalkair & Ophéli

An Urban Gardening Survival Guide

Published by

BOOM! BOX™

Written by
Cookie Kalkair & Ophélie Damblé

Illustrated by
Cookie Kalkair

Translated by
Edward Gauvin

Lettered by
Jim Campbell

English Edition Editor
Shannon Watters

English Edition Assistant Editor
Kenzie Rzonca

English Edition Designer
Scott Newman

Original Edition Editor
Célina Salvador

Original Cover and Interior Design
Maqsimum Création

"Ophélie Explains It All" Page Design
Manon Fargeat and Maud Bachotet

BOOm! BOX™ STEINKIS

GUERILLA GREEN, April 2021. Published by BOOM! Box, a division of Boom Entertainment, Inc. GUERILLA GREEN is ™ & © 2019 Steinkis Groupe. All rights reserved. Used under license. BOOM! Box™ and the BOOM! Box logo are trademarks of Boom Entertainment, Inc., registered in various countries and categories. All characters, events, and institutions depicted herein are fictional. Any similarity between any of the names, characters, persons, events, and/or institutions in this publication to actual names, characters, and persons, whether living or dead, events, and/or institutions is unintended and purely coincidental. BOOM! Box does not read or accept unsolicited submissions of ideas, stories, or artwork.

BOOM! Studios, 5670 Wilshire Boulevard, Suite 400, Los Angeles, CA 90036-5679. Printed in China. First Printing.

ISBN: 978-1-68415-663-4, eISBN: 978-1-64668-148-8

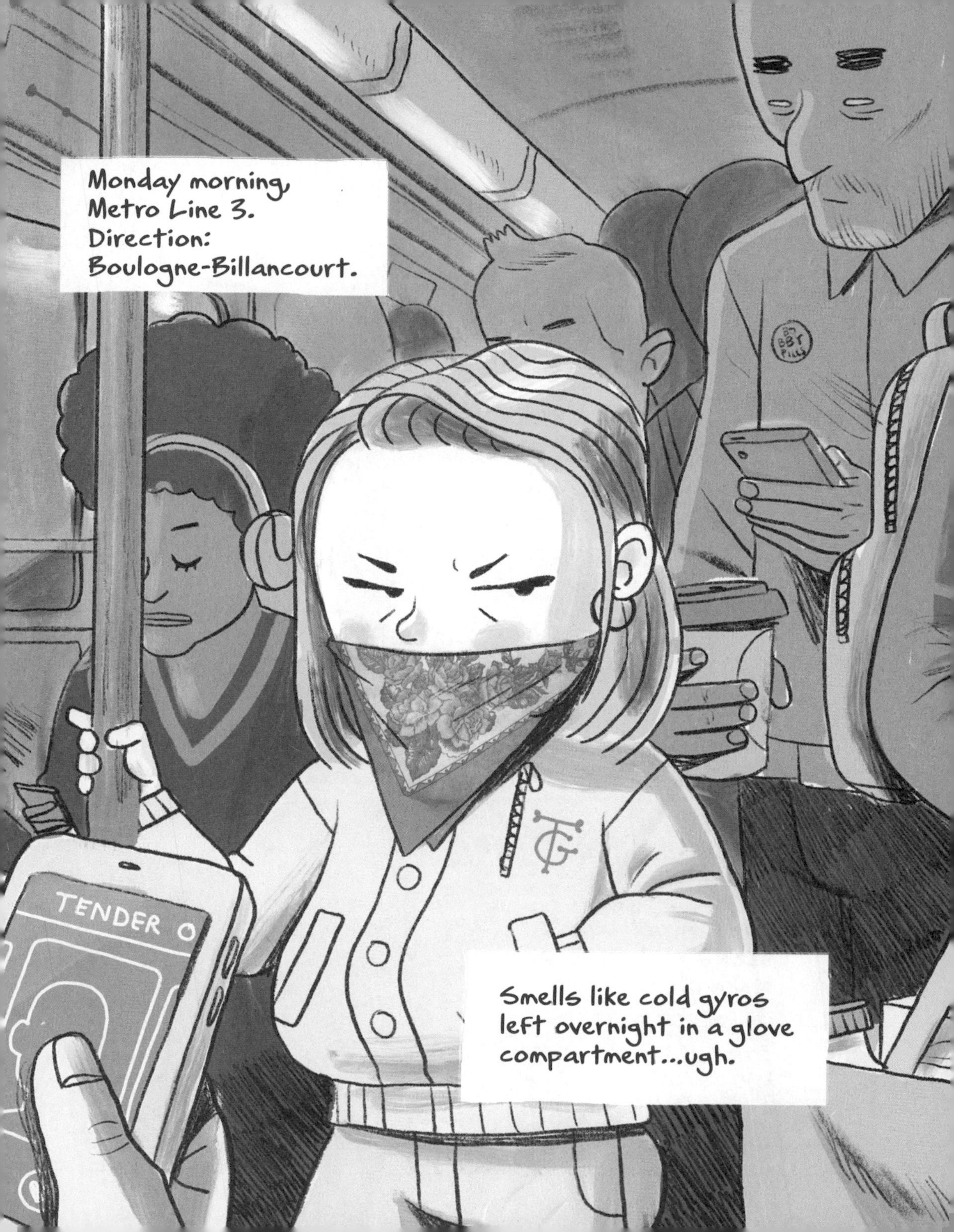
Monday morning, Metro Line 3. Direction: Boulogne-Billancourt.
TENDER
Smells like cold gyros left overnight in a glove compartment...ugh.

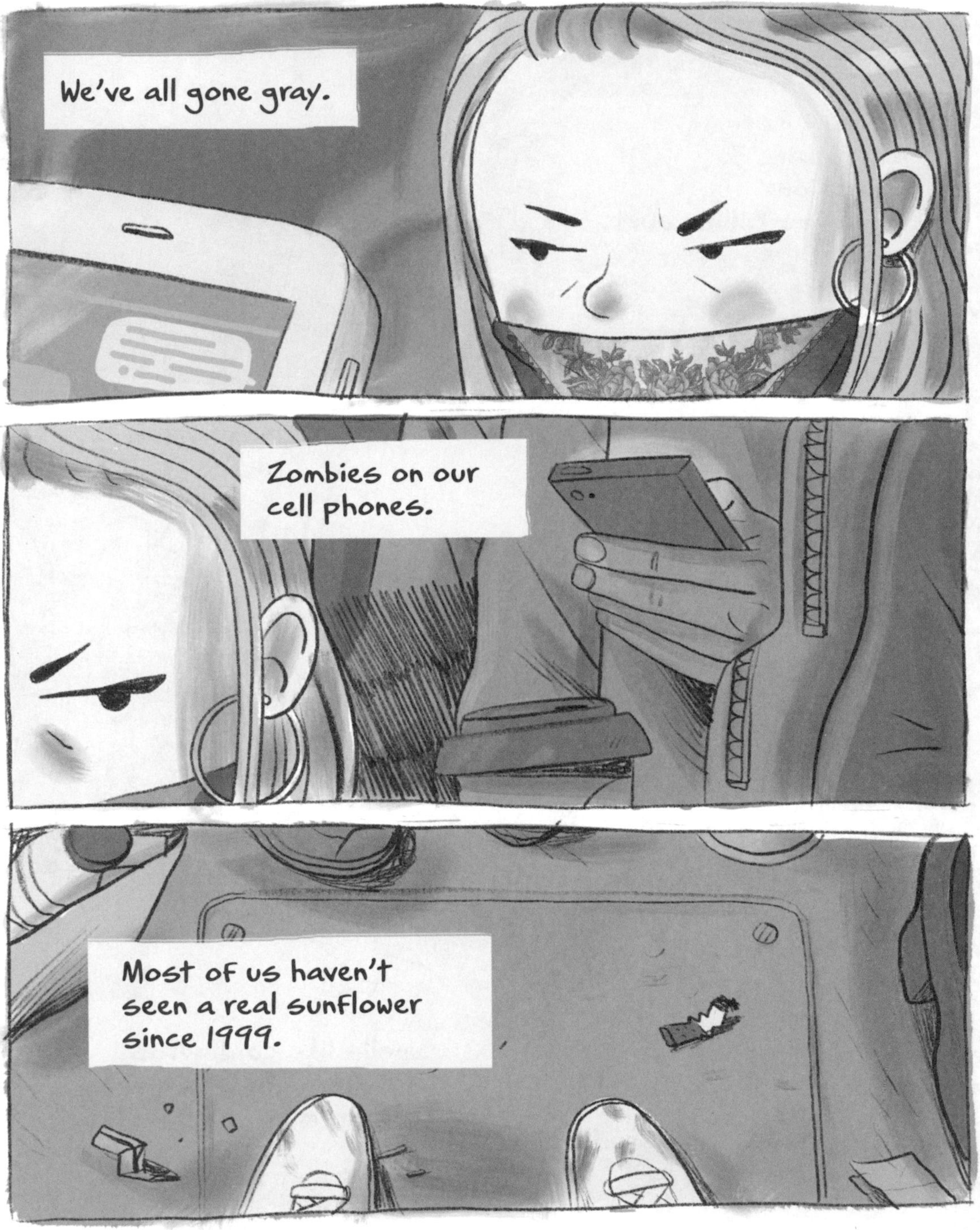
We've all gone gray.
Zombies on our cell phones.
Most of us haven't seen a real sunflower since 1999.

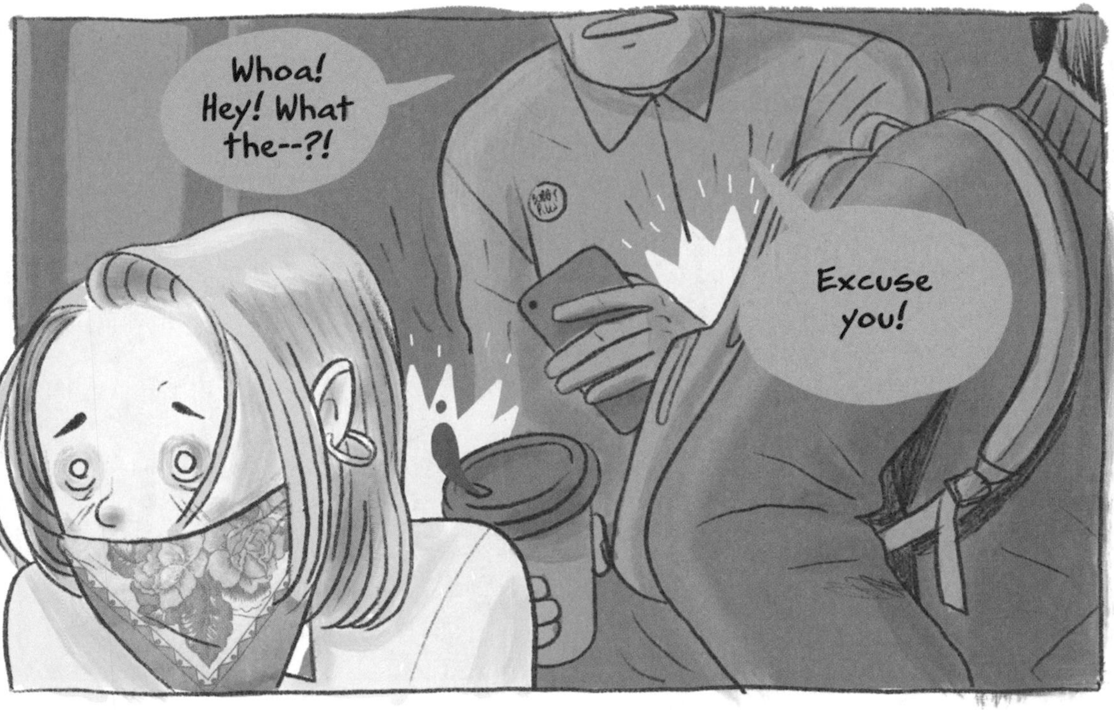
Whoa!
Hey! What
the--?!
Excuse
you!
BOBBY PILLS

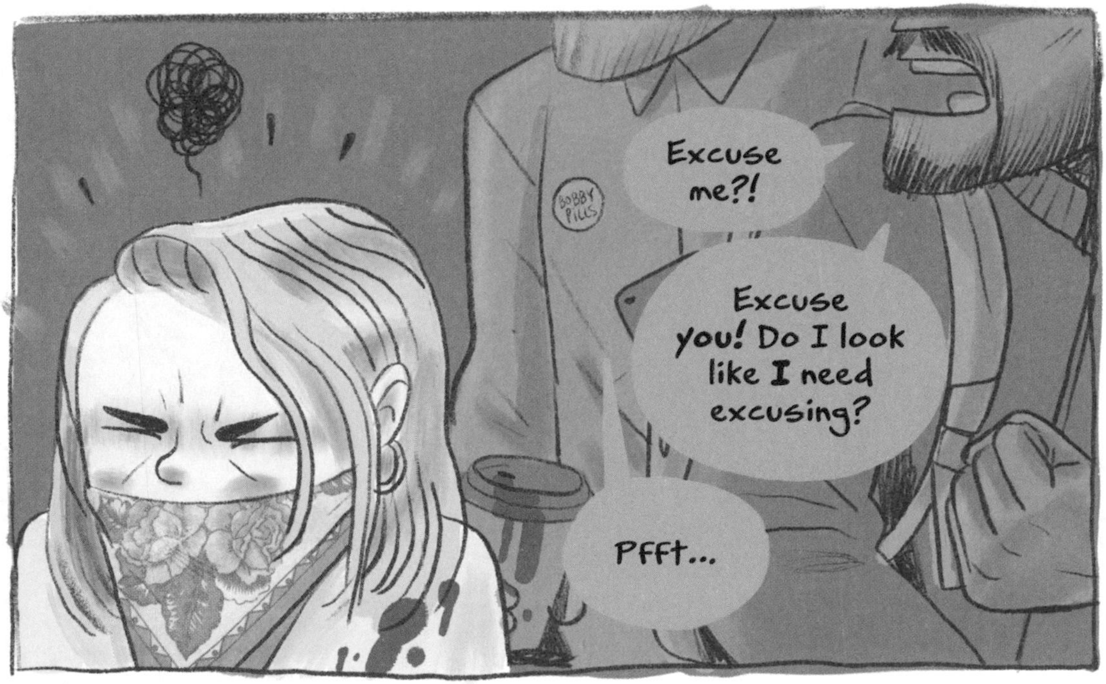
BOBBY PILLS
Excuse
me?!
Excuse
you! Do I look
like **I** need
excusing?
Pfft...

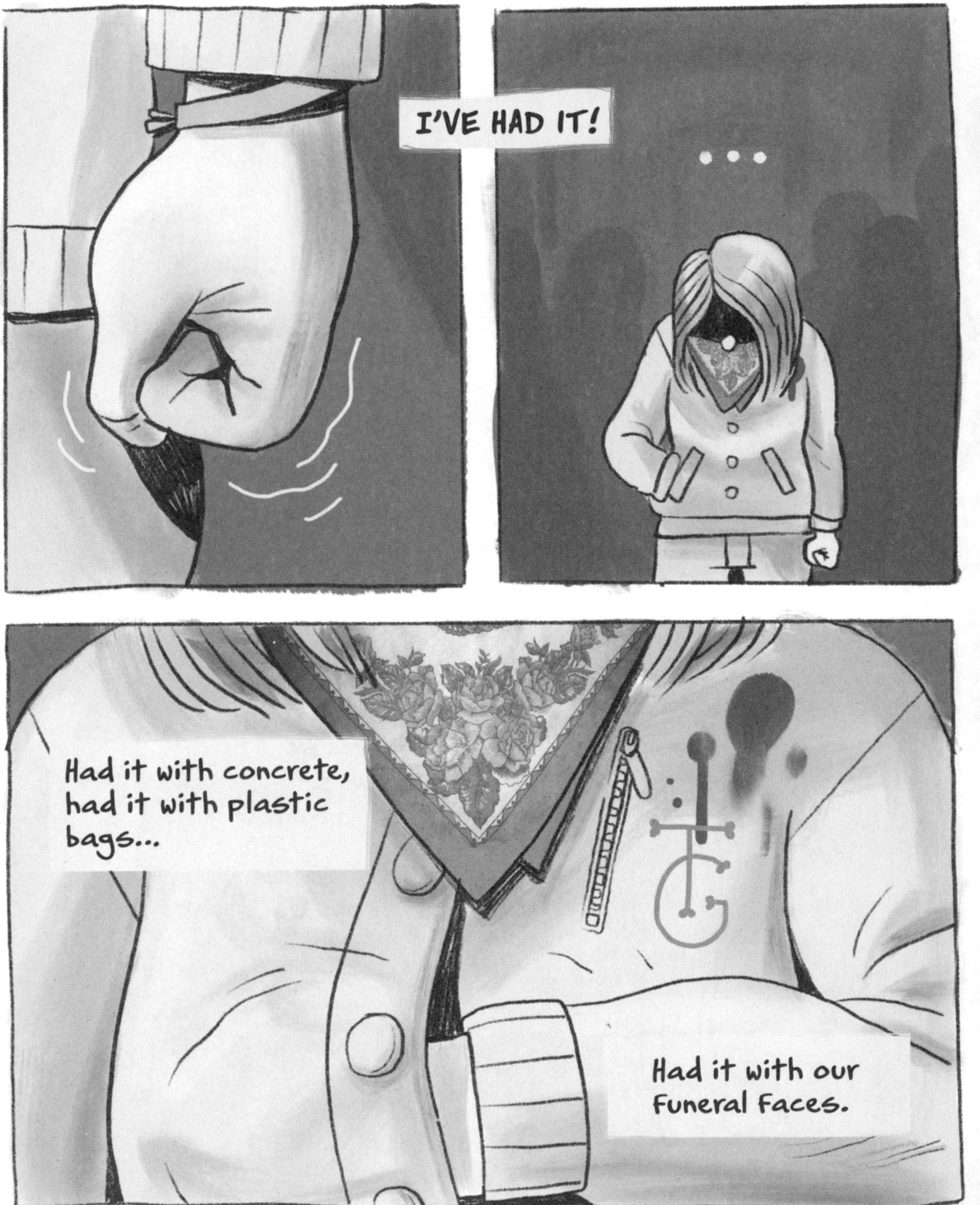
I'VE HAD IT!
• • •
Had it with concrete, had it with plastic bags...
Had it with our Funeral Faces.

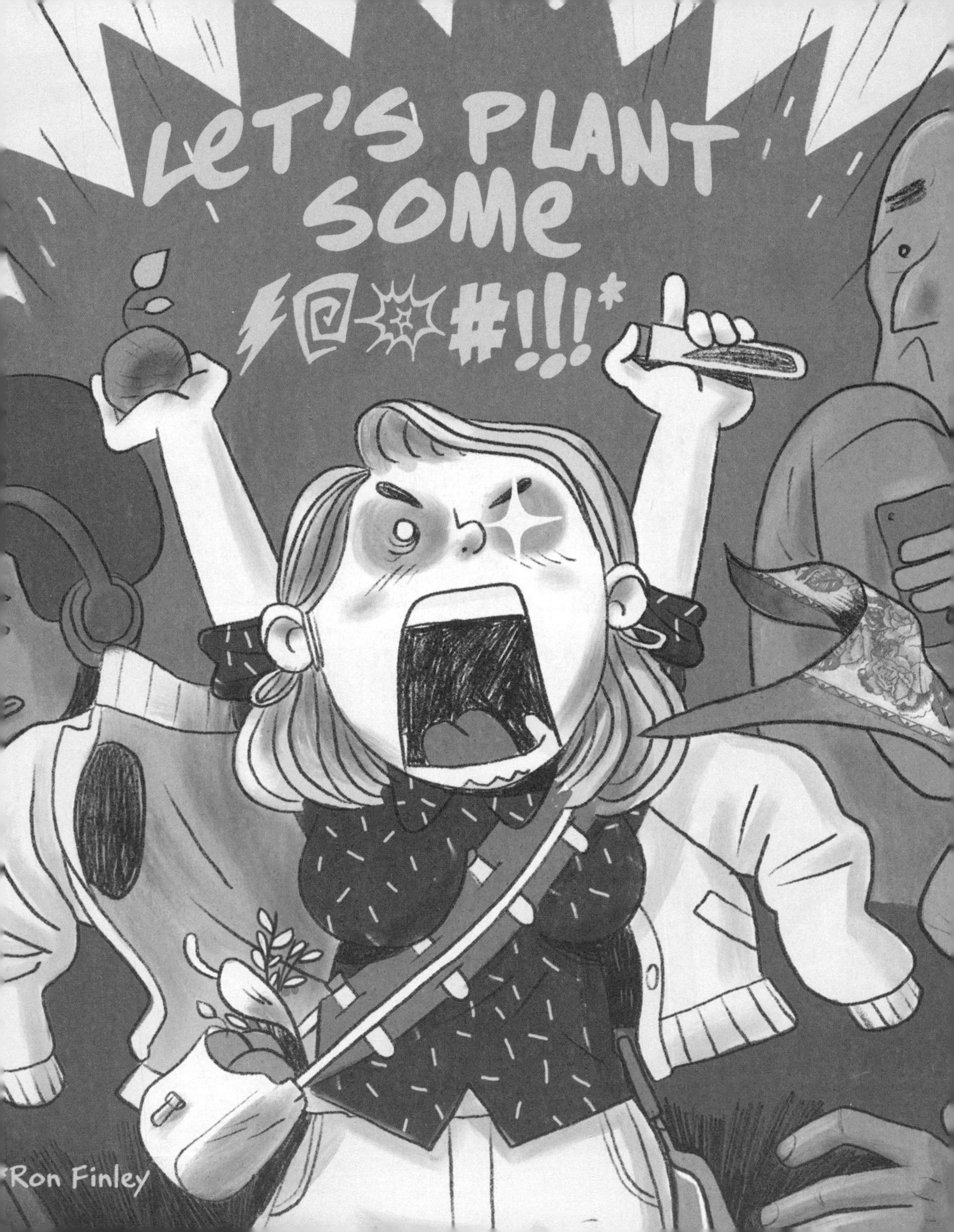
LET'S PLANT SOME
#!!!*
Ron Finley

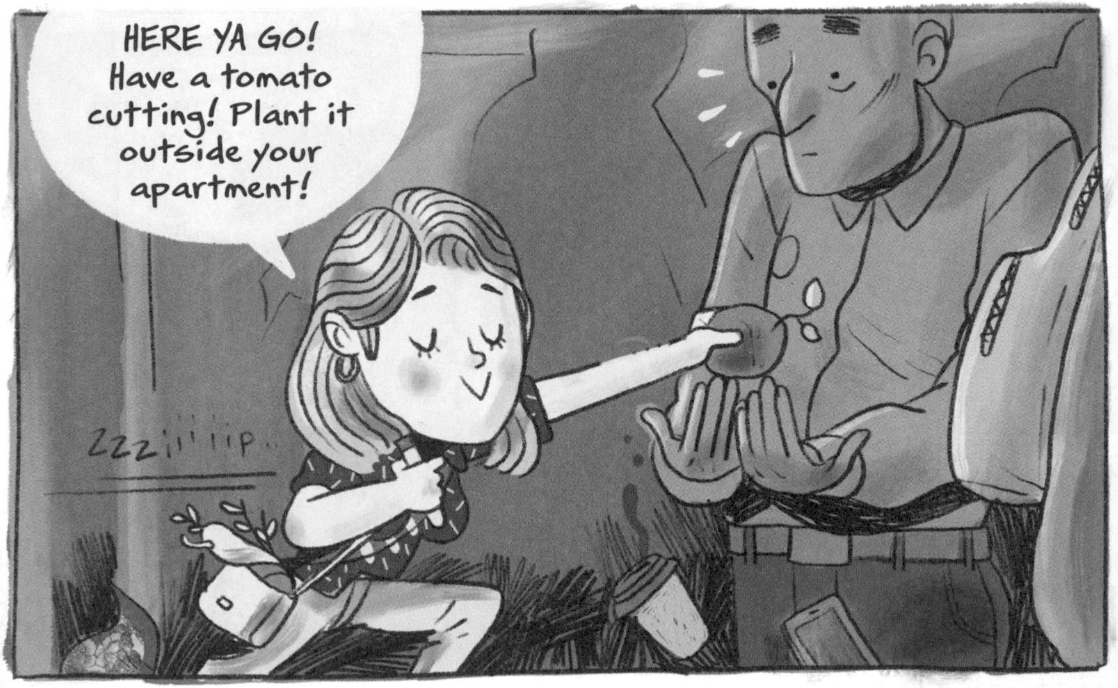
HERE YA GO! Have a tomato cutting! Plant it outside your apartment!
Zzziiiiip..

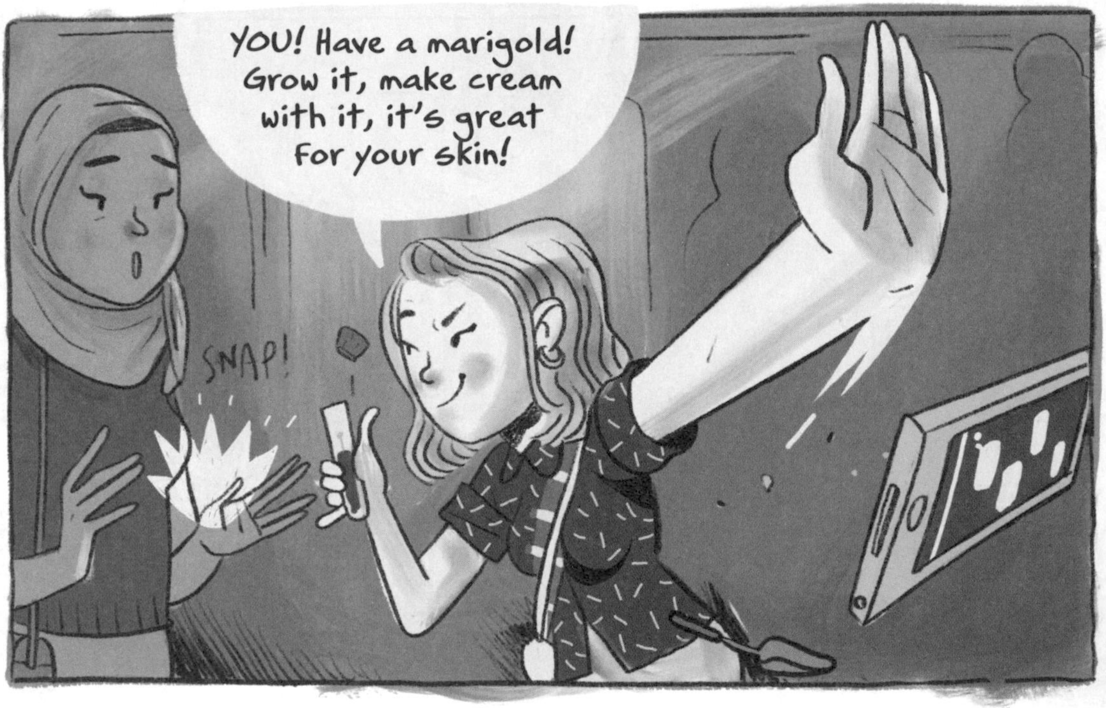
YOU! Have a marigold! Grow it, make cream with it, it's great for your skin!
SNAP!

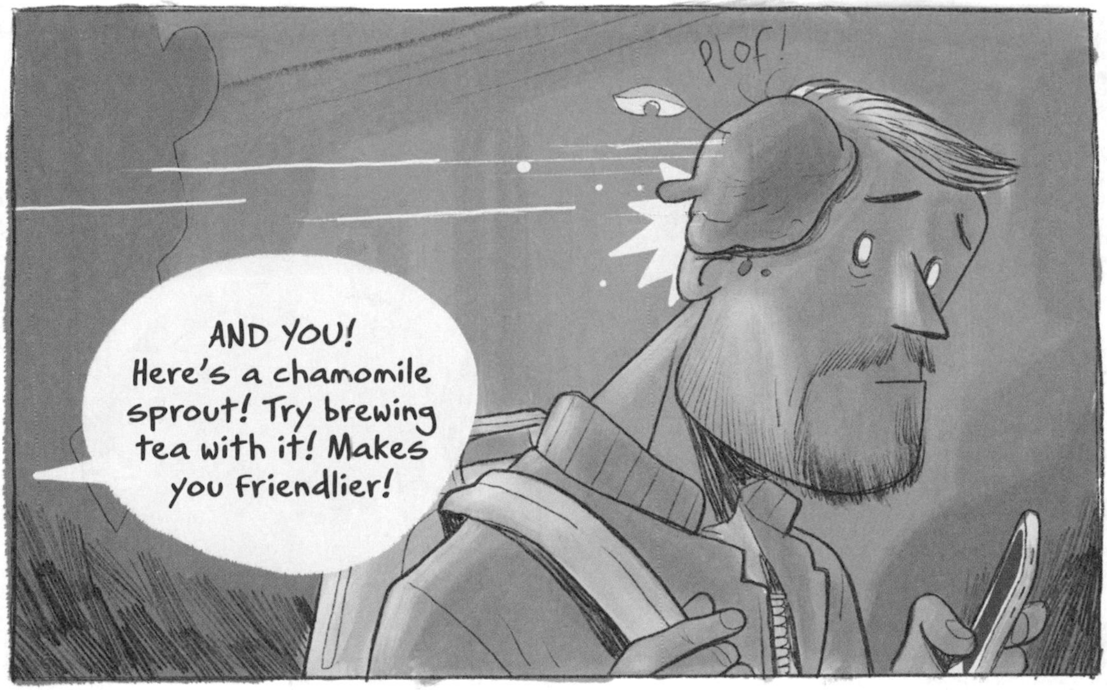
PLOF!
AND YOU! Here's a chamomile sprout! Try brewing tea with it! Makes you friendlier!

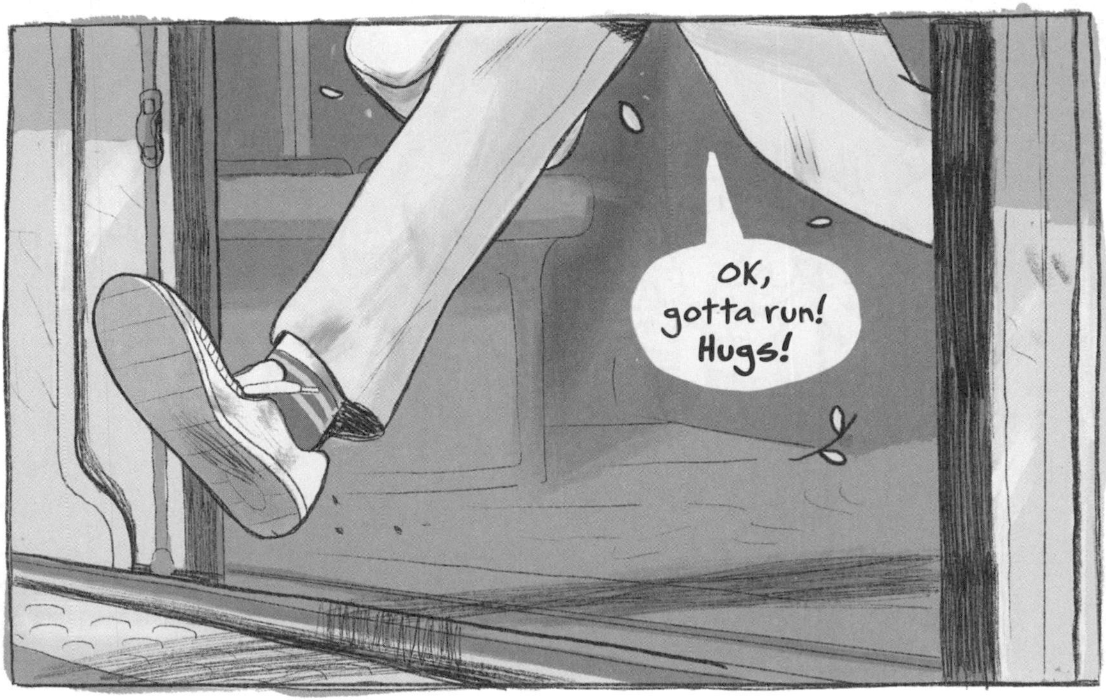
OK, gotta run! Hugs!

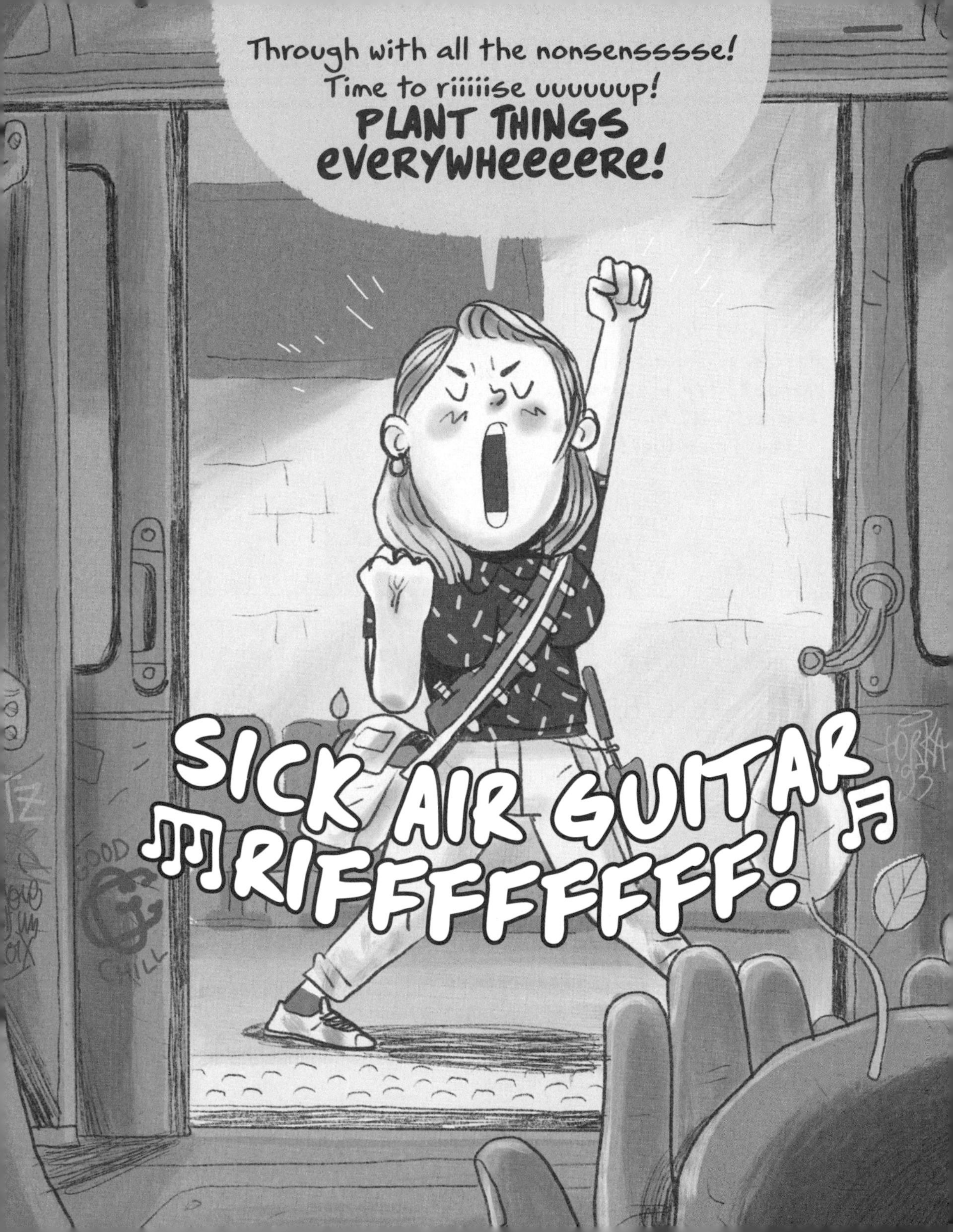
Through with all the nonsensssse! Time to riiiiise uuuuuup! PLANT THINGS EVERYWHEEEERE!
SICK AIR GUITAR RIFFFFFFFF!

Cookie Kalkair & Ophélie Damblé

Guerilla Green

An Urban Gardening Survival Guide

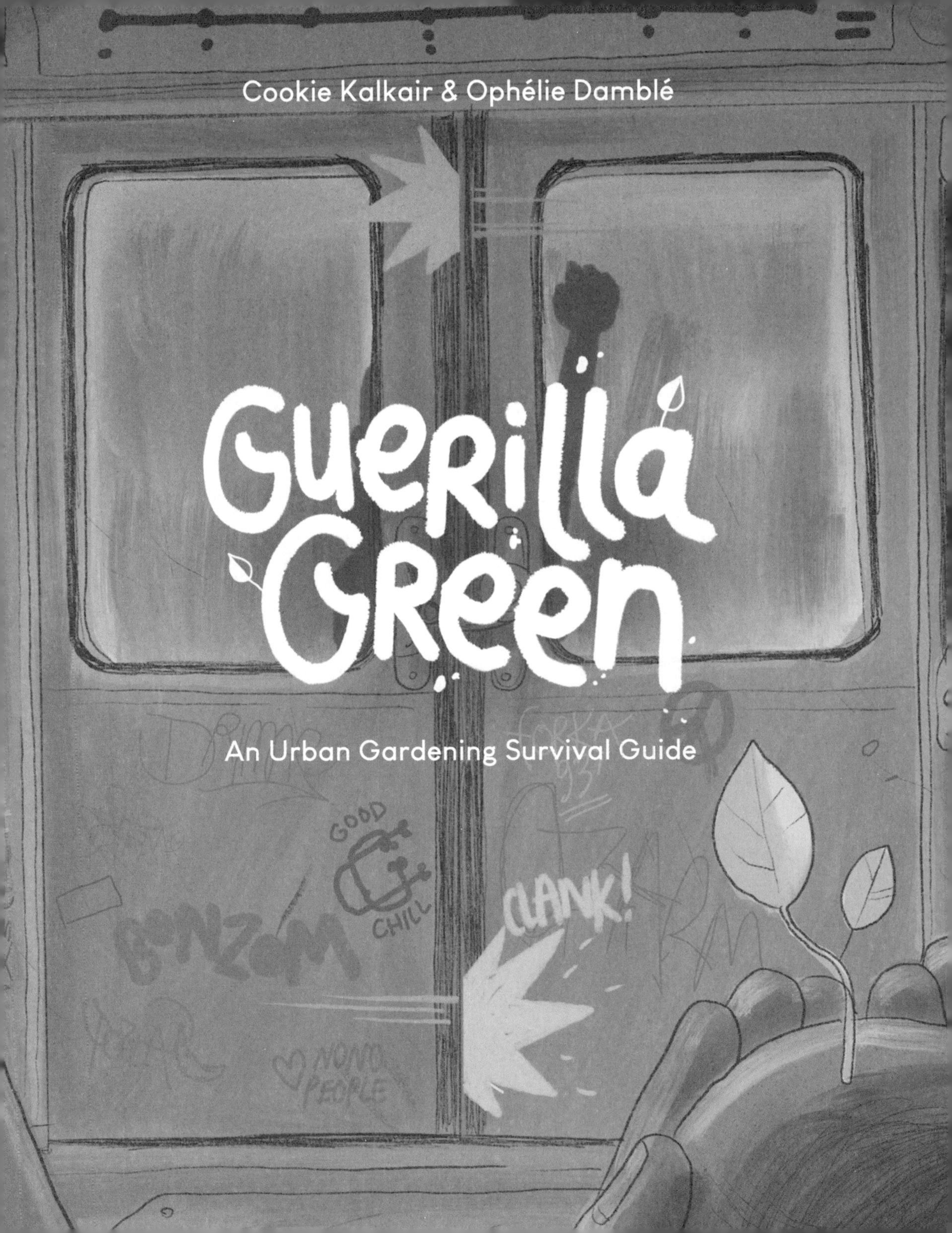
GOOD
CHILL
CLANK!

GREEN GUERILLAS:
ROOTS

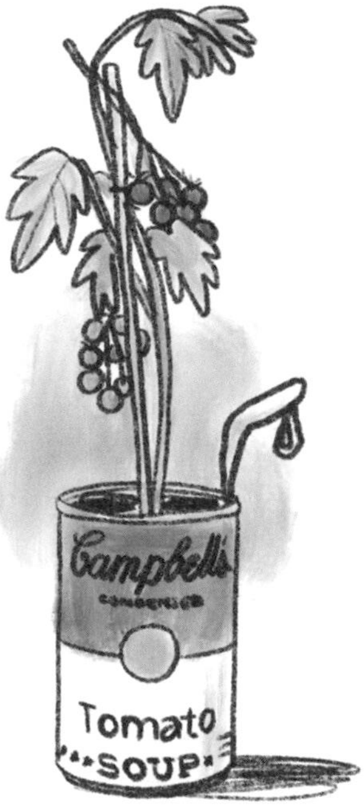
Campbell's
Tomato
SOUP

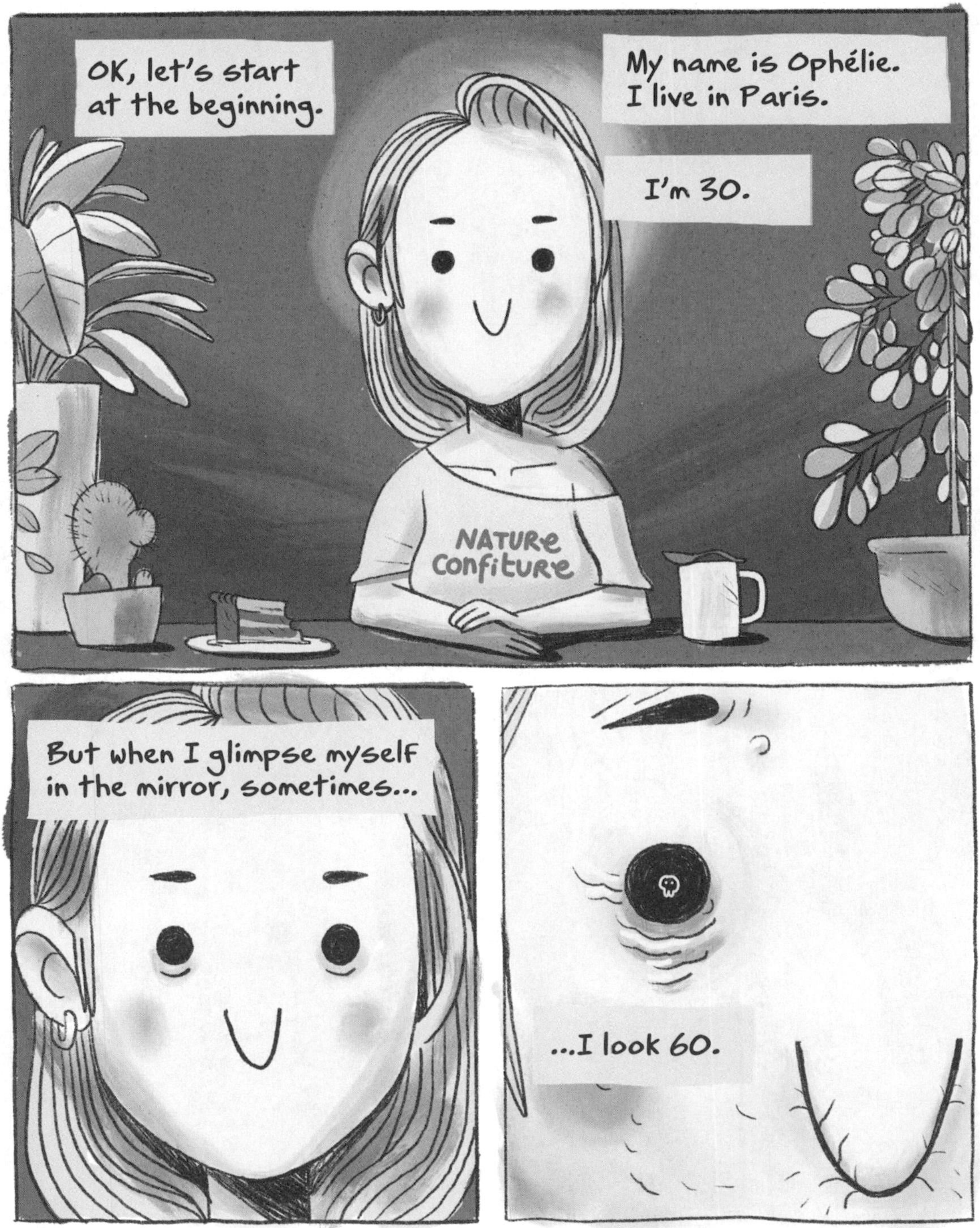
OK, let's start at the beginning.
My name is Ophélie. I live in Paris.
I'm 30.
NATURe Confiture
But when I glimpse myself in the mirror, sometimes...
...I look 60.

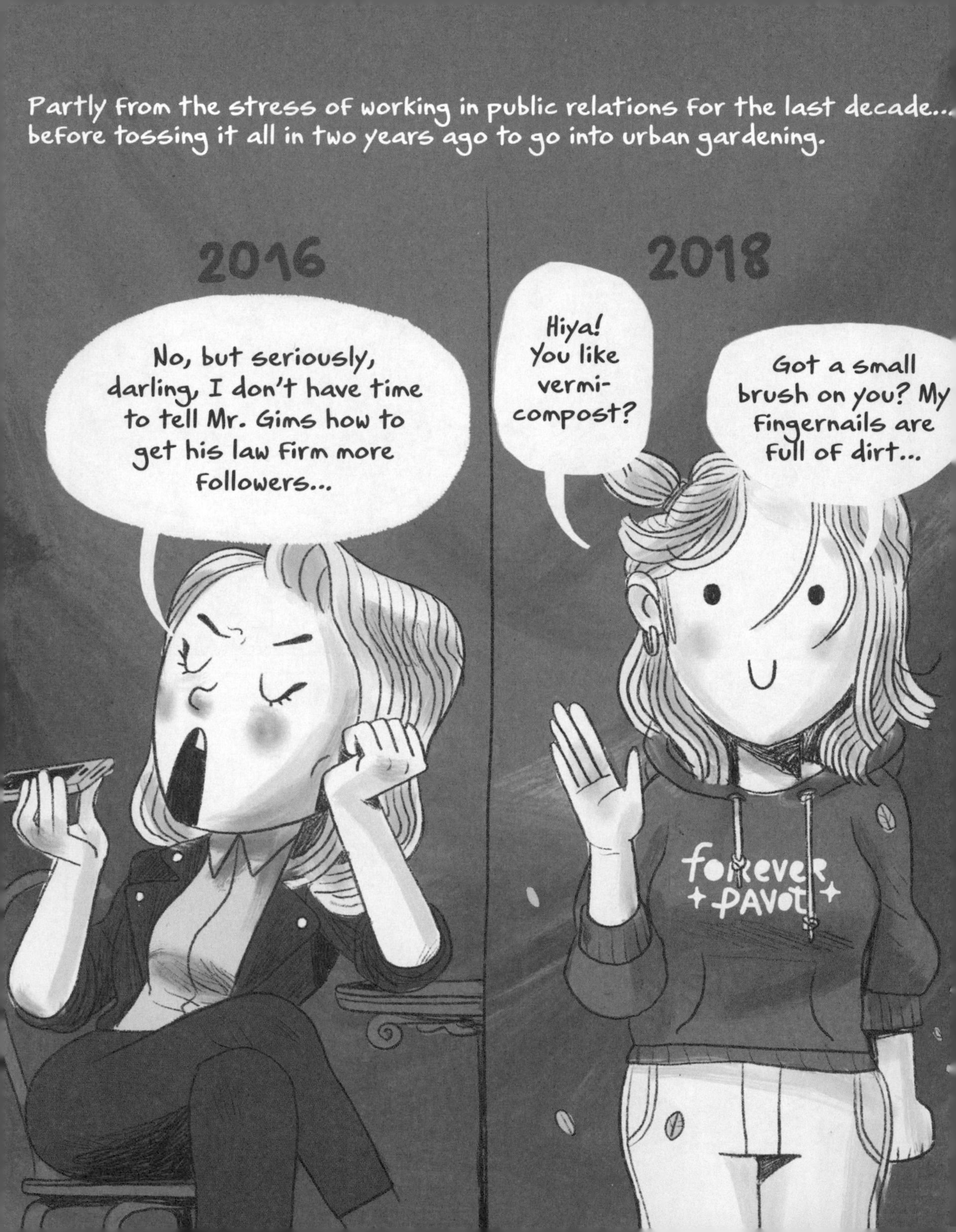
Partly from the stress of working in public relations for the last decade...
before tossing it all in two years ago to go into urban gardening.
2016
No, but seriously, darling, I don't have time to tell Mr. Gims how to get his law firm more followers...
2018
Hiya! You like vermi-compost?
Got a small brush on you? My fingernails are full of dirt...
forever PAVOT

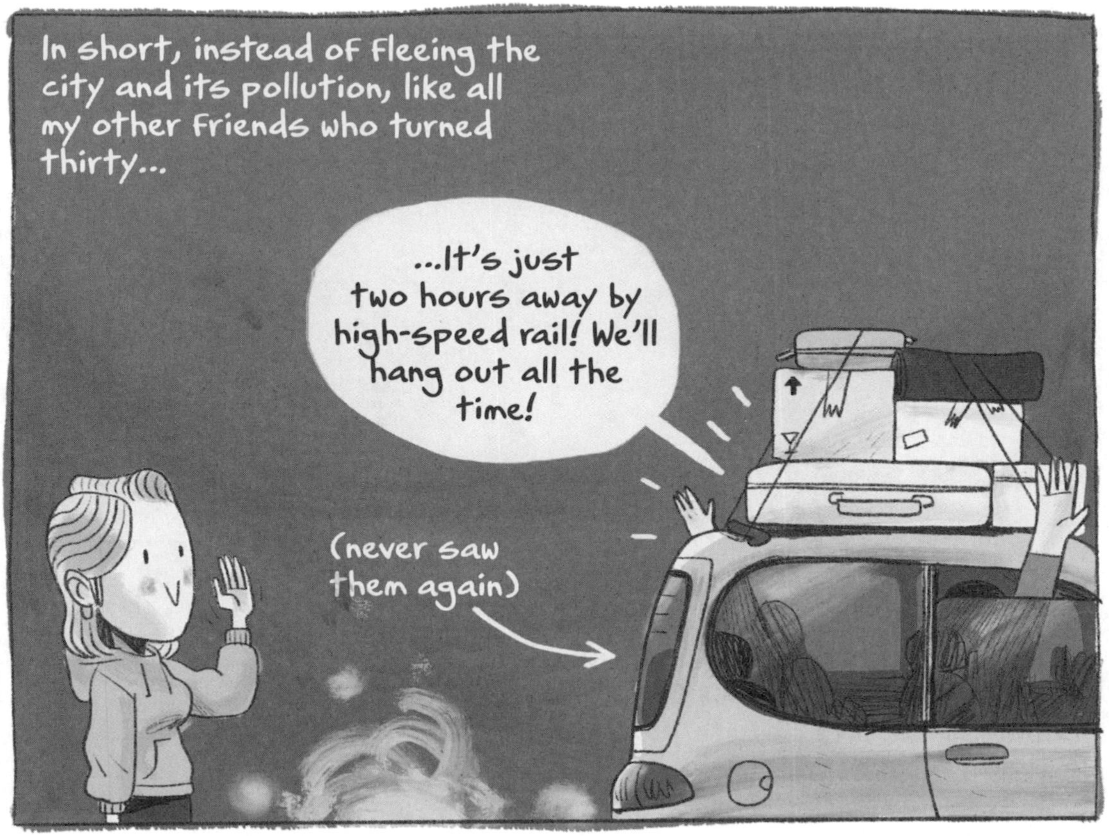
In short, instead of fleeing the city and its pollution, like all my other friends who turned thirty...
...It's just two hours away by high-speed rail! We'll hang out all the time!
(never saw them again)

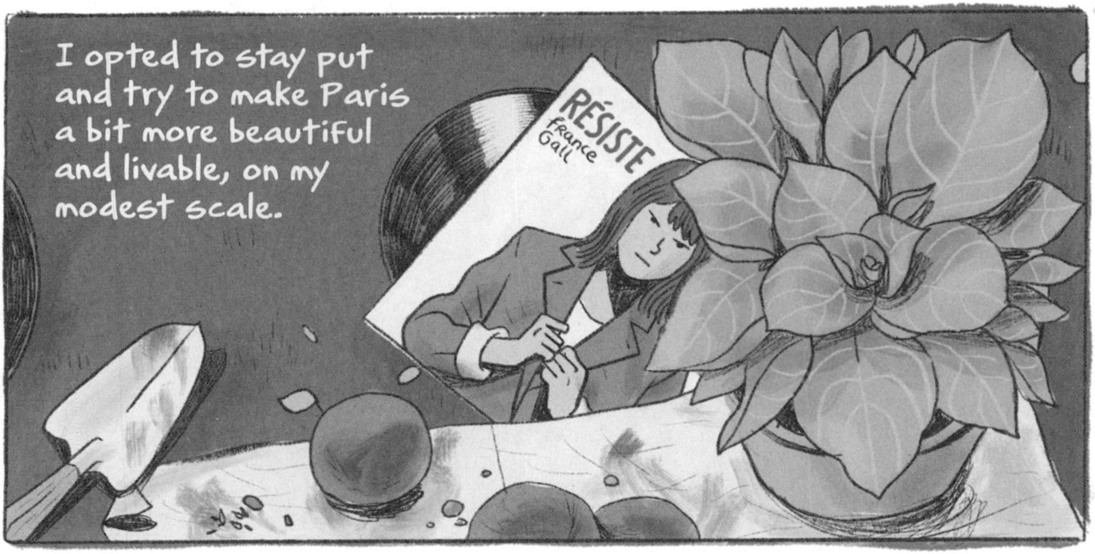
I opted to stay put and try to make Paris a bit more beautiful and livable, on my modest scale.
RÉSISTE
France Gall

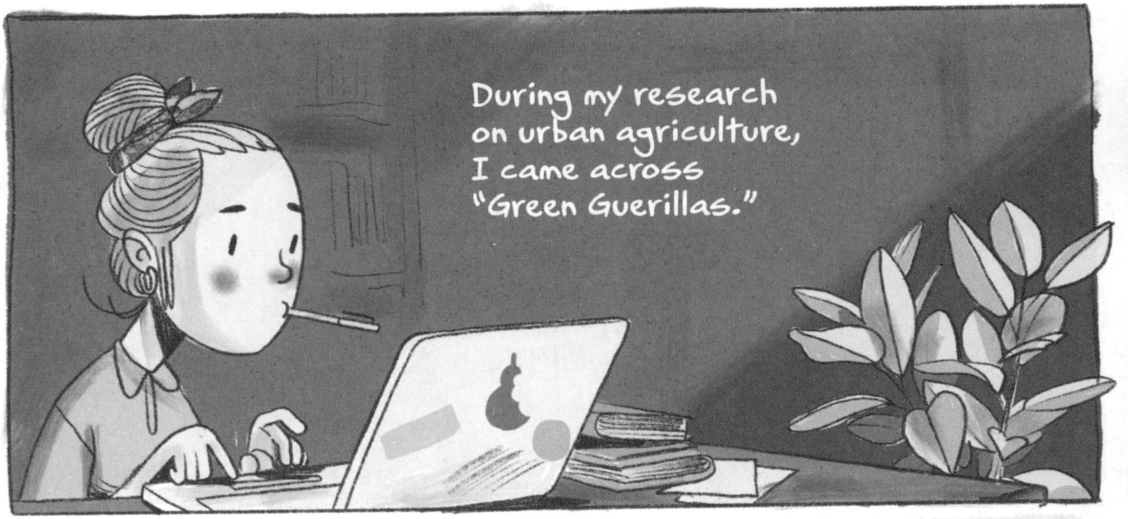
During my research on urban agriculture, I came across "Green Guerillas."

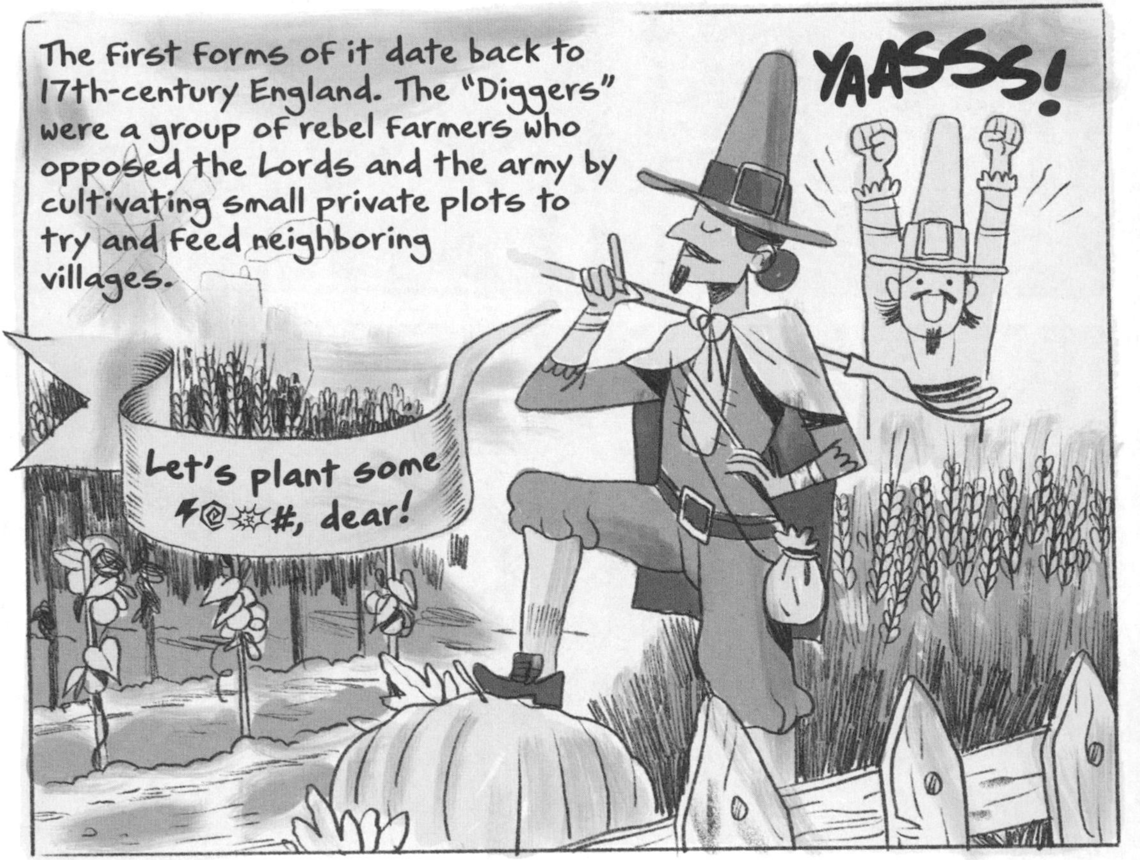
The first forms of it date back to 17th-century England. The "Diggers" were a group of rebel farmers who opposed the Lords and the army by cultivating small private plots to try and feed neighboring villages.
YAASSS!
Let's plant some #@##, dear!

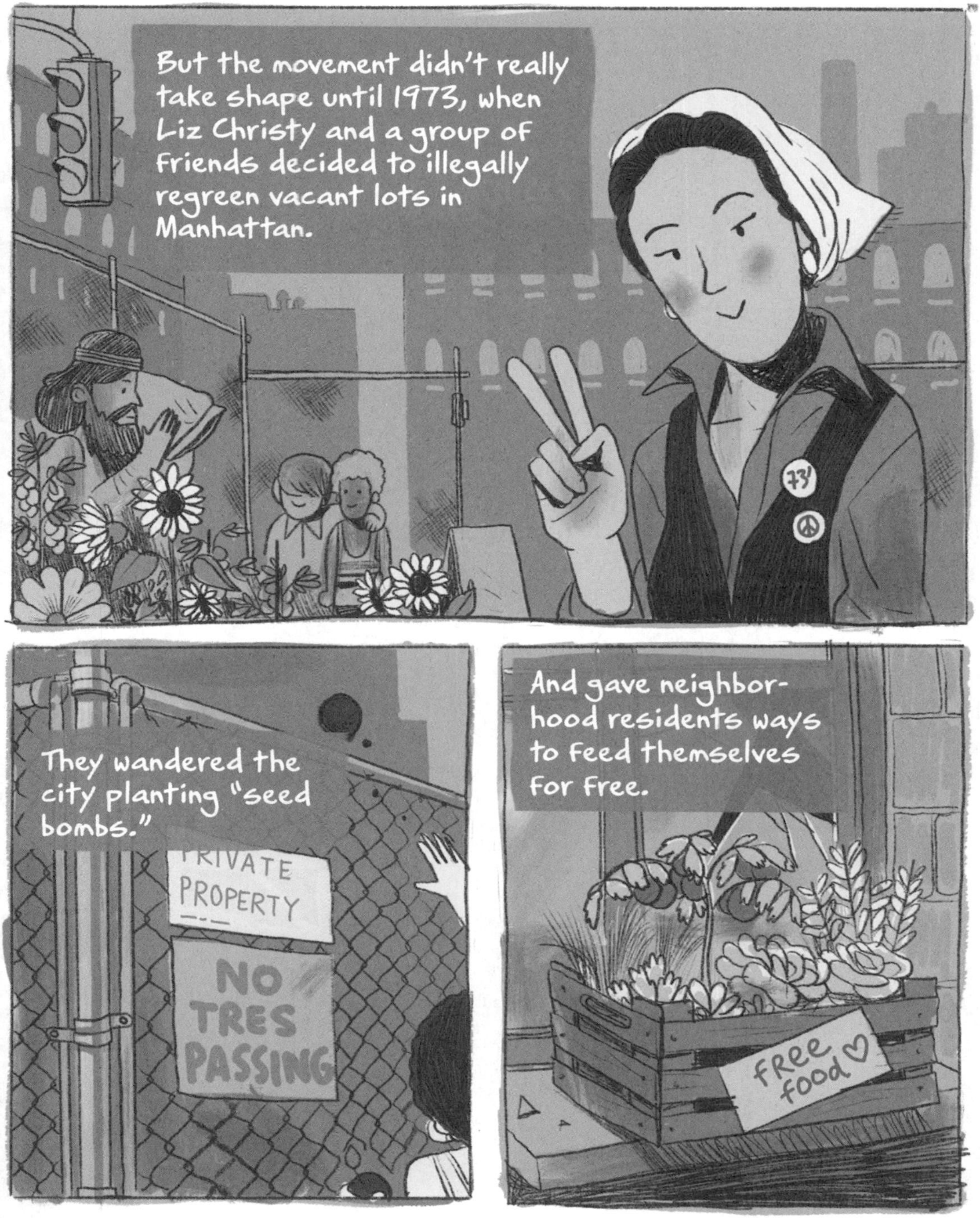
But the movement didn't really take shape until 1973, when Liz Christy and a group of friends decided to illegally regreen vacant lots in Manhattan.
73'
They wandered the city planting "seed bombs."
PRIVATE PROPERTY
NO TRES PASSING
And gave neighbor-hood residents ways to feed themselves for free.
free food

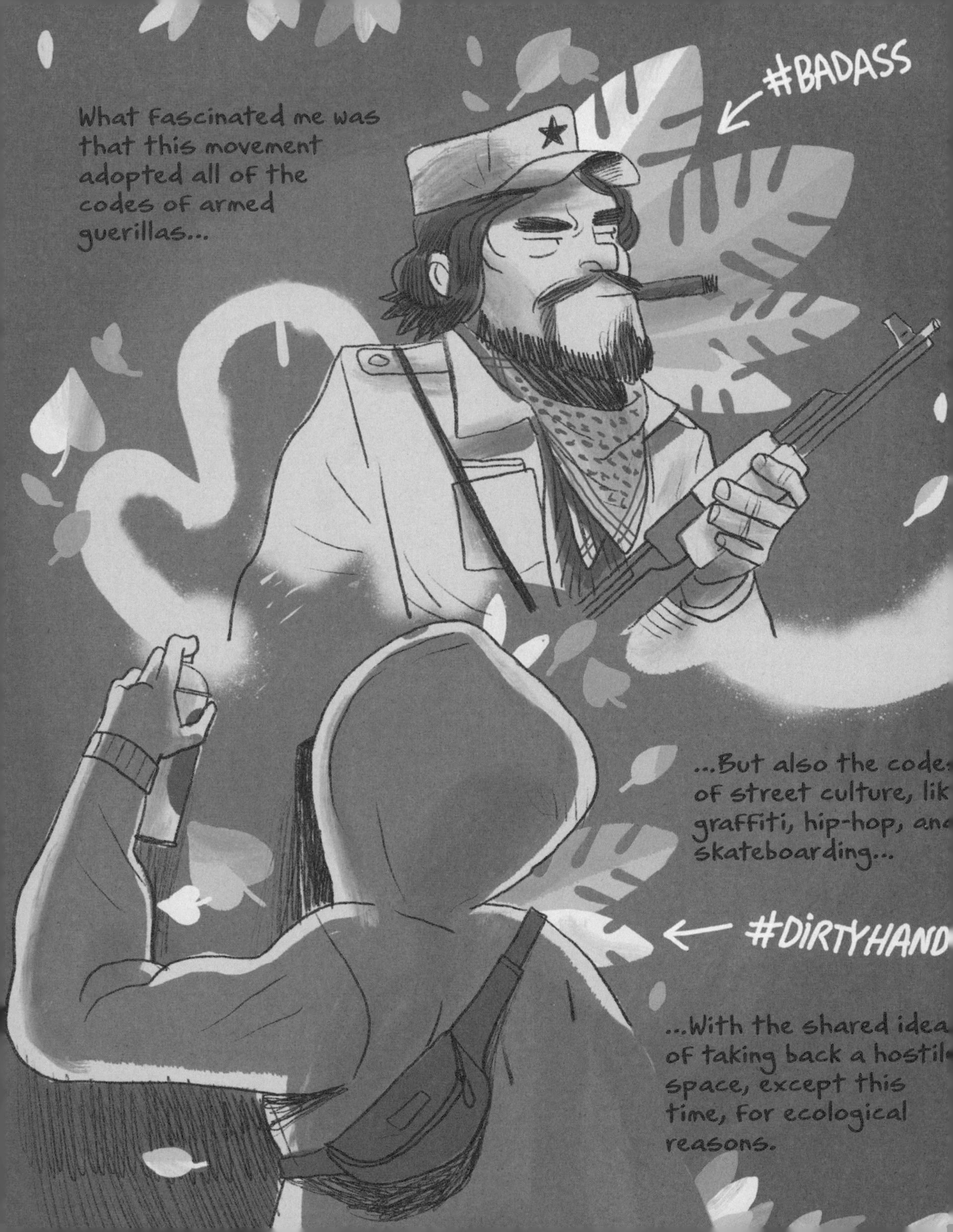
What fascinated me was that this movement adopted all of the codes of armed guerillas...
#BADASS
...But also the codes of street culture, like graffiti, hip-hop, and skateboarding...
#DIRTYHAND
...With the shared idea of taking back a hostile space, except this time, for ecological reasons.

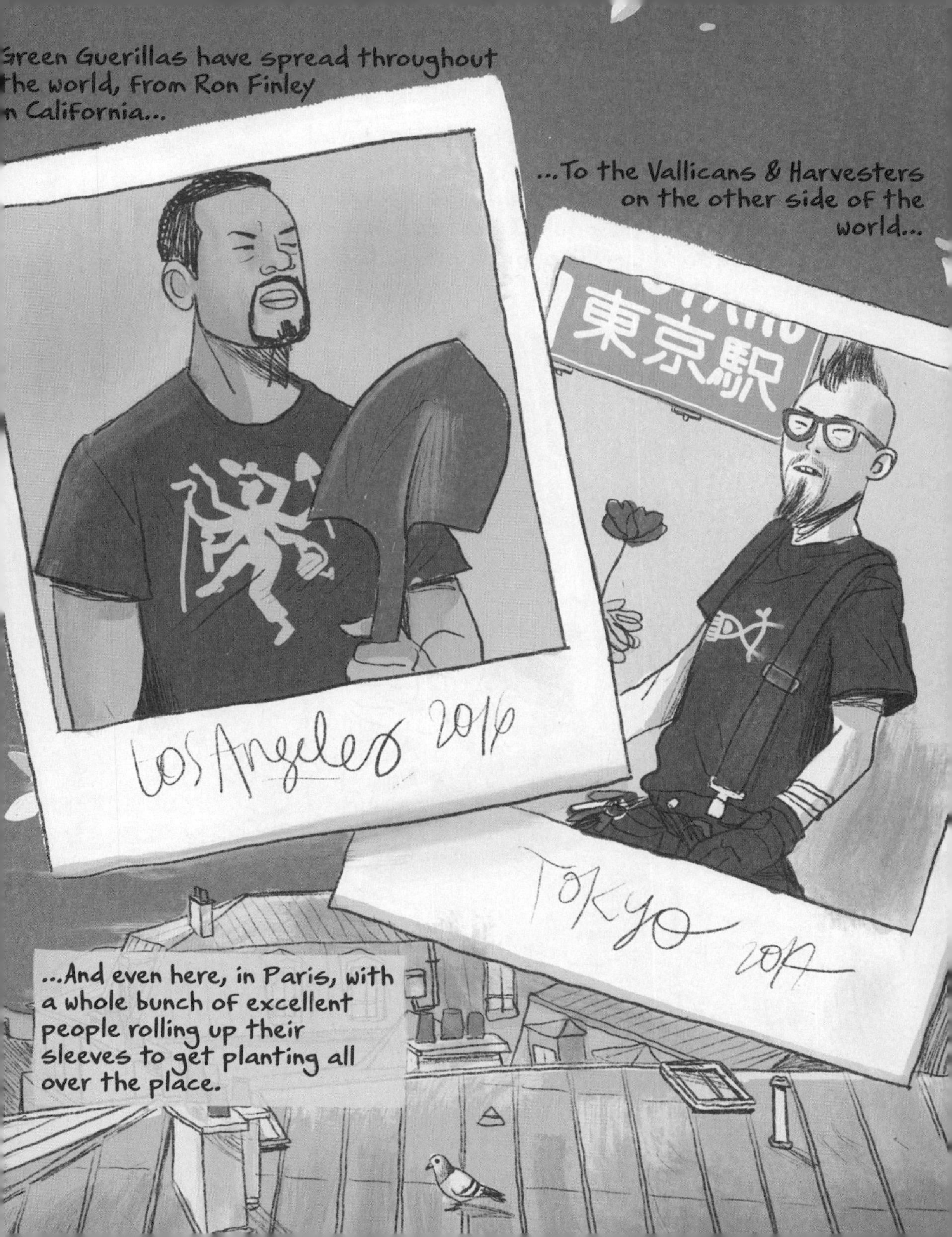
Green Guerillas have spread throughout the world, from Ron Finley in California...
...To the Vallicans & Harvesters on the other side of the world...
東京駅
Los Angeles 2016
Tokyo 2017
...And even here, in Paris, with a whole bunch of excellent people rolling up their sleeves to get planting all over the place.

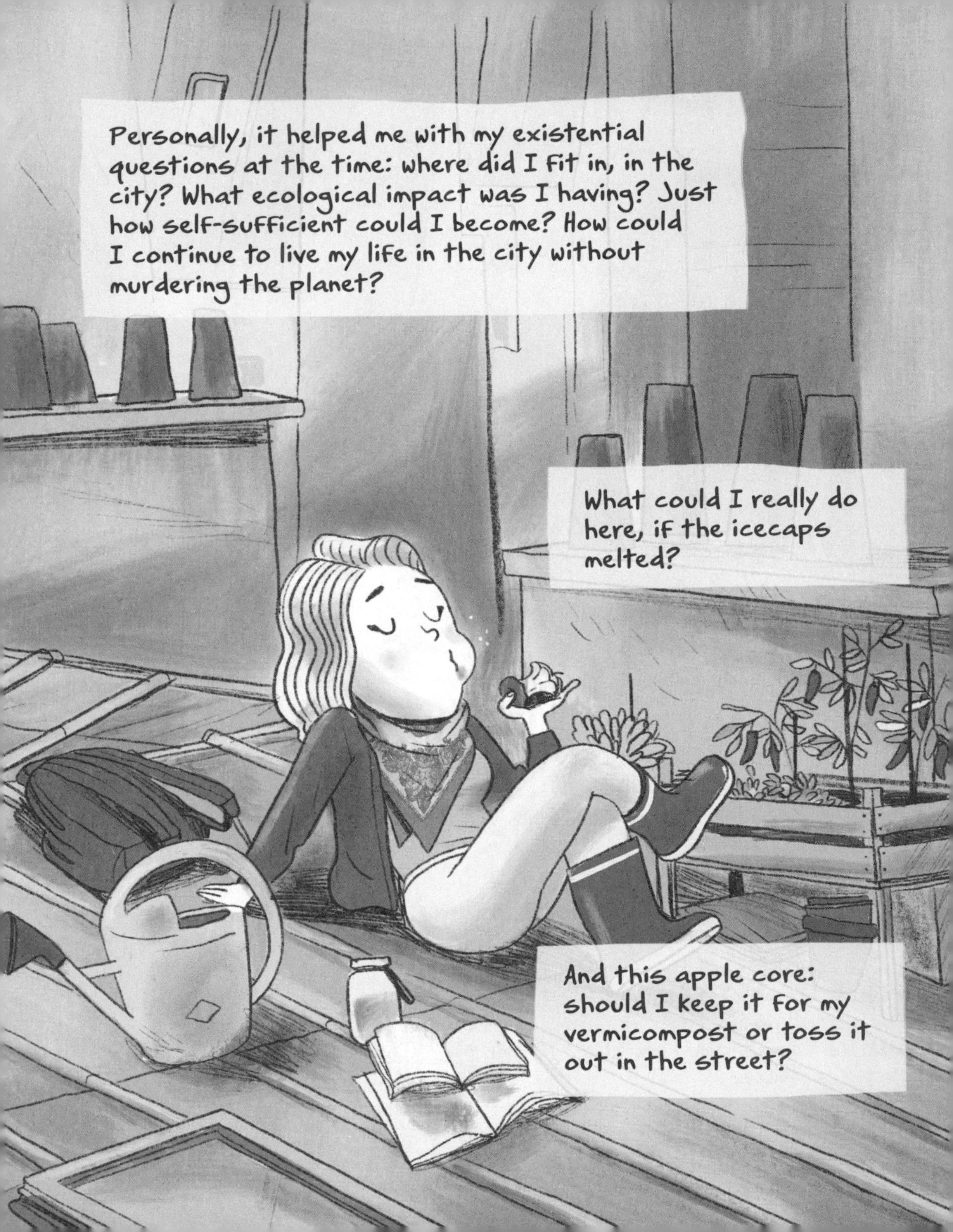
Personally, it helped me with my existential questions at the time: where did I fit in, in the city? What ecological impact was I having? Just how self-sufficient could I become? How could I continue to live my life in the city without murdering the planet?
What could I really do here, if the icecaps melted?
And this apple core: should I keep it for my vermicompost or toss it out in the street?

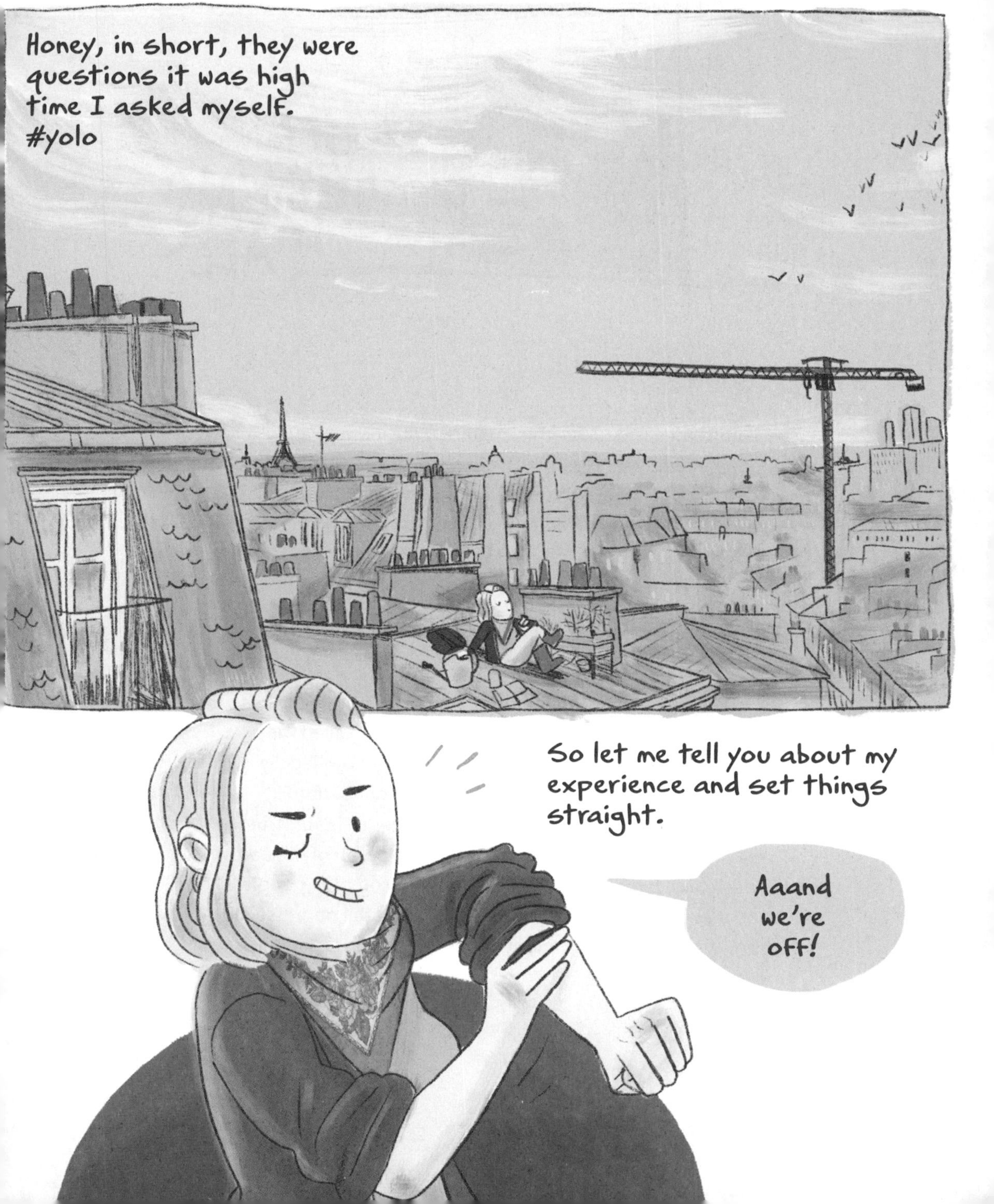
Honey, in short, they were questions it was high time I asked myself. #yolo
So let me tell you about my experience and set things straight.
Aaand we're off!

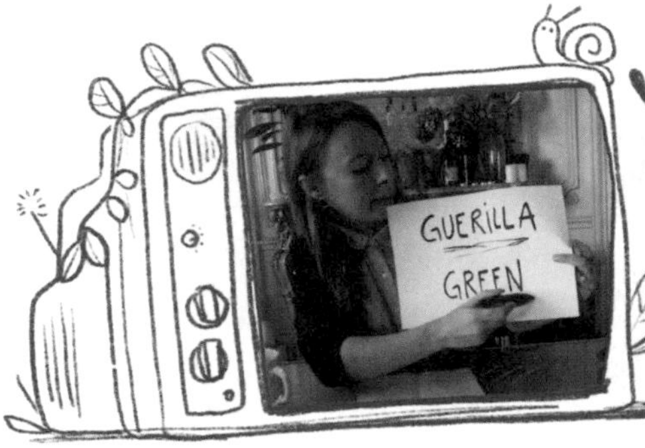
GUERILLA
GREEN

OPHÉLIE EXPLAINS IT ALL

HOW DID GREEN GUERILLAS COME ABOUT?

Guerilla means "little war" in Spanish (cute, right?). Guerillas act independently for their own causes. And "green"? Well, that's the color of sweet peas, lettuce, kale—in short, plants. So this is a war, but one with flowers and goodies to eat!

A LITTLE BIT OF HISTORY

England—17th century
The king just got decapitated, famine is rearing its ugly head, and there's no more land to cultivate. A group called the "Diggers" performs the first Green Guerilla act by illegally occupying communal land to grow things on. Gerrard Winstanley, cofounder of the Diggers, writes in 1650: "True religion and undefiled is this, to make restitution of the Earth which hath been taken and held from the common people by the power of Conquests formerly and so set the oppressed free." Diggers were swiftly brought before the courts and banned from access to the land.

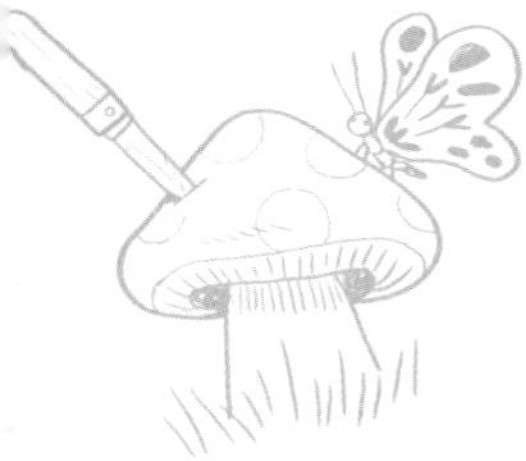

New York—1973

Painter Liz Christie turned a street corner one day and saw a tomato plant growing in an abandoned lot littered with trash. It was a revelation. With a little help from her friends, she decided to turn the vacant lot into a park. Together, they spent a year clearing and replanting the lot. It was Liz who coined the term "Green Guerillas" (it was either that or "Radical Rhizomes"!), largely inspired by Che Guevara, who had died just a few years earlier. Today, the park has become a community garden that bears Liz Christie's name.

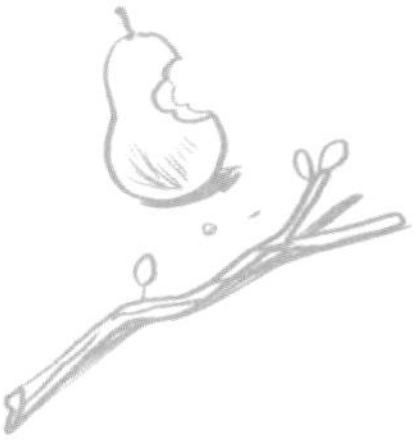

The Green Guerilla movement is rife with other anecdotes, like the one about the group of young Californians who took over an empty lot at the University of California Berkeley and made it into a community garden. In 1969, Ronald Reagan, then governor of California, got involved and sent out a police unit to invade the park. The result: one casualty and over a hundred wounded. #ACAB!

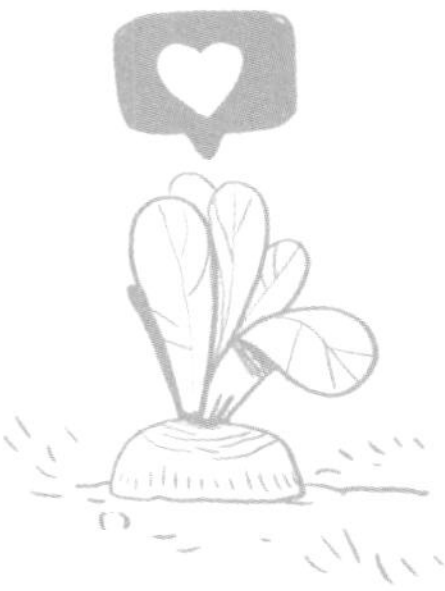

CLEANING UP YOUR CITY: A HOW-TO GUIDE

OK, so, the big question: "Why, exactly, should people start planting stuff everywhere?"
Stay right there! I've got at least five good reasons for ya!
#001

Some to improve the city...
...others to improve your own life and the lives of those around you.

DIET

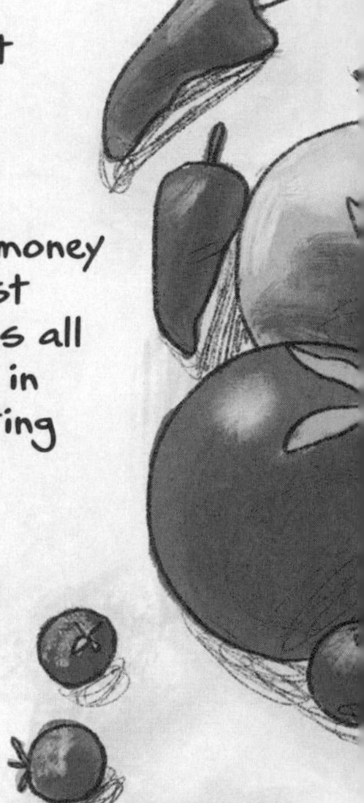

Food! Look, you and I both know we can't live without it. It's kind of like drinking water or having a roof over your head.

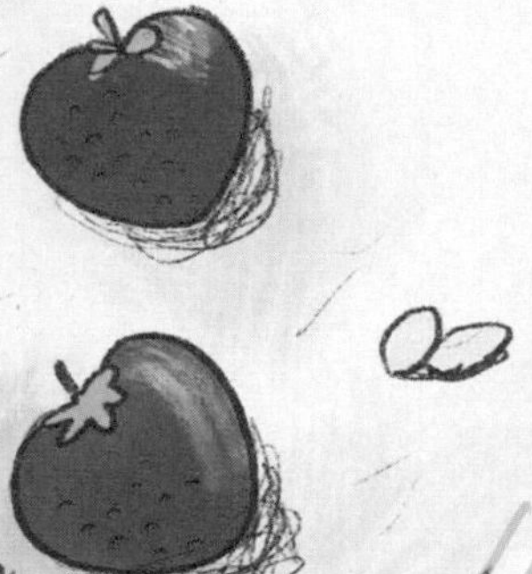

Whether you've got Steve Jobs money coming in or you're a student just scraping by, food is what ties us all together. Planting edible things in public places makes healthy eating accessible to one and all.

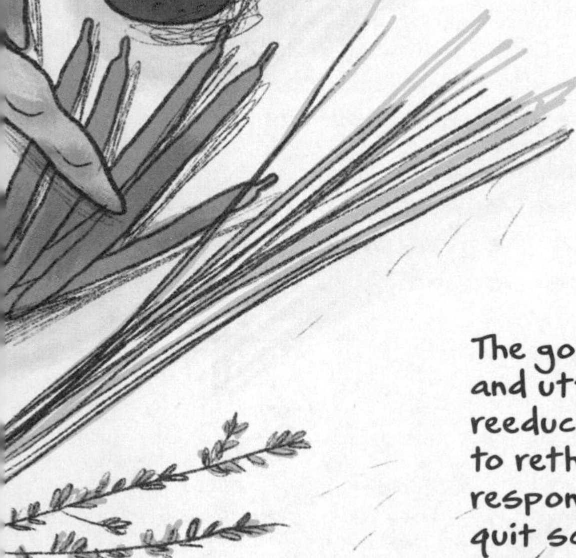

The goal isn't necessarily complete and utter self-sufficiency, but rather reeducating people and encouraging them to rethink their relationship to nature, be responsible for their communities, and quit scarfing Slim Jims or chicken nuggets alone in their studios.

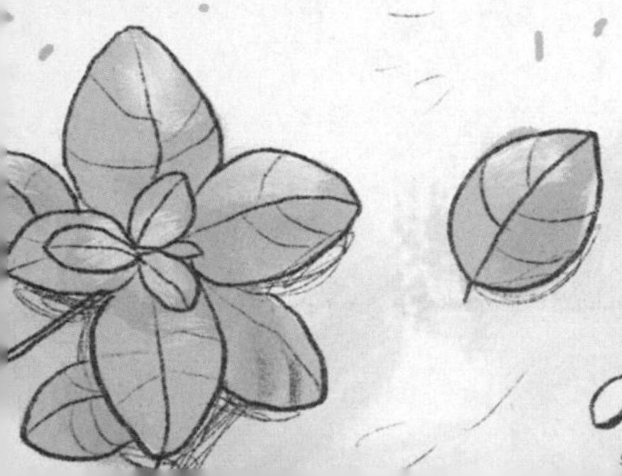

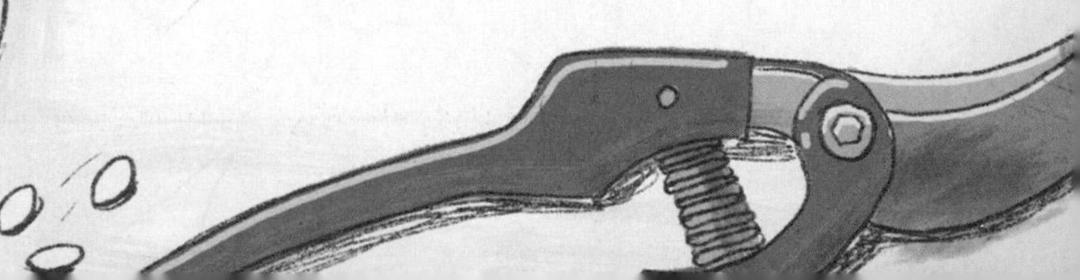

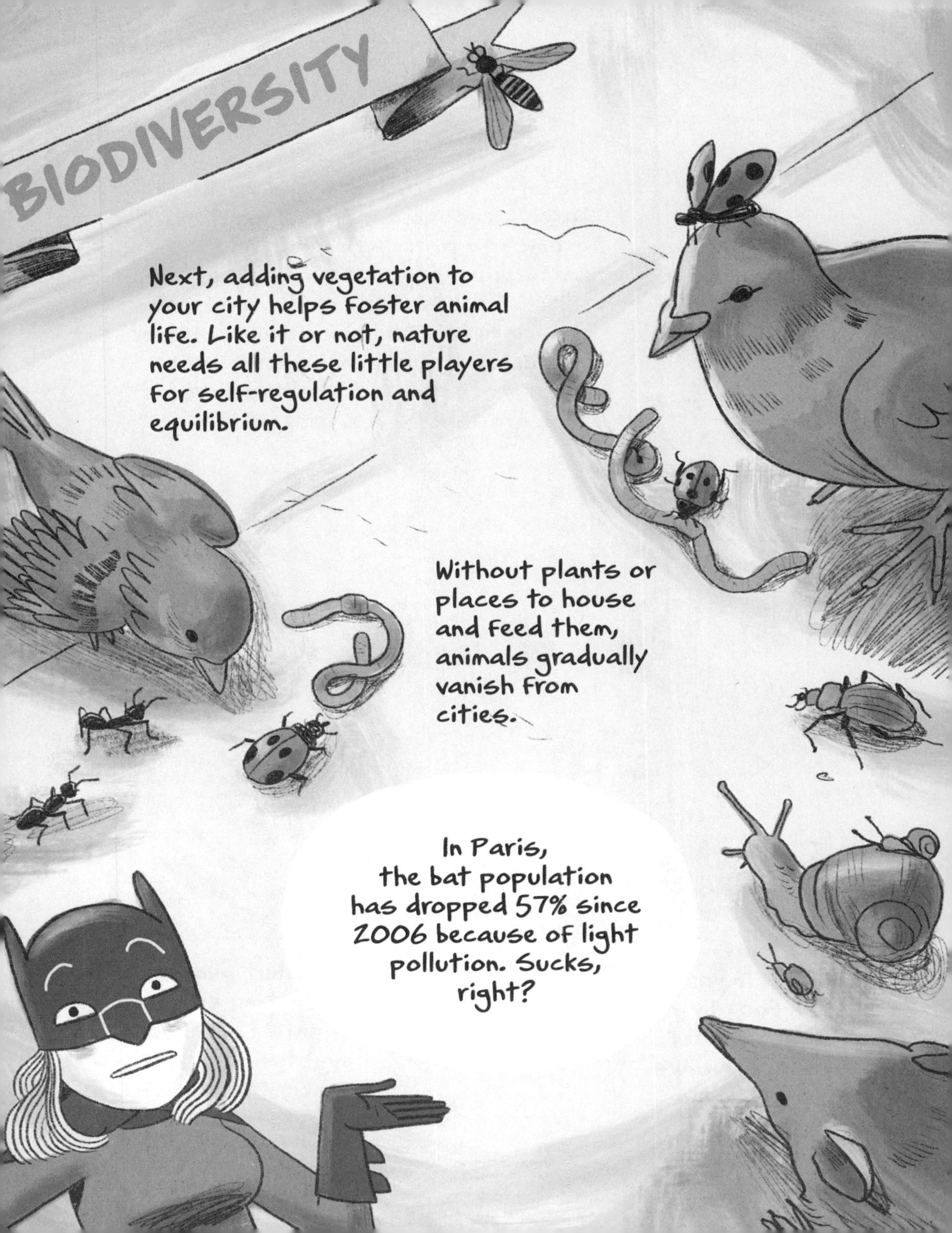
BIODIVERSITY
Next, adding vegetation to your city helps foster animal life. Like it or not, nature needs all these little players for self-regulation and equilibrium.
Without plants or places to house and feed them, animals gradually vanish from cities.
In Paris, the bat population has dropped 57% since 2006 because of light pollution. Sucks, right?

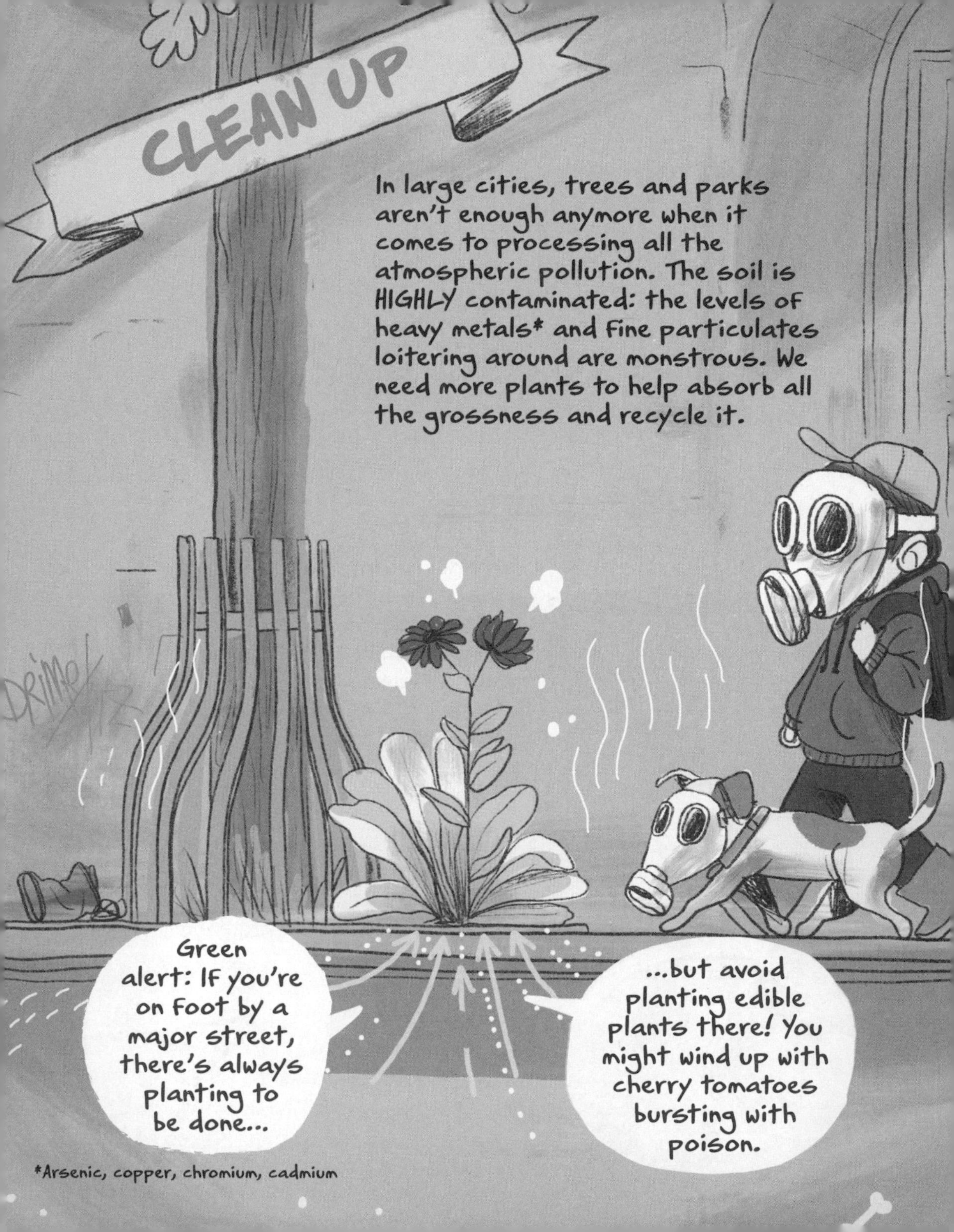
CLEAN UP
In large cities, trees and parks aren't enough anymore when it comes to processing all the atmospheric pollution. The soil is HIGHLY contaminated: the levels of heavy metals* and fine particulates loitering around are monstrous. We need more plants to help absorb all the grossness and recycle it.
Green alert: If you're on foot by a major street, there's always planting to be done...
...but avoid planting edible plants there! You might wind up with cherry tomatoes bursting with poison.
*Arsenic, copper, chromium, cadmium

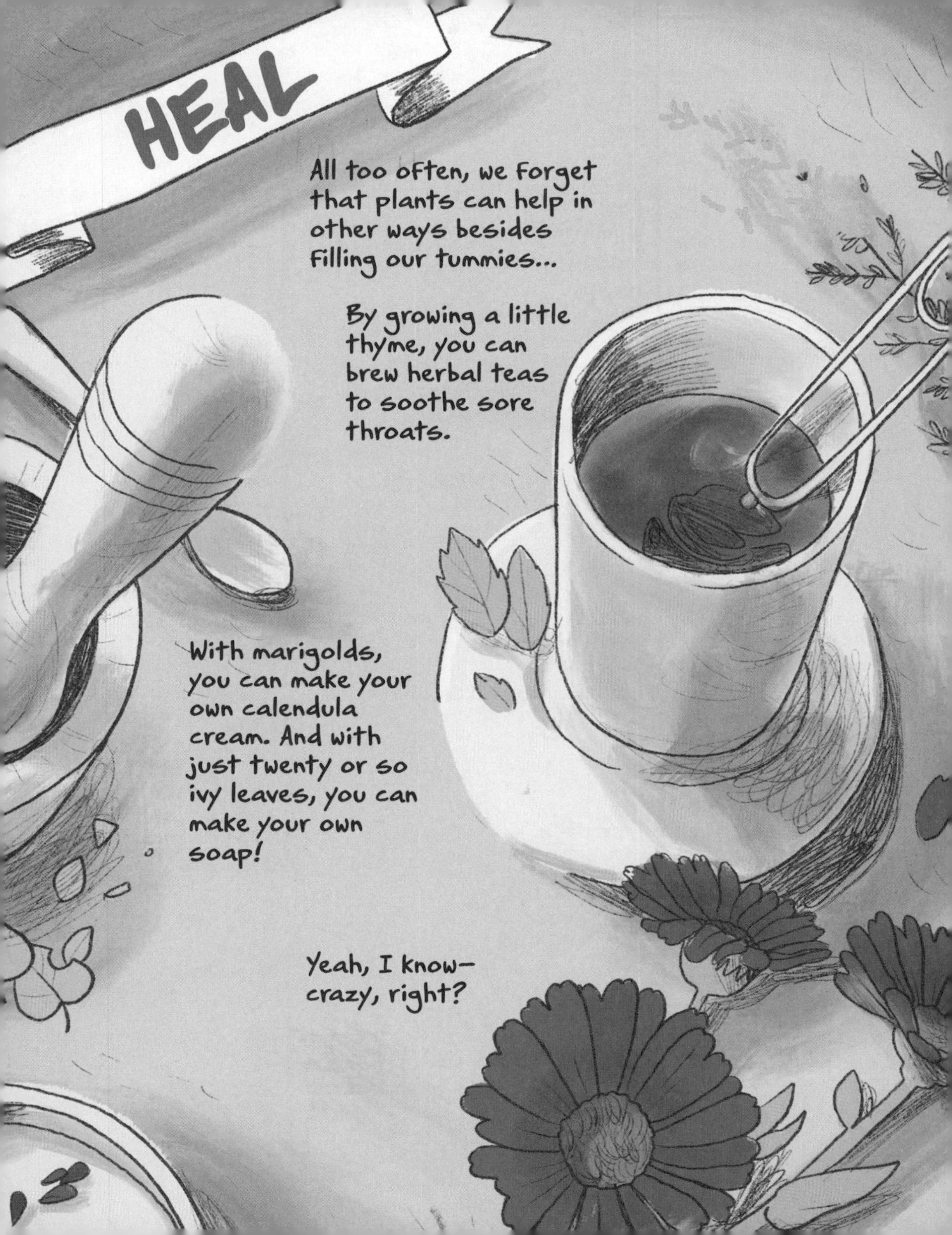
HEAL
All too often, we forget that plants can help in other ways besides filling our tummies...
By growing a little thyme, you can brew herbal teas to soothe sore throats.
With marigolds, you can make your own calendula cream. And with just twenty or so ivy leaves, you can make your own soap!
Yeah, I know—crazy, right?

PACIFY

Look, it sounds dumb, but plants make people happy.

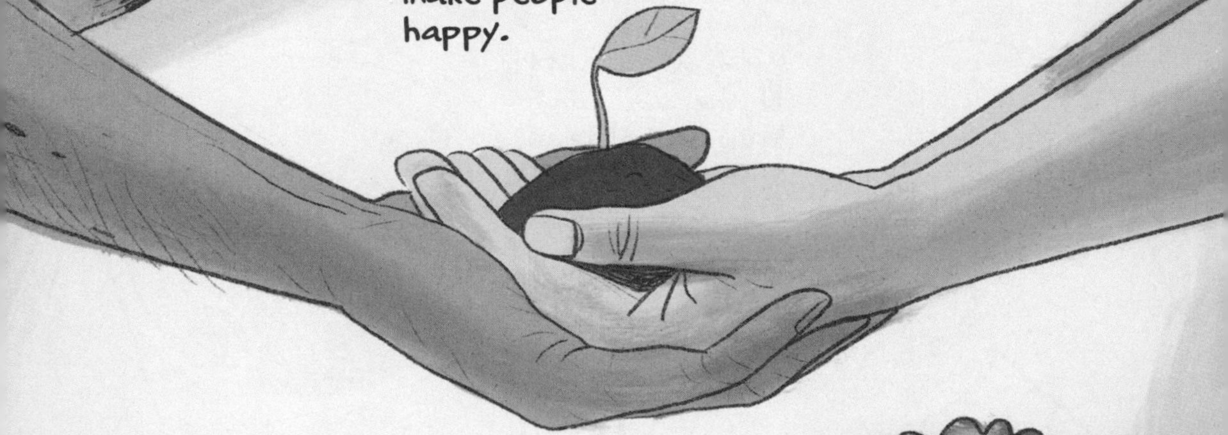

They're way less hassle to care for than pets, and have the same beneficial effect on your mental health and well-being!

It's been proven time and again: gardening is a source of relaxation and personal fulfillment accessible to one and all. Your kids, your grandparents—everyone needs it!

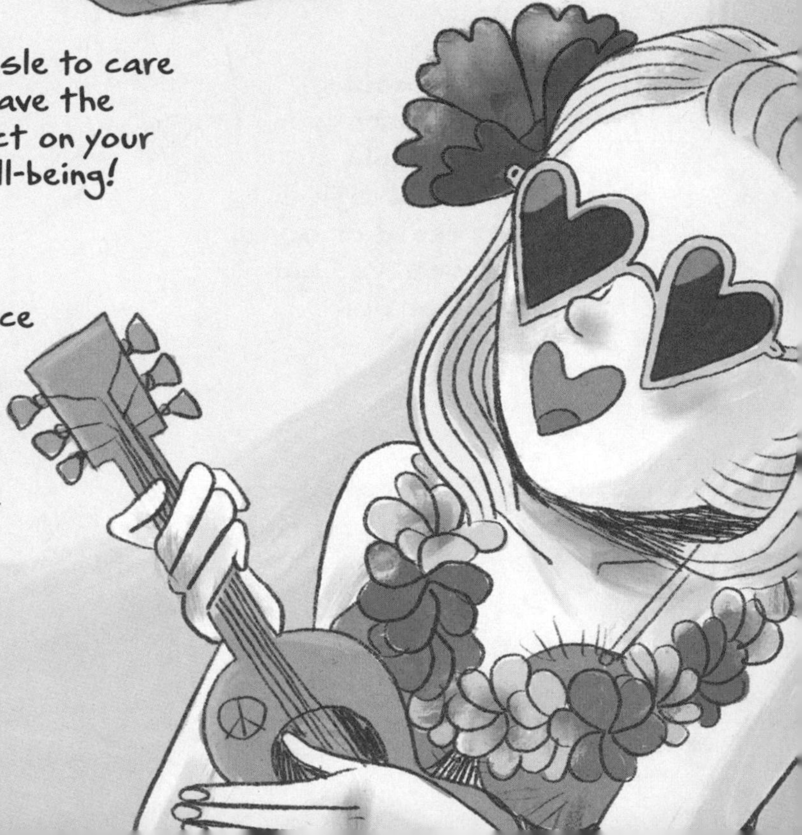

*World Scientists' Warning to Humanity: A Second Notice, Bioscience.

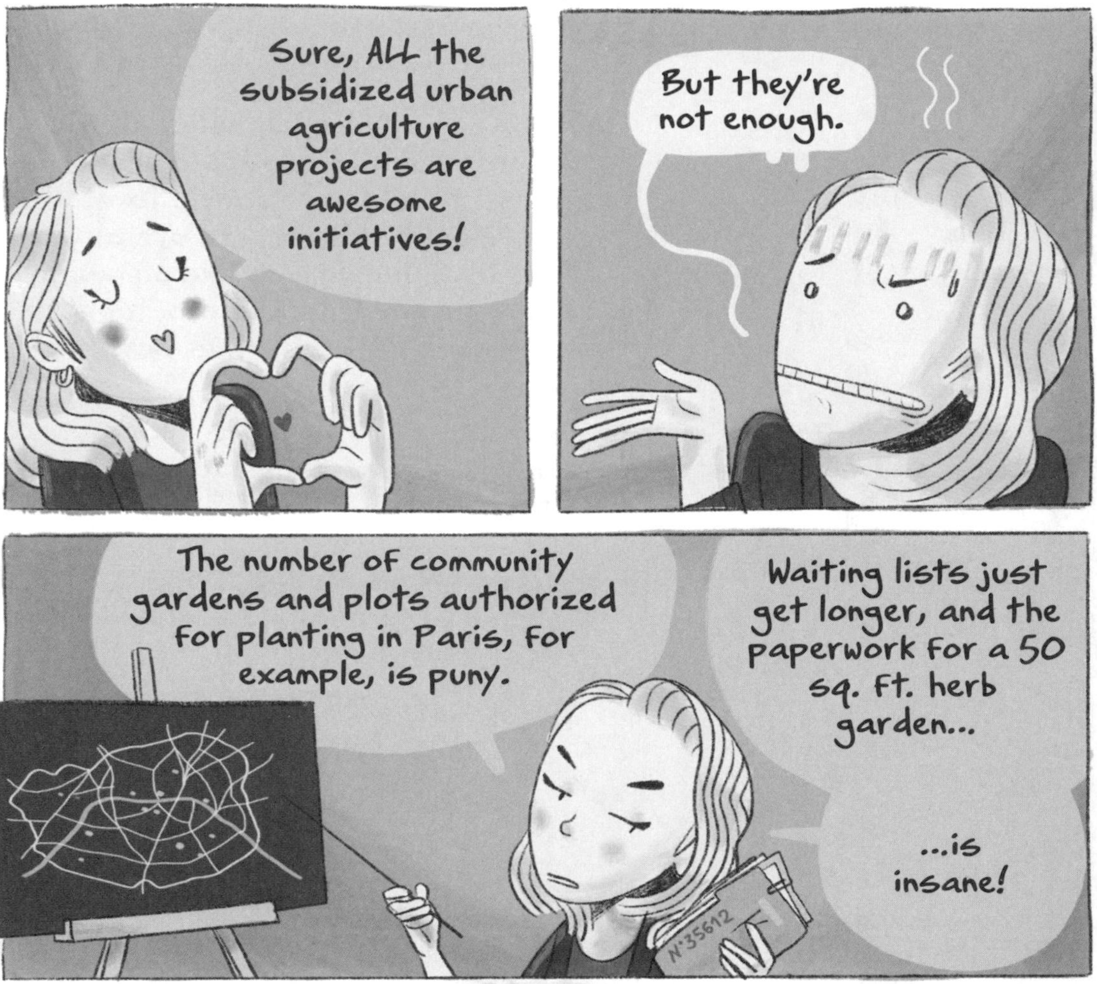
Sure, ALL the subsidized urban agriculture projects are awesome initiatives!
But they're not enough.
The number of community gardens and plots authorized for planting in Paris, for example, is puny.
Waiting lists just get longer, and the paperwork for a 50 sq. ft. herb garden...
...is insane!
N°35612

The Green Guerilla ideal is to think of the ENTIRE city as a potential garden.

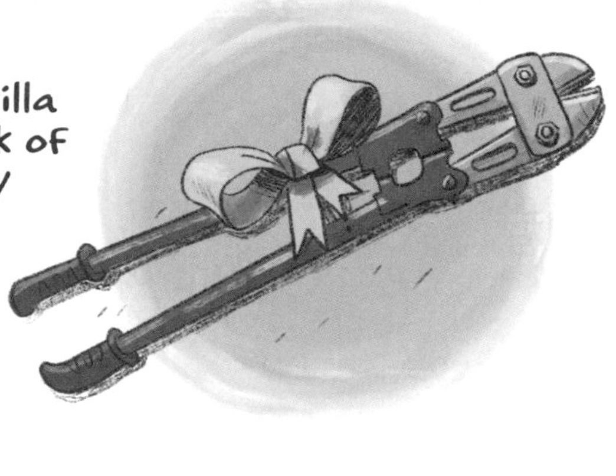

To go out there and cultivate any viable space: a parking lot, a traffic circle, a vacant lot... without waiting for permission!

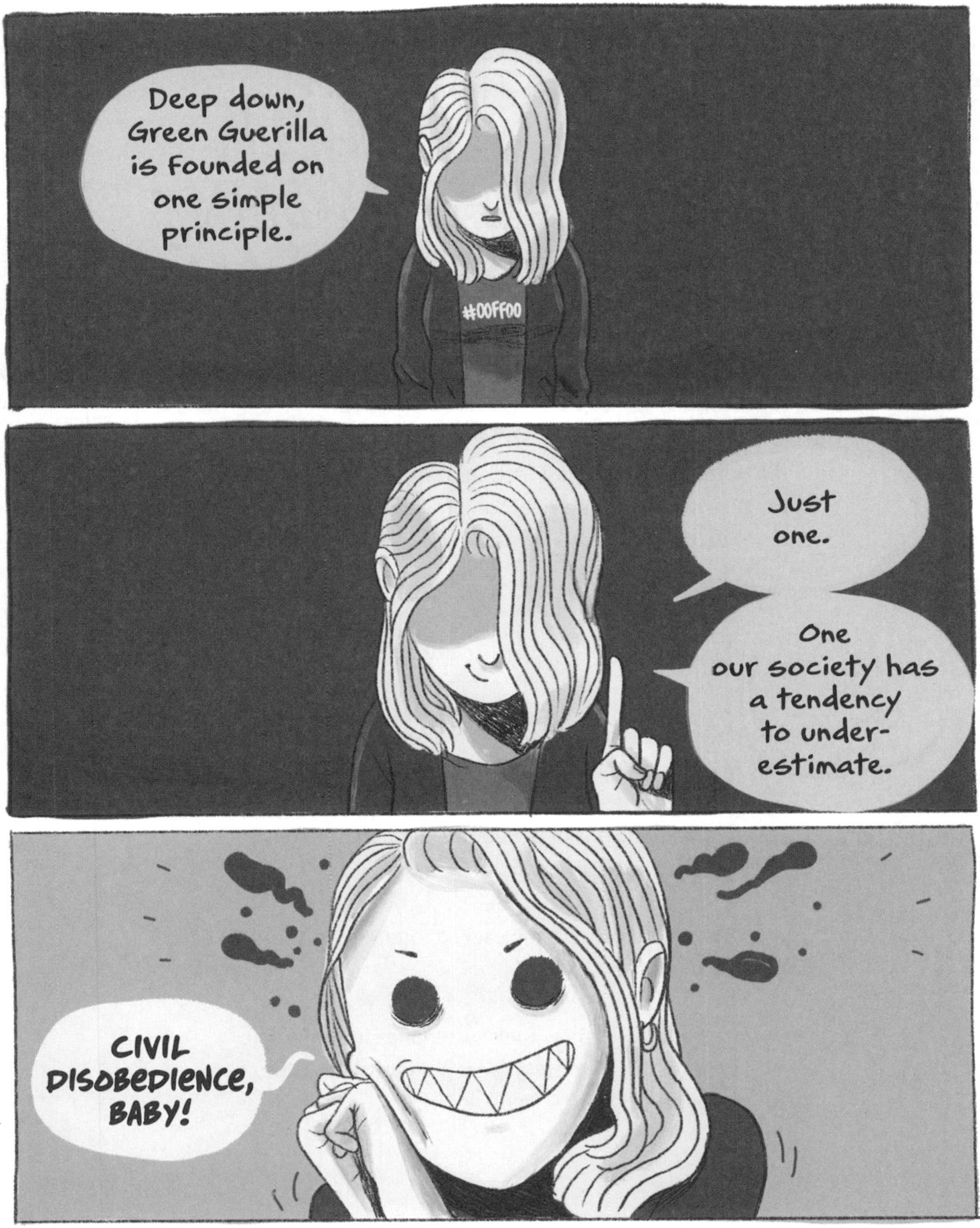
Deep down, Green Guerilla is founded on one simple principle.
#00FF00
Just one.
One our society has a tendency to under-estimate.
CIVIL DISOBEDIENCE, BABY!

OPHÉLIE EXPLAINS IT ALL

CLEANING UP YOUR CITY: A HOW-TO GUIDE

In the Buisseau Community Gardens north of Paris, I met Anne Barbillon (Caution: she's a scientist!). Trained as an agronomist, and policy officer for AgroParisTech, she conducts research on urban agriculture.

WHAT IS POLLUTION?

It's the direct or indirect introduction of substances or heat, mostly from human activity, into the soil, air, or water, which can be harmful to the health of humans and ecosystems.
There are different kinds of pollution: pollution from heavy metals, light pollution, even sound pollution.

In cities, things are very closely packed together, and sources of pollution can pile up.

Now, since vegetables draw their sustenance from the soil, air, and water, if one of these three is polluted, vegetables can become polluted as well.

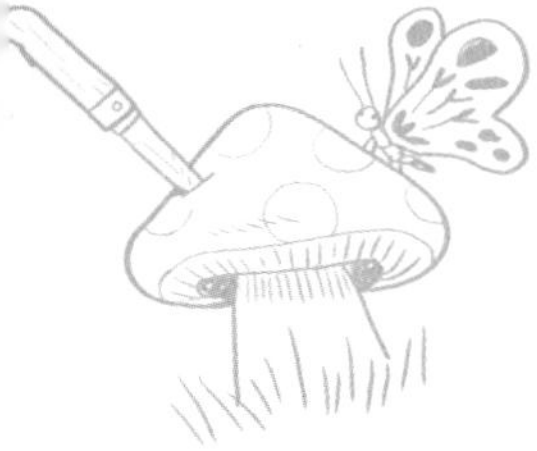

In short, if you're not sure about the soil where you are, you're better off growing things in planters lined with geotextile fabrics, so that the healthy substrate inside won't risk contact or contamination from the soil beneath.

The substrate is the medium in which vegetables grow: soil, or just as easily water, in the case of hydroponics.

It is also possible, before sowing your vegetables, to purify the soil with certain containing or decontaminant species. This is known as phytoremediation.

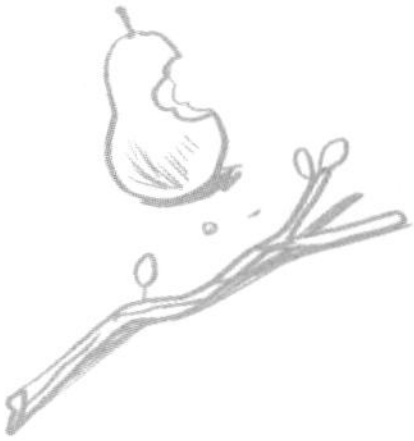

Sadly, just washing your vegetables isn't enough! That might get rid of atmospheric sediments, but if your vegetables grew in soil polluted by heavy metals, washing them won't change a thing You may notice that vegetables will absorb more or less of certain kinds of pollutants. For instance, fruits absorb far fewer heavy metals than root vegetables or leafy greens.

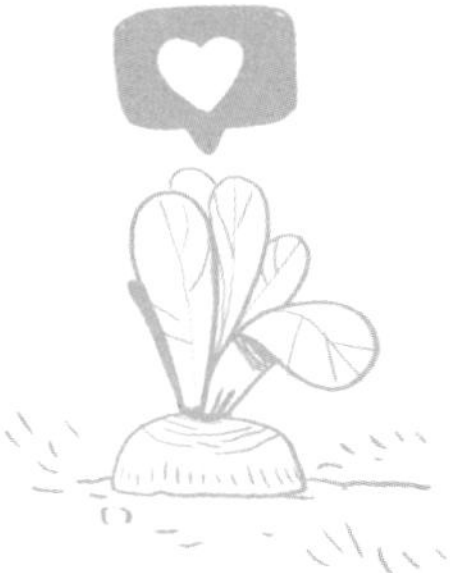

THE ART OF DISOBEDIENCE

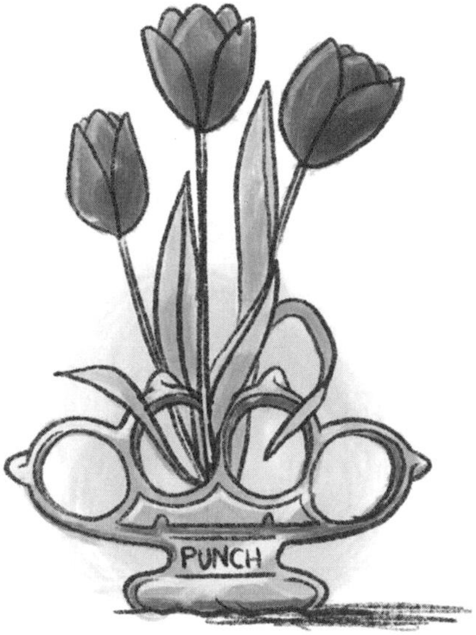
PUNCH

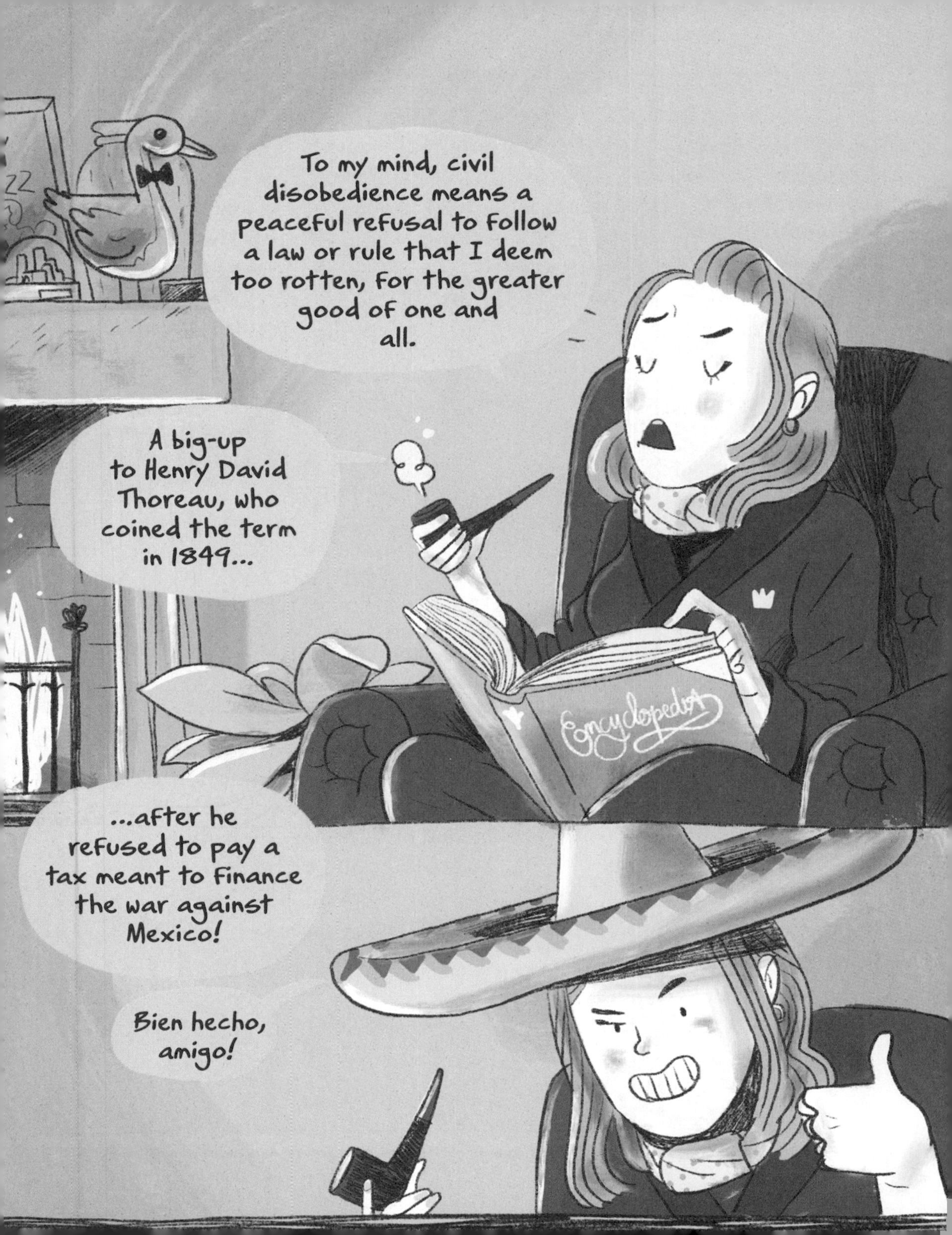
To my mind, civil disobedience means a peaceful refusal to follow a law or rule that I deem too rotten, for the greater good of one and all.
A big-up to Henry David Thoreau, who coined the term in 1849...
Encyclopedia
...after he refused to pay a tax meant to finance the war against Mexico!
Bien hecho, amigo!

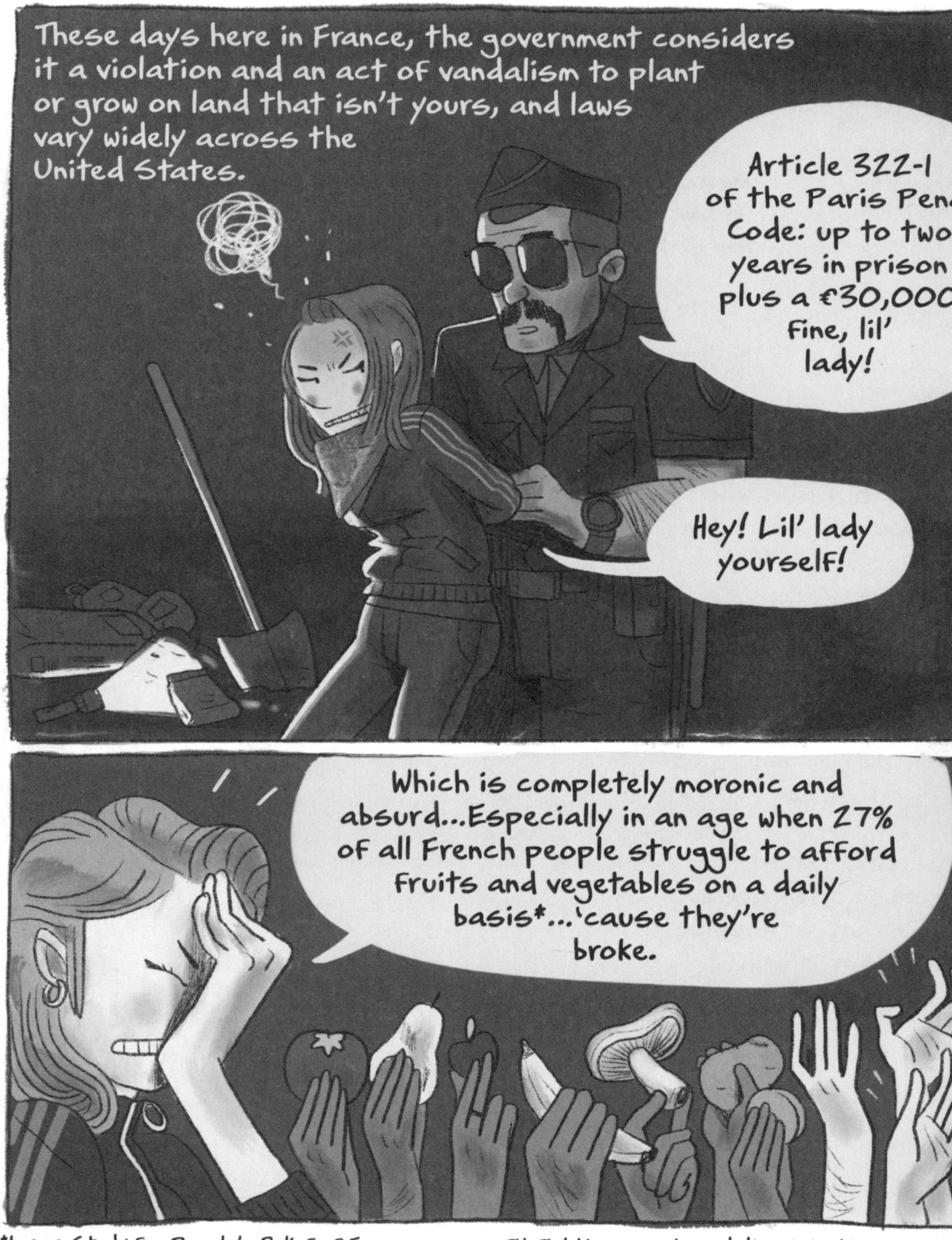
These days here in France, the government considers it a violation and an act of vandalism to plant or grow on land that isn't yours, and laws vary widely across the United States.
Article 322-1 of the Paris Penal Code: up to two years in prison plus a €30,000 fine, lil' lady!
Hey! Lil' lady yourself!
Which is completely moronic and absurd...Especially in an age when 27% of all French people struggle to afford fruits and vegetables on a daily basis*...'cause they're broke.

*Ipsos Study for People's Relief of France, a nonprofit fighting poverty and discrimination.

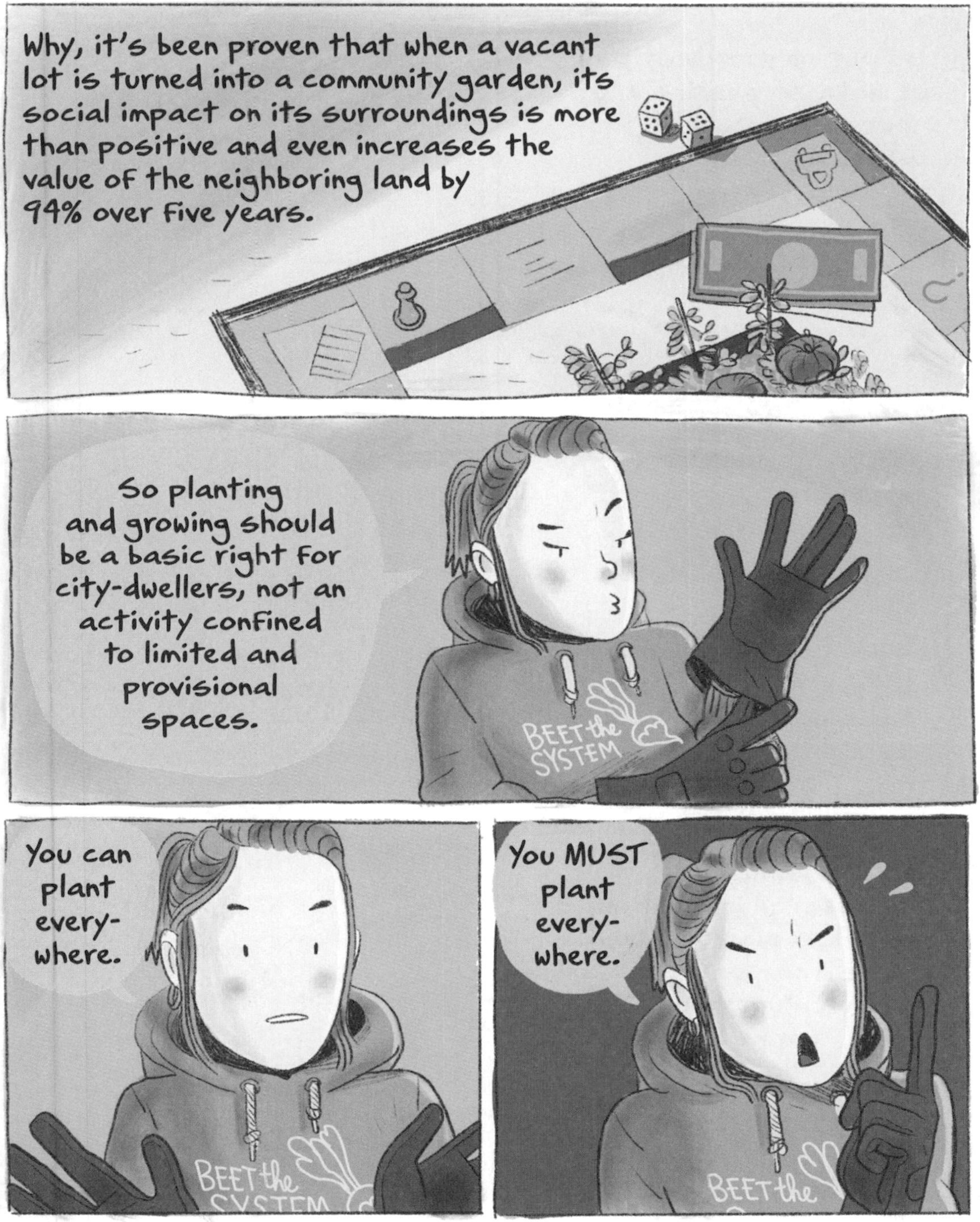
Why, it's been proven that when a vacant lot is turned into a community garden, its social impact on its surroundings is more than positive and even increases the value of the neighboring land by 94% over five years.
So planting and growing should be a basic right for city-dwellers, not an activity confined to limited and provisional spaces.
BEET the SYSTEM
You can plant every-where.
You MUST plant every-where.

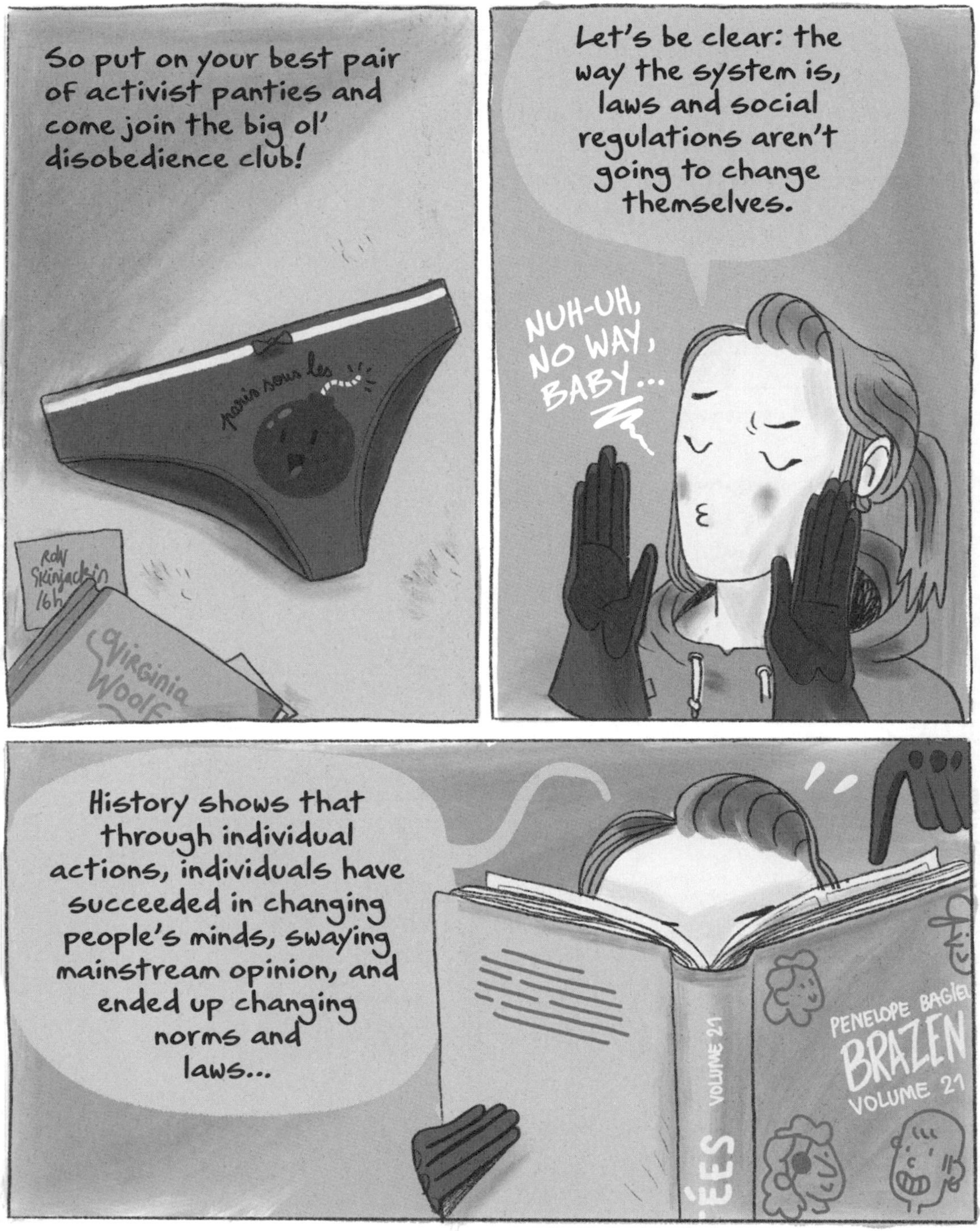
So put on your best pair of activist panties and come join the big ol' disobedience club!
Virginia Woolf
Let's be clear: the way the system is, laws and social regulations aren't going to change themselves.
NUH-UH, NO WAY, BABY...
History shows that through individual actions, individuals have succeeded in changing people's minds, swaying mainstream opinion, and ended up changing norms and laws...
VOLUME 21
PENELOPE BAGIEU
BRAZEN
VOLUME 21

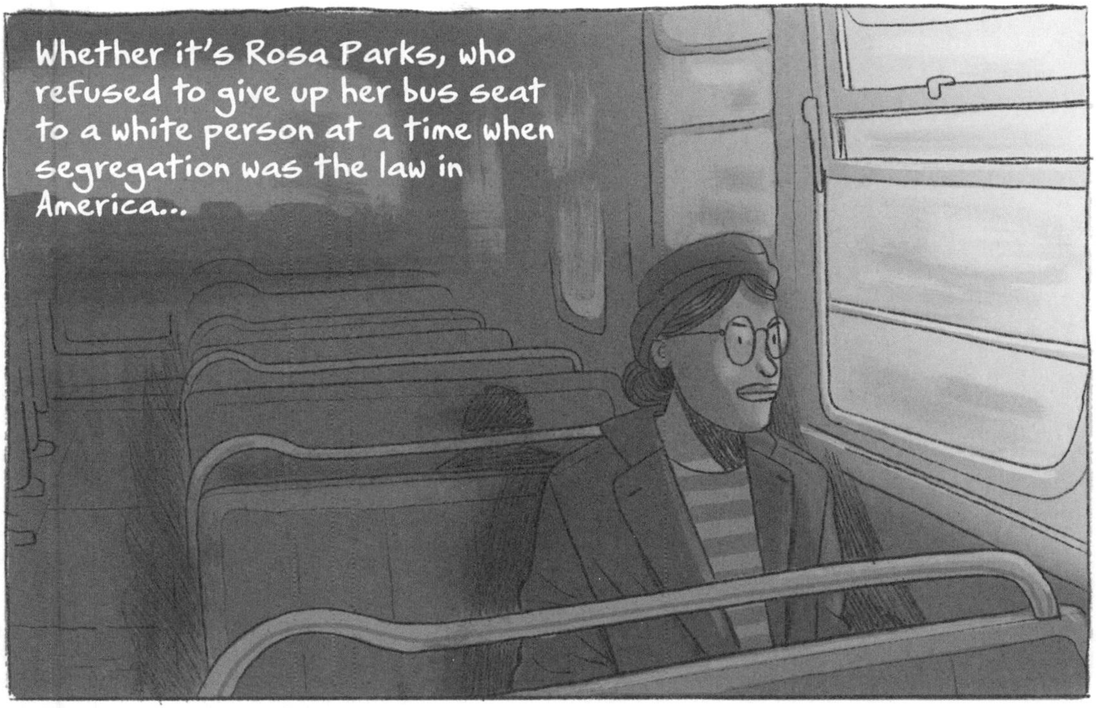
Whether it's Rosa Parks, who refused to give up her bus seat to a white person at a time when segregation was the law in America...

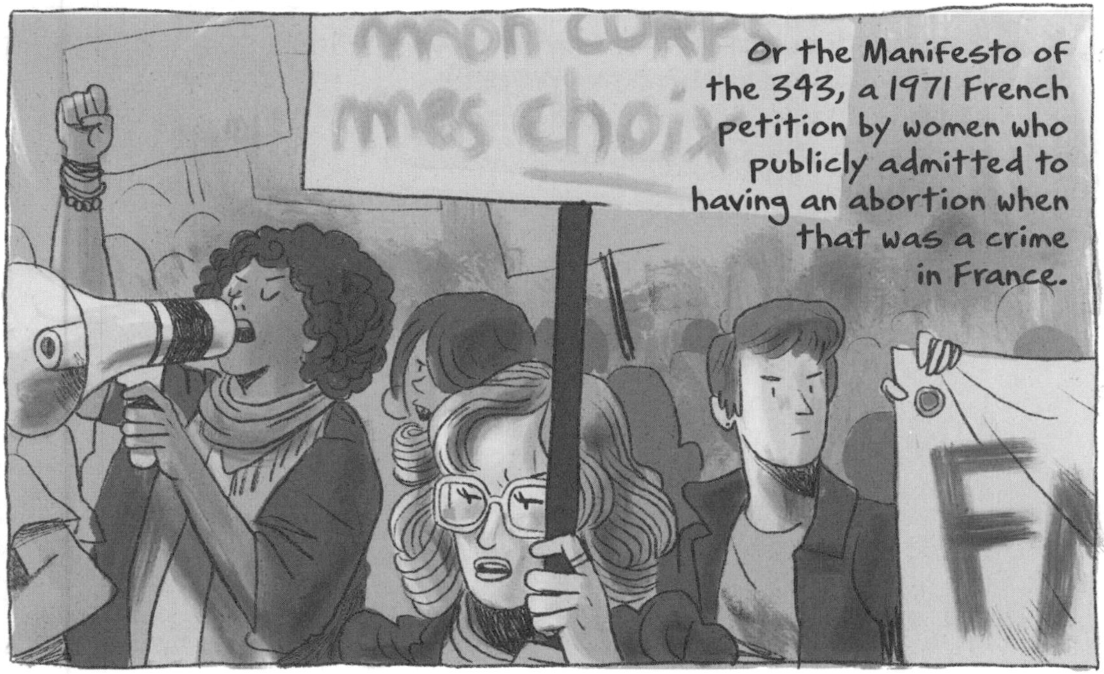
mes choix
Or the Manifesto of the 343, a 1971 French petition by women who publicly admitted to having an abortion when that was a crime in France.

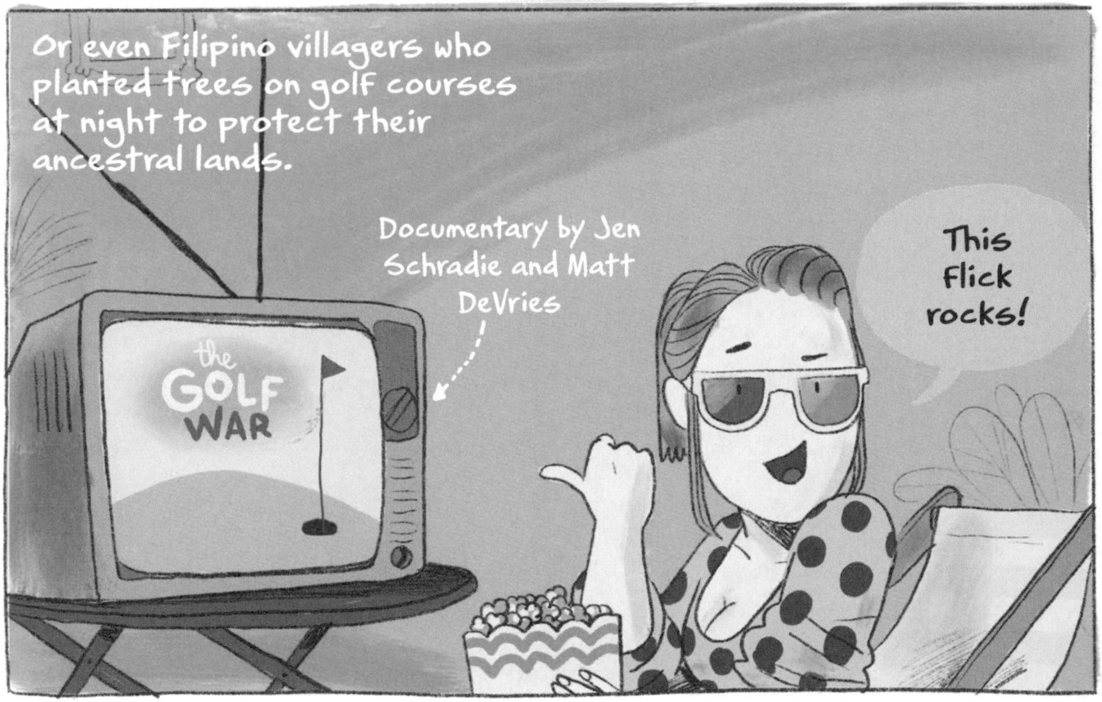
Or even Filipino villagers who planted trees on golf courses at night to protect their ancestral lands.
Documentary by Jen Schradie and Matt DeVries
the GOLF WAR
This Flick rocks!

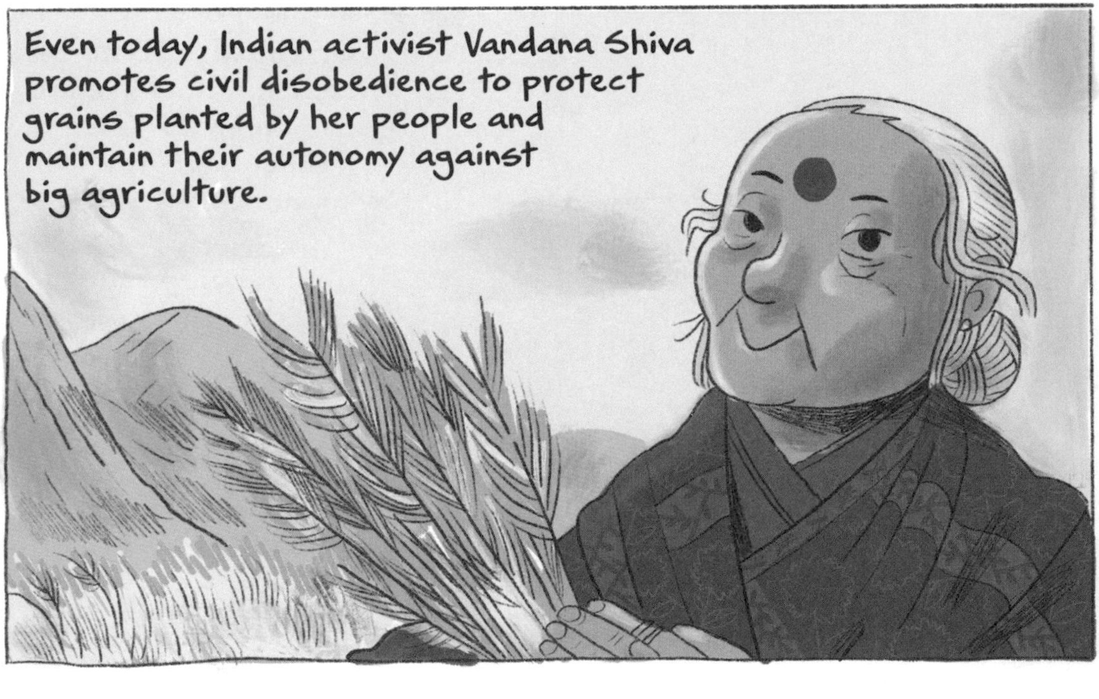
Even today, Indian activist Vandana Shiva promotes civil disobedience to protect grains planted by her people and maintain their autonomy against big agriculture.

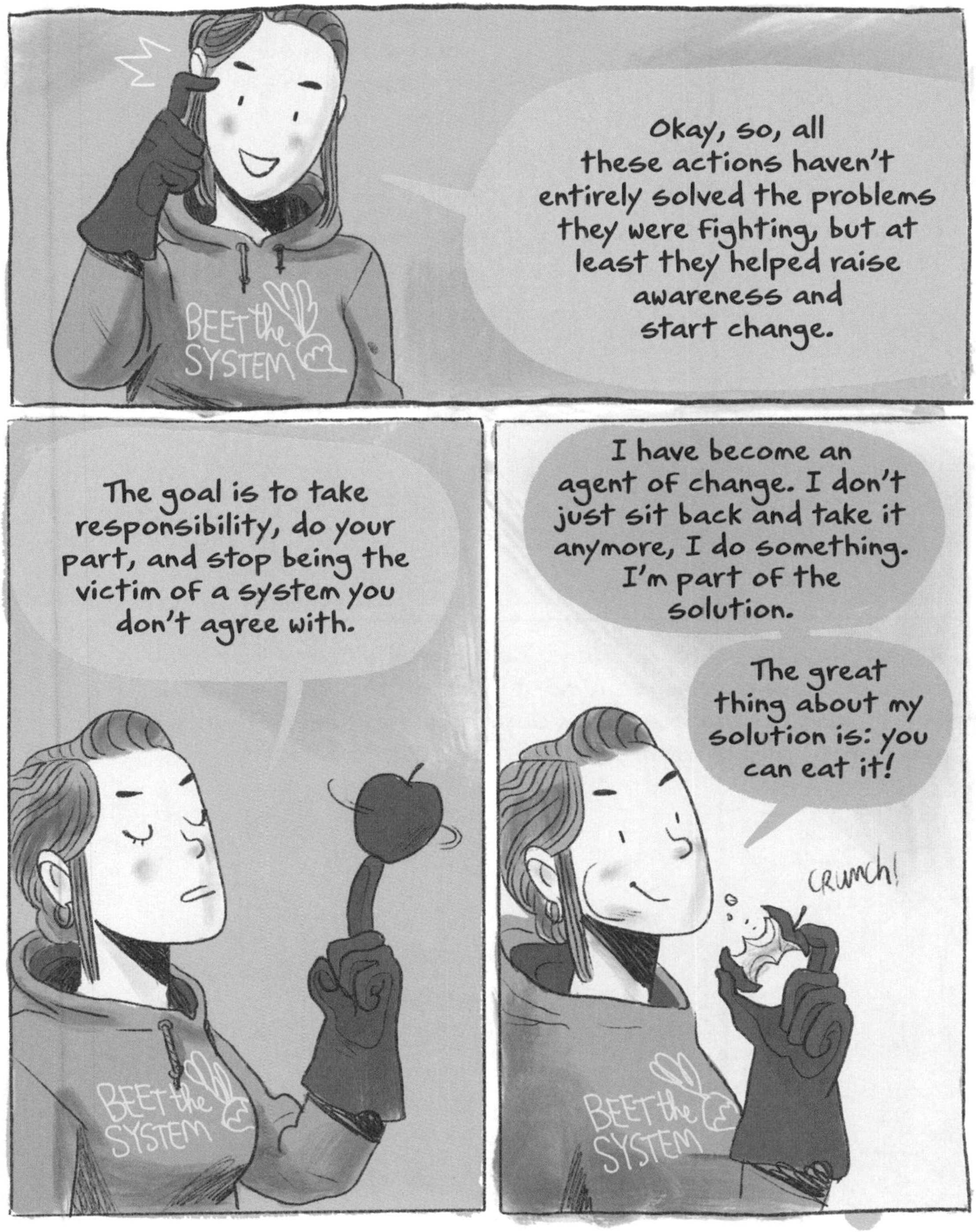
Okay, so, all these actions haven't entirely solved the problems they were fighting, but at least they helped raise awareness and start change.
BEET the SYSTEM
The goal is to take responsibility, do your part, and stop being the victim of a system you don't agree with.
BEET the SYSTEM
I have become an agent of change. I don't just sit back and take it anymore, I do something. I'm part of the solution.
The great thing about my solution is: you can eat it!
CRUNCH!
BEET the SYSTEM

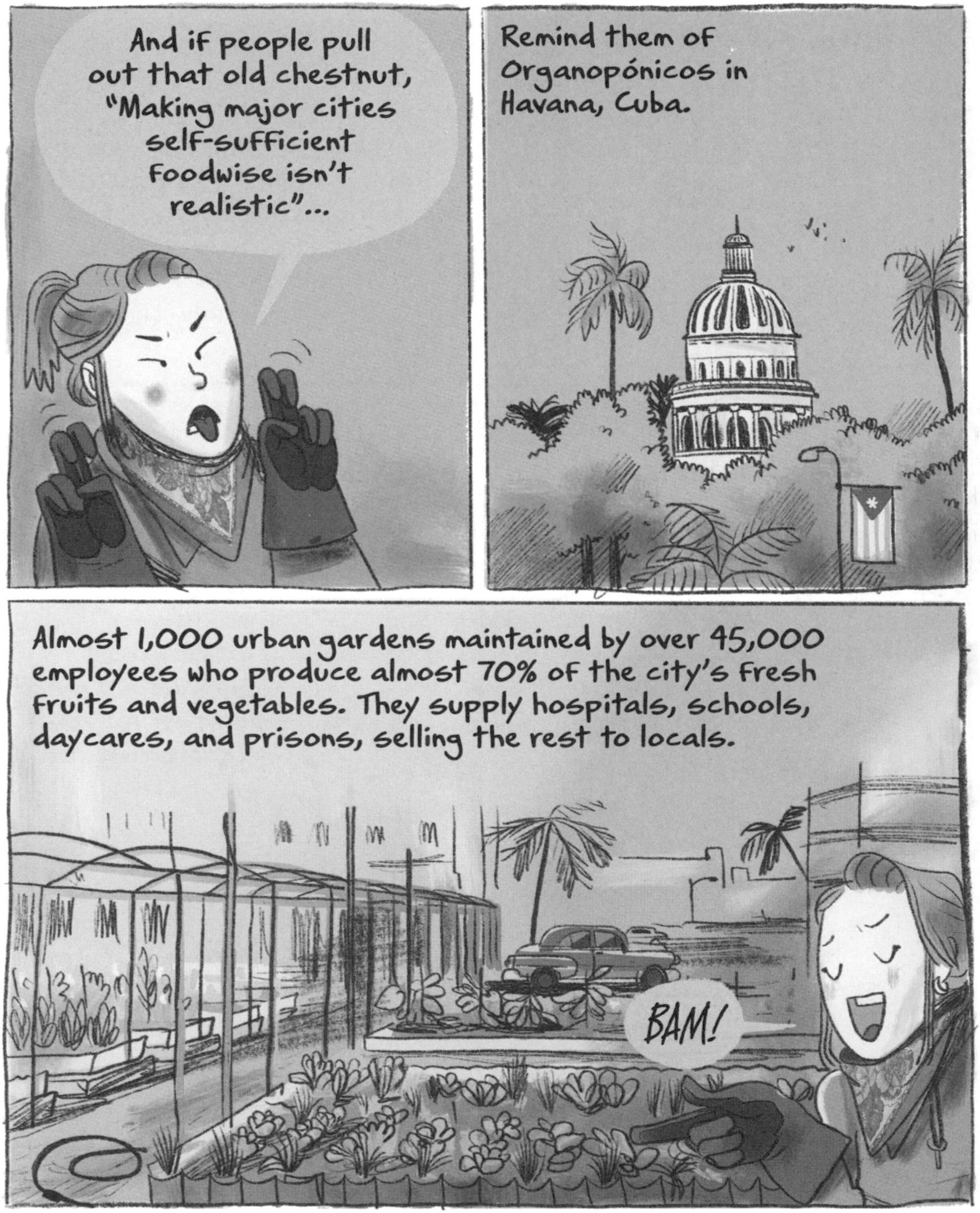
And if people pull out that old chestnut, "Making major cities self-sufficient foodwise isn't realistic"...
Remind them of Organopónicos in Havana, Cuba.
Almost 1,000 urban gardens maintained by over 45,000 employees who produce almost 70% of the city's fresh fruits and vegetables. They supply hospitals, schools, daycares, and prisons, selling the rest to locals.
BAM!

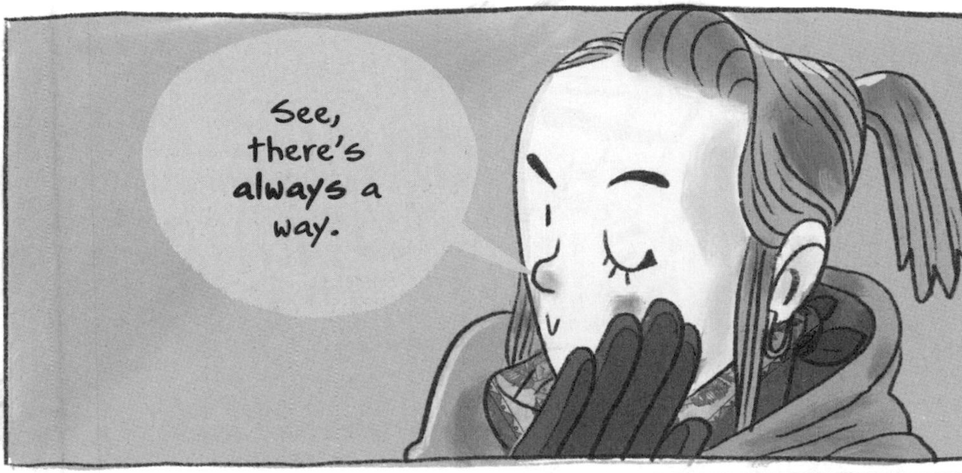
See, there's always a way.

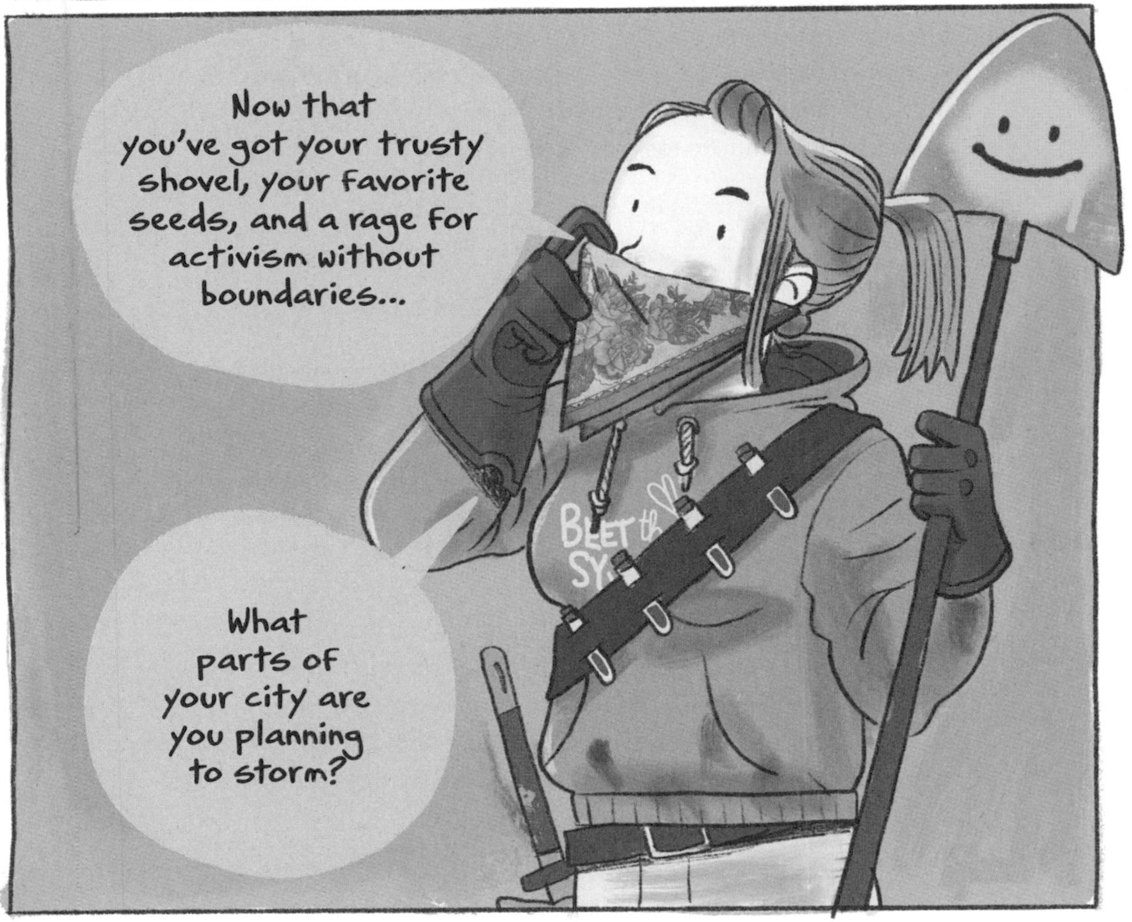
Now that you've got your trusty shovel, your favorite seeds, and a rage for activism without boundaries...
What parts of your city are you planning to storm?

OPHÉLIE EXPLAINS IT ALL

THE ART OF DISOBEDIENCE

Sometimes, being a Green Guerilla means breaking the law. Civil disobedience is peaceful refusal to follow a law or regulation you believe is harmful to the greater good.

THREE CAUSES THAT DESERVE SOME DISOBEYING

Seed Freedom
Seeds are a rather special legislative case. Certain varieties are recorded in a European catalogue, while many others aren't, and thus cannot be marketed by producers. In a single century, 75% of our edible species have disappeared! That is why it is important to support all seed producers struggling to preserve this natural wealth.

Medicinal Herbs
Herbalists are no longer a recognized profession in France. The rare die-hard herbalists are regularly attacked for practicing medicine illegally. My friend Julie, an apprentice herbalist and nursery owner, tells me about medicinal herbs that can be used

for daily self-care. For example, sage has antiseptic, hormonal, digestive, and anti-inflammatory properties. There is a list of one hundred some legal medicinal herbs, but many other varieties— by definition, illegal—also exist.

Extinction of Living Species

I met a member of the civil disobedience movement Extinction Rebellion, which aims to use nonviolent civil disobedience to compel government action to avoid tipping points in social and ecological collapse. Their primary goal is to bring politicians and the media to recognize the gravity of the situation. According to them, civil disobedience involves five levels of risk:

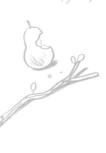

1: Zero Risk— Calling out to people in the subway;
2: Small Risk— Chalk tagging, could result in charges of defacement of public property;
3 to 5: Significant Risk— Blocking strategic bridges or major roads or disrupting a meeting of a publicly-traded company, could result in court trials or police custody.

On March 24, 2019, the French branch of Extinction Rebellion became official before the French government and the media during Declaration of Rebellion Day (JDR).

THE BEST SPOTS FOR
GOING GUERILLA GREEN

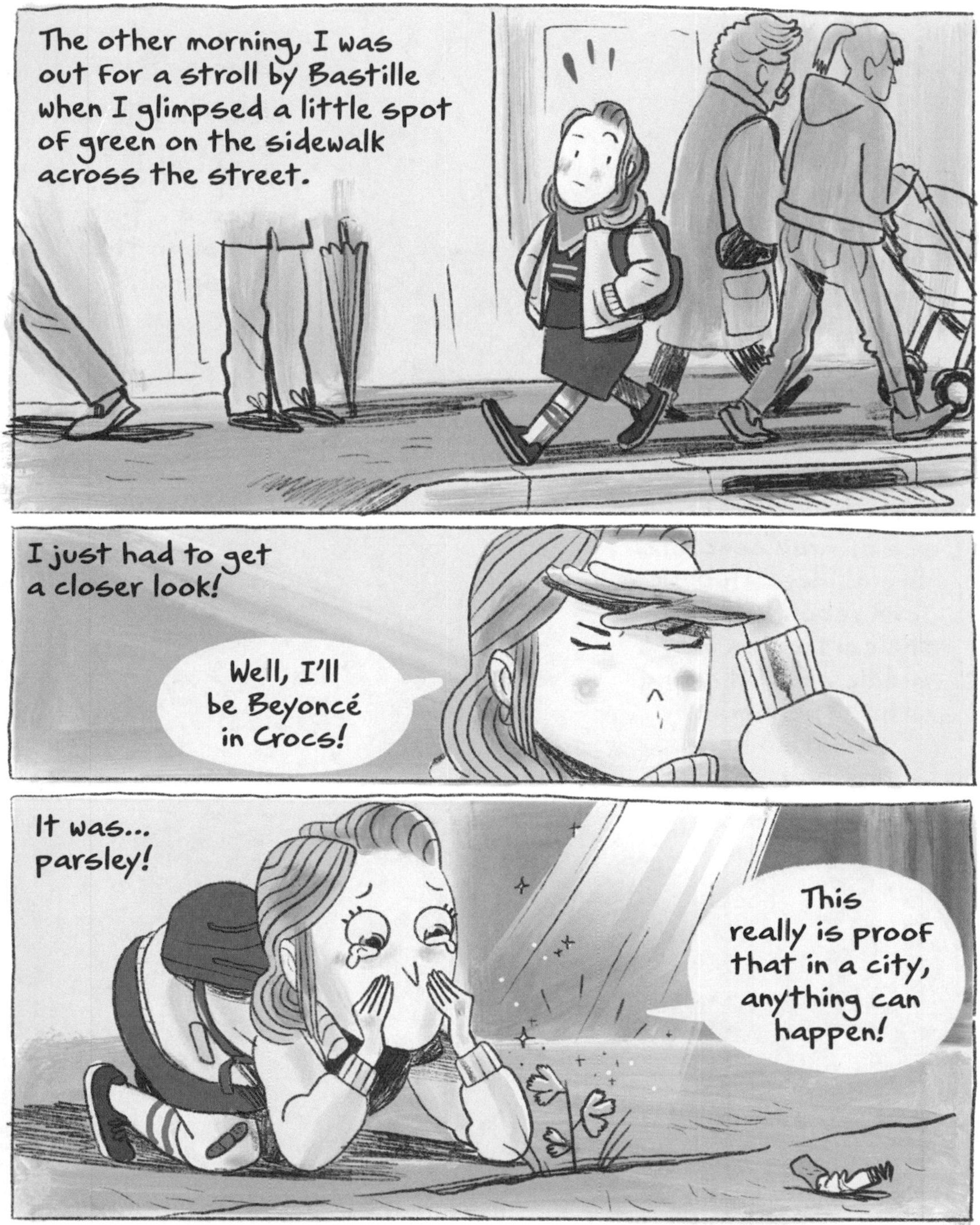
The other morning, I was out for a stroll by Bastille when I glimpsed a little spot of green on the sidewalk across the street.
I just had to get a closer look!
Well, I'll be Beyoncé in Crocs!
It was... parsley!
This really is proof that in a city, anything can happen!

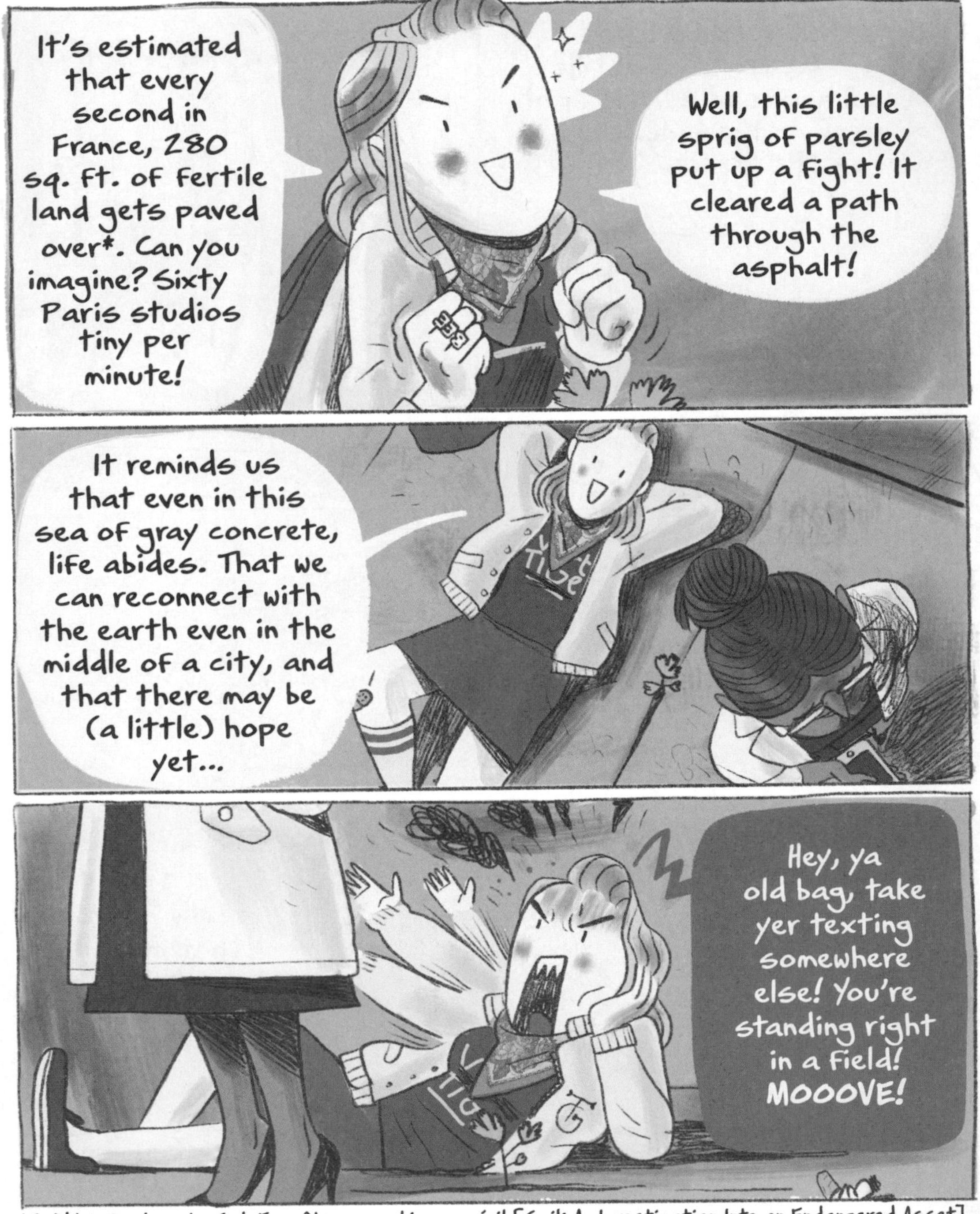
It's estimated that every second in France, 280 sq. ft. of fertile land gets paved over*. Can you imagine? Sixty Paris studios tiny per minute!
Well, this little sprig of parsley put up a fight! It cleared a path through the asphalt!
It reminds us that even in this sea of gray concrete, life abides. That we can reconnect with the earth even in the middle of a city, and that there may be (a little) hope yet...
Hey, ya old bag, take yer texting somewhere else! You're standing right in a field! MOOOVE!

*Frédéric Denhez, Le Sol, Enquête sur un bien en péril [Soil: An Investigation Into an Endangered Asset]. (Flammarion, 2018)

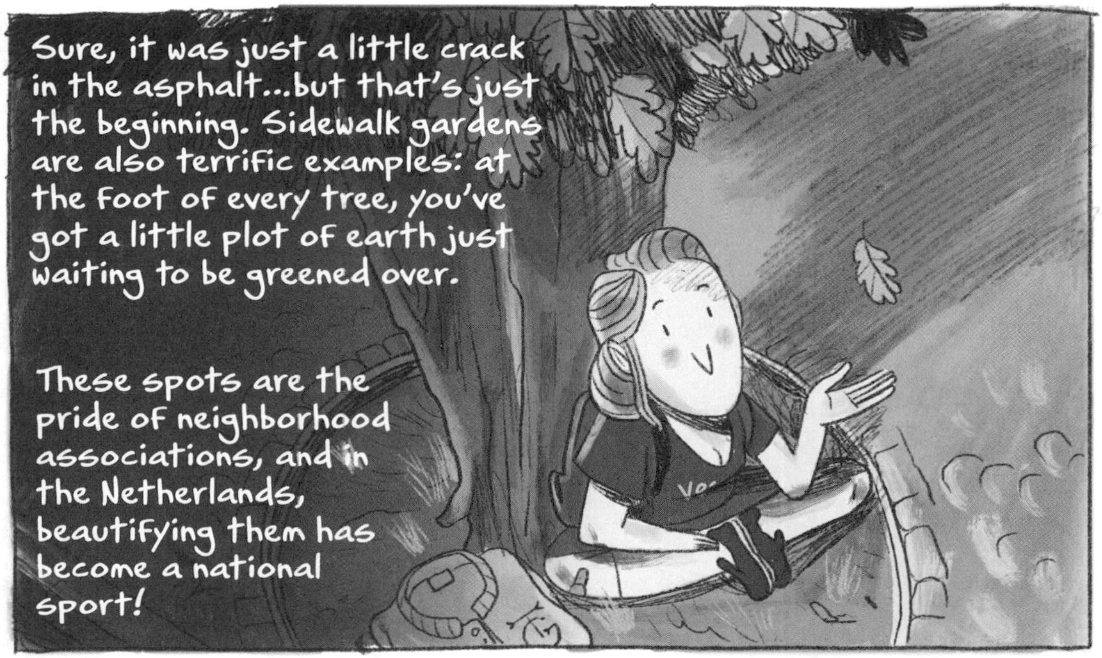
Sure, it was just a little crack in the asphalt...but that's just the beginning. Sidewalk gardens are also terrific examples: at the foot of every tree, you've got a little plot of earth just waiting to be greened over.
These spots are the pride of neighborhood associations, and in the Netherlands, beautifying them has become a national sport!

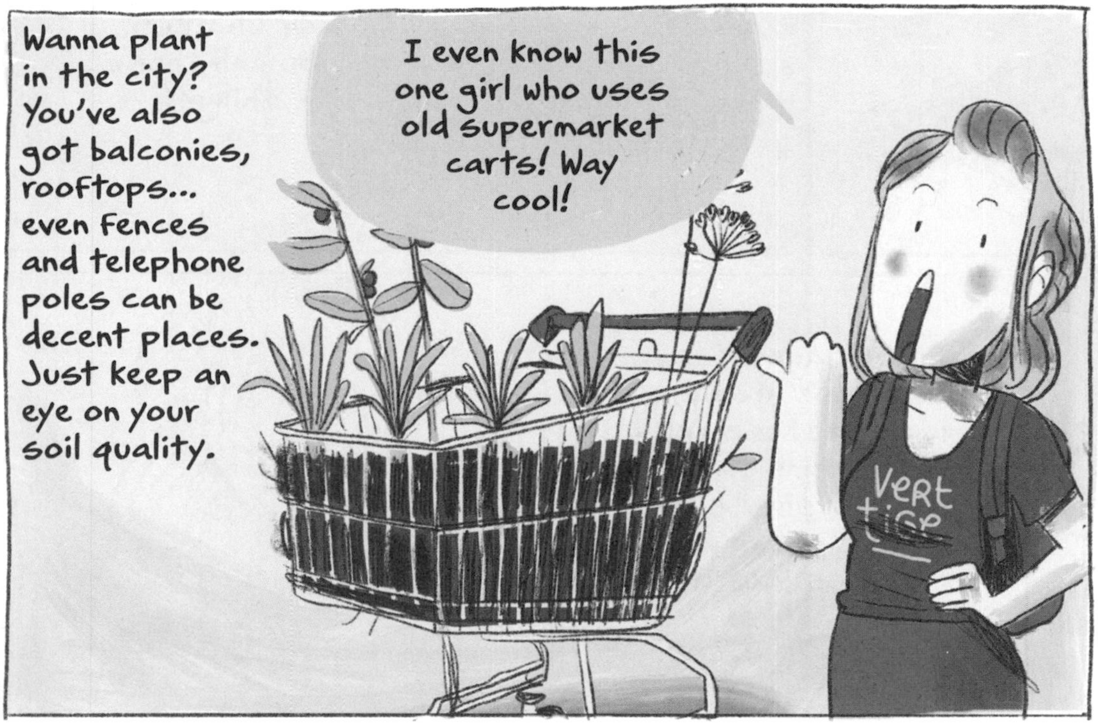
Wanna plant in the city? You've also got balconies, rooftops... even fences and telephone poles can be decent places. Just keep an eye on your soil quality.
I even know this one girl who uses old supermarket carts! Way cool!
Vert tige

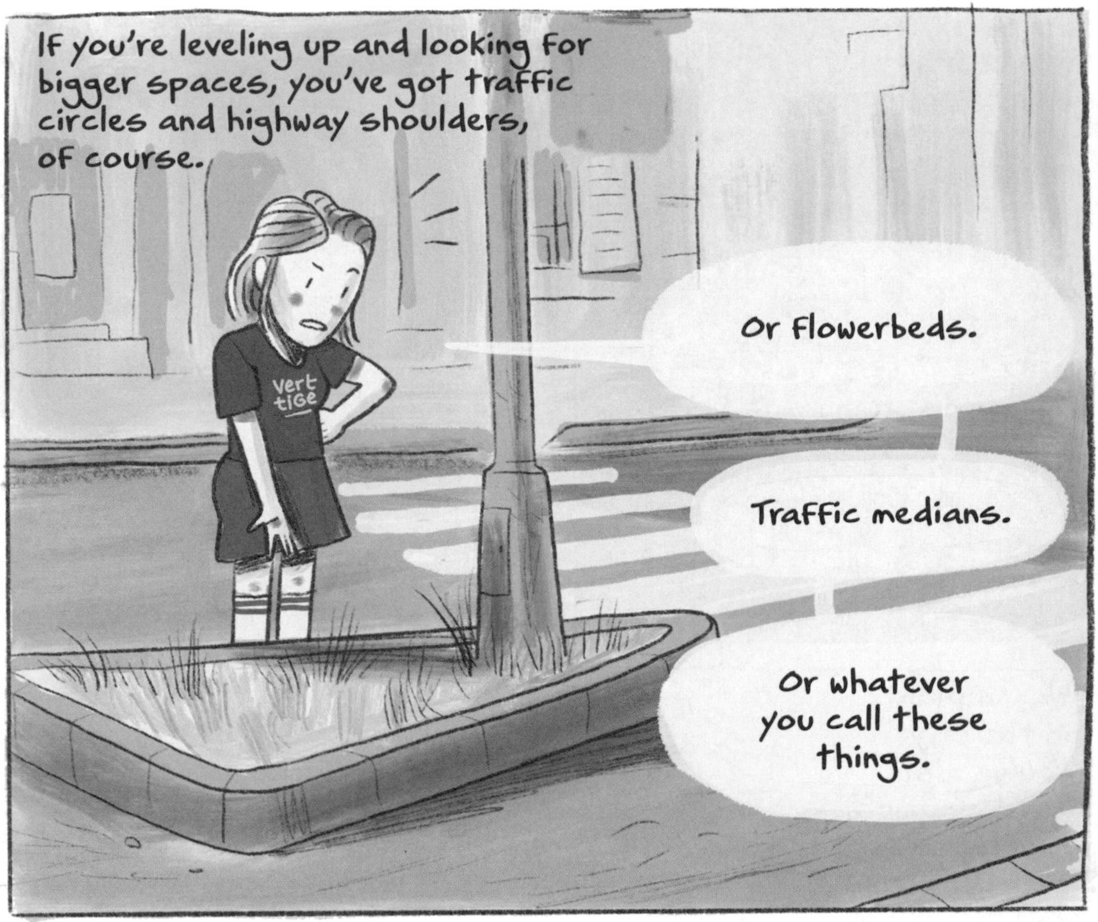
If you're leveling up and looking for bigger spaces, you've got traffic circles and highway shoulders, of course.
Or Flowerbeds.
Traffic medians.
Or whatever you call these things.
Vert tiGe

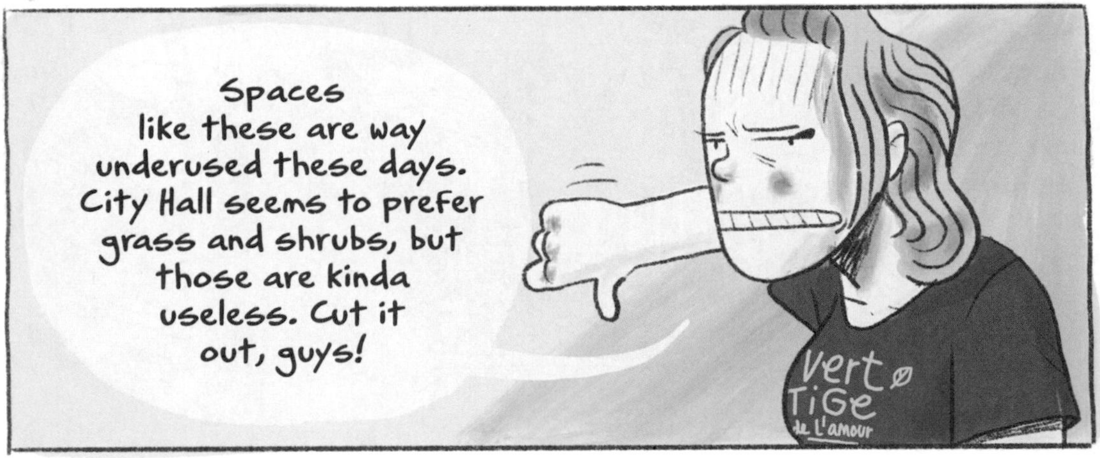
Spaces like these are way underused these days. City Hall seems to prefer grass and shrubs, but those are kinda useless. Cut it out, guys!
Vert TiGe

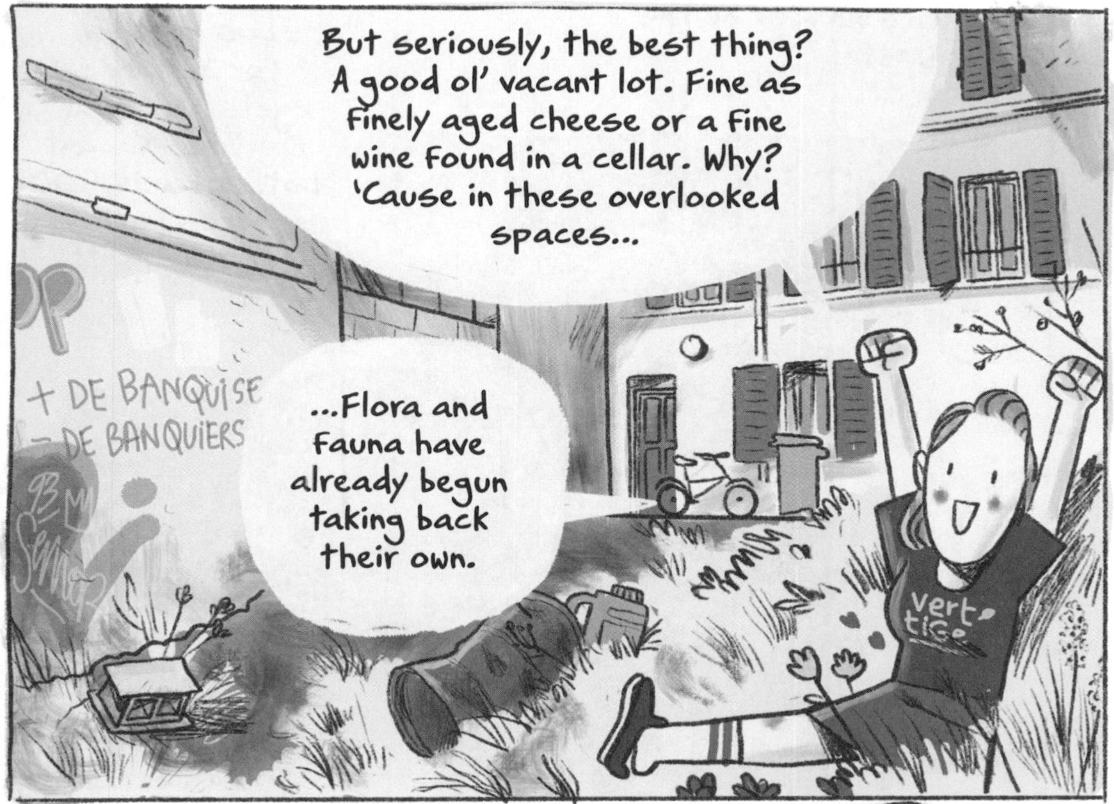
But seriously, the best thing? A good ol' vacant lot. Fine as finely aged cheese or a fine wine found in a cellar. Why? 'Cause in these overlooked spaces...
+ DE BANQUISE
DE BANQUIERS
...Flora and Fauna have already begun taking back their own.
vert tige

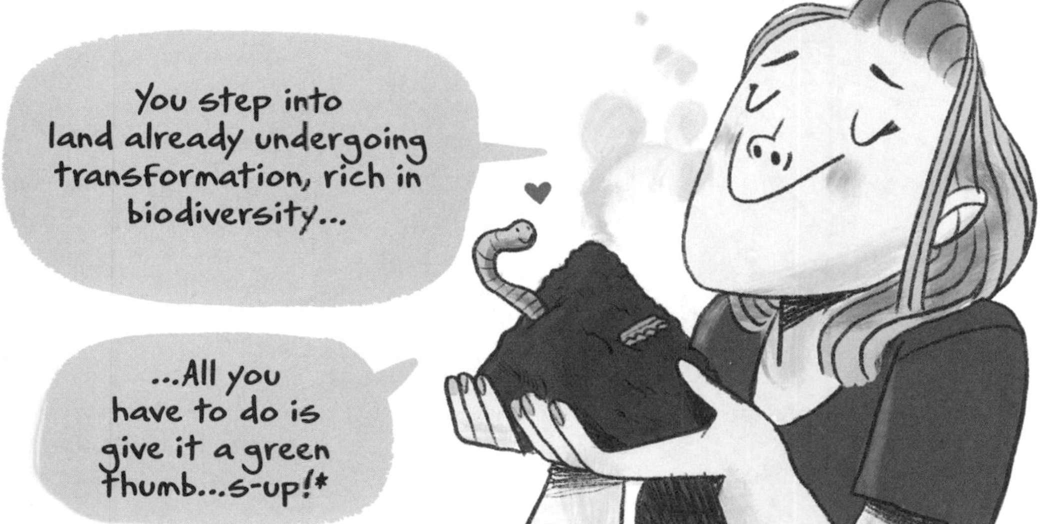
You step into land already undergoing transformation, rich in biodiversity...
...All you have to do is give it a green thumb...s-up!*

pecial Jury Prize for Best Eco-Wordplay, 2013

When you add up all these areas in your city, it gives an idea of the extent of the waste!
Los Angeles, for instance, gets an Oscar for Best Vacant Lots: over 17,500 acres in the metro area*!
17,500 acres
los angeles
central park
Ron Finley ran the numbers... that's more than 20 times the size of Central Park!
Big enough for 725 million tomato plants!
Kinda burns you up inside, don't it?
WEIRD SCIENCE
* Most were abandoned after the 1965 Watts Uprisin

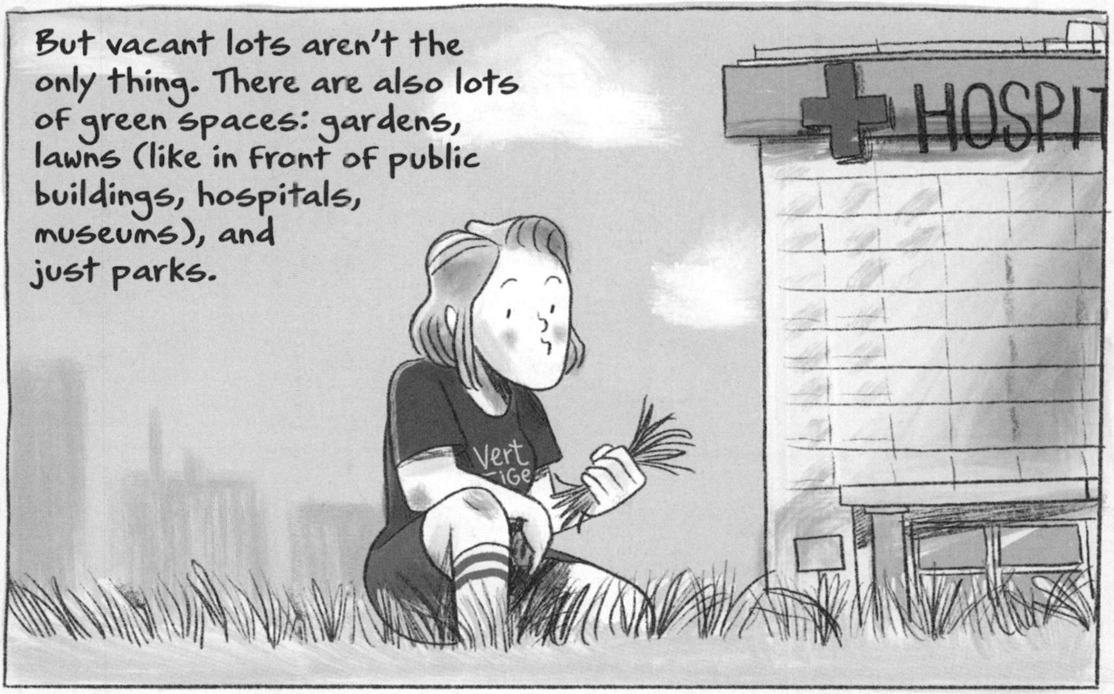
But vacant lots aren't the only thing. There are also lots of green spaces: gardens, lawns (like in front of public buildings, hospitals, museums), and just parks.
HOSPIT
Vert

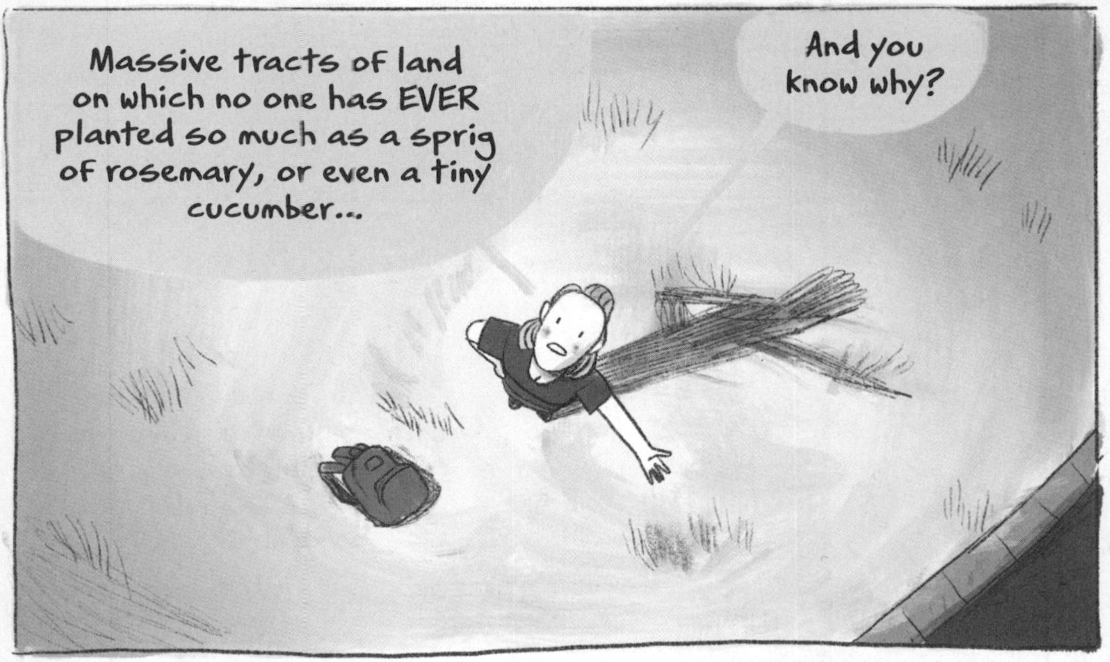
Massive tracts of land on which no one has EVER planted so much as a sprig of rosemary, or even a tiny cucumber...
And you know why?

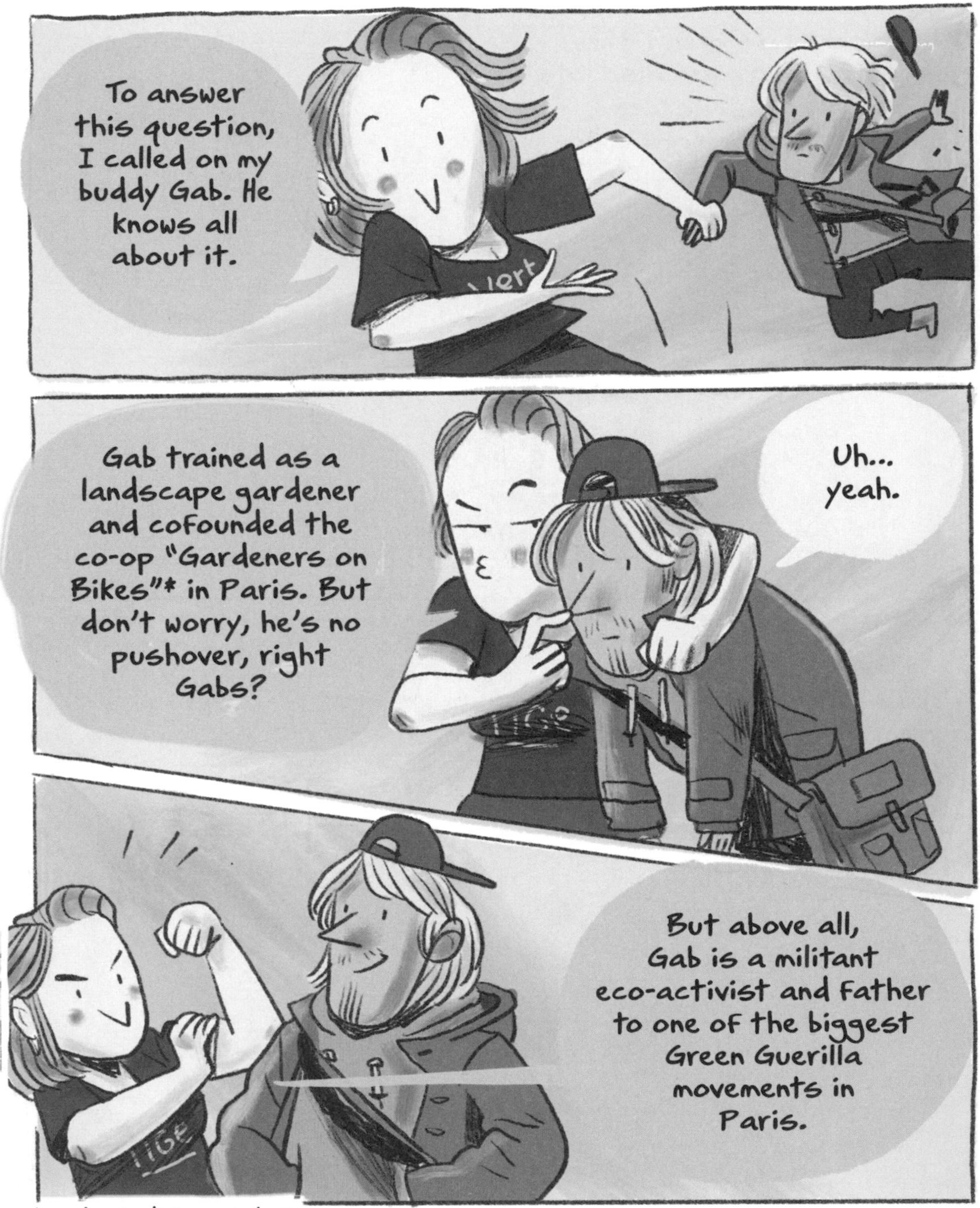
To answer this question, I called on my buddy Gab. He knows all about it.
Vert
Gab trained as a landscape gardener and cofounded the co-op "Gardeners on Bikes"* in Paris. But don't worry, he's no pushover, right Gabs?
Uh... yeah.
But above all, Gab is a militant eco-activist and father to one of the biggest Green Guerilla movements in Paris.

*www.les-jardiniers-a-velo.fr

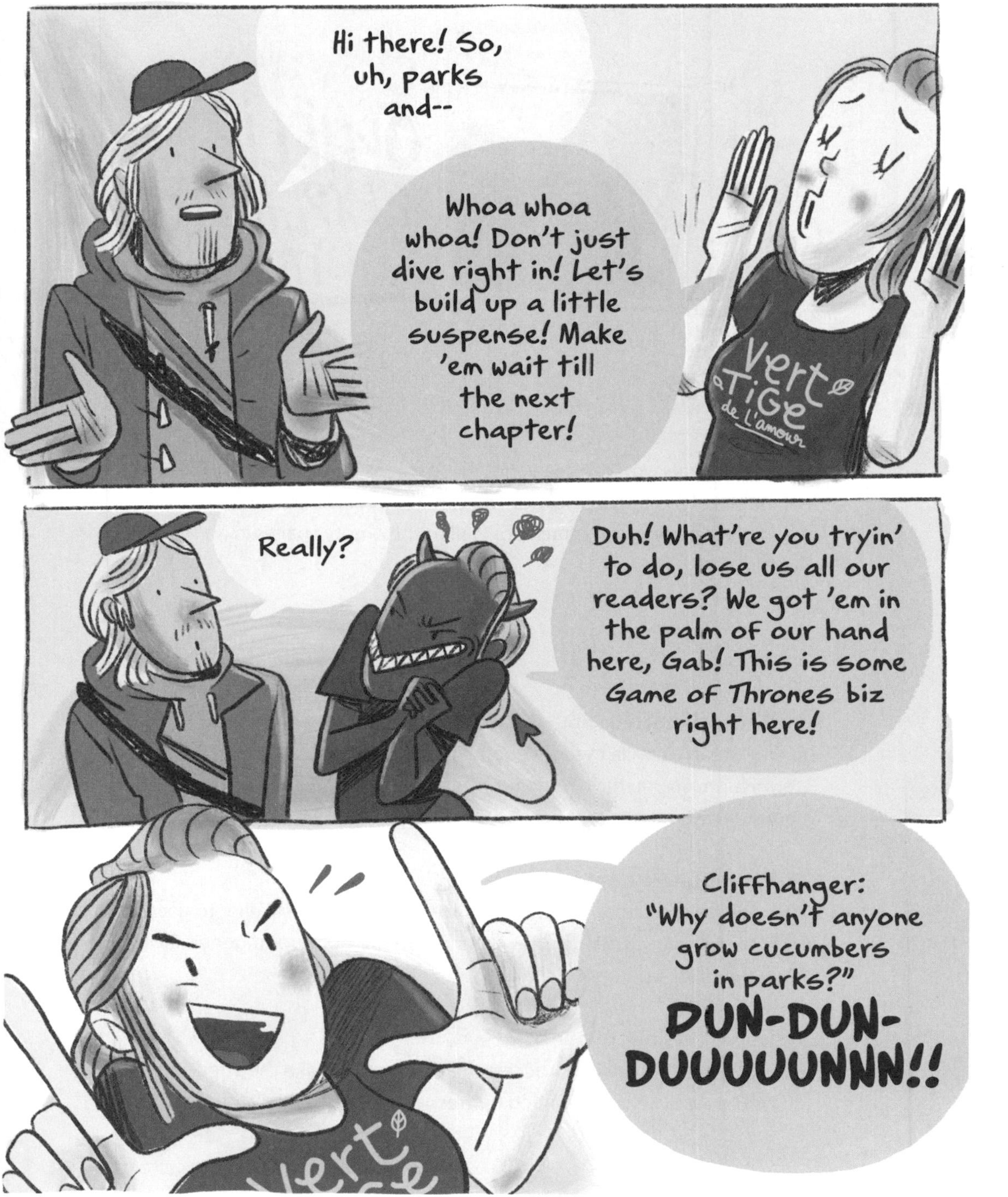

Hi there! So, uh, parks and--
Whoa whoa whoa! Don't just dive right in! Let's build up a little suspense! Make 'em wait till the next chapter!
Vert TiGe de l'amour
Really?
Duh! What're you tryin' to do, lose us all our readers? We got 'em in the palm of our hand here, Gab! This is some Game of Thrones biz right here!
Cliffhanger: "Why doesn't anyone grow cucumbers in parks?" DUN-DUN-DUUUUUNNN!!

"OPHÉLIE EXPLAINS IT ALL"

THE BEST SPOTS FOR GOING GUERILLA GREEN

If you look closely, you can see vegetable gardens at the base of trees in town. It's a beginning. But you can go Green Guerilla in all sorts of places, from a tiny crack in a wall to the empty spaces in an industrial area.

A FEW TIPS FOR PICKING THE PERFECT BATTLEGROUND

1. Pick an unexpected spot.
Going Green Guerilla means veggifying the city without asking permission. So you have to go for somewhere unexpected, not a community garden: we're here to vandalize!

2. Pick somewhere close to home.
If you pick a spot close to where you live or work, you're likelier to pass by more regularly, check on how your plants are doing, and generally, keep the place up better.

3. Pick an accessible, public spot.
Public places that are easily accessed are preferable, like the street. First off, you're less likely to get fined for trespassing on private property.

And second of all, such places give you a chance to interact with curious passersby and tell them what you're up to. Maybe you can win over converts to the guerilla cause!

4. Case the joint.

Before you engage in open battle, inspect the field thoroughly. Is it shady or sunny? Is there a breeze? Will you have to bring in soil? All these questions will influence your choice of plants and even neighborhoods.

Once you've found your ideal spot, remember: you can veggify everything (or almost everything) on the way there, too! For instance, you can hang window boxes on fences, flowerpots on gutters, plant flowers and produce in the middle of dried-out hedges and shrubs that haven't been cared for, etc.

Careful, though! The idea isn't to destroy the urban environment, but rather to invest in and enrich it. Don't go planting a tree in a crack in a wall!

LOOK FOR UNEXPECTED OPPORTUNITIES

I met Gabs from Guerilla Gardening France in the parking lot of a supermarket in Montesson. For a few years now, the group has been taking various actions to prevent urbanization from encroaching on the small farms around the city. They struggle to find alternative ways to citify these areas and create a border between the city and farming zones. To do so, they plant seeds wherever they can—even in the middle of roundabouts.

LAWNS ARE
FOR LOSERS

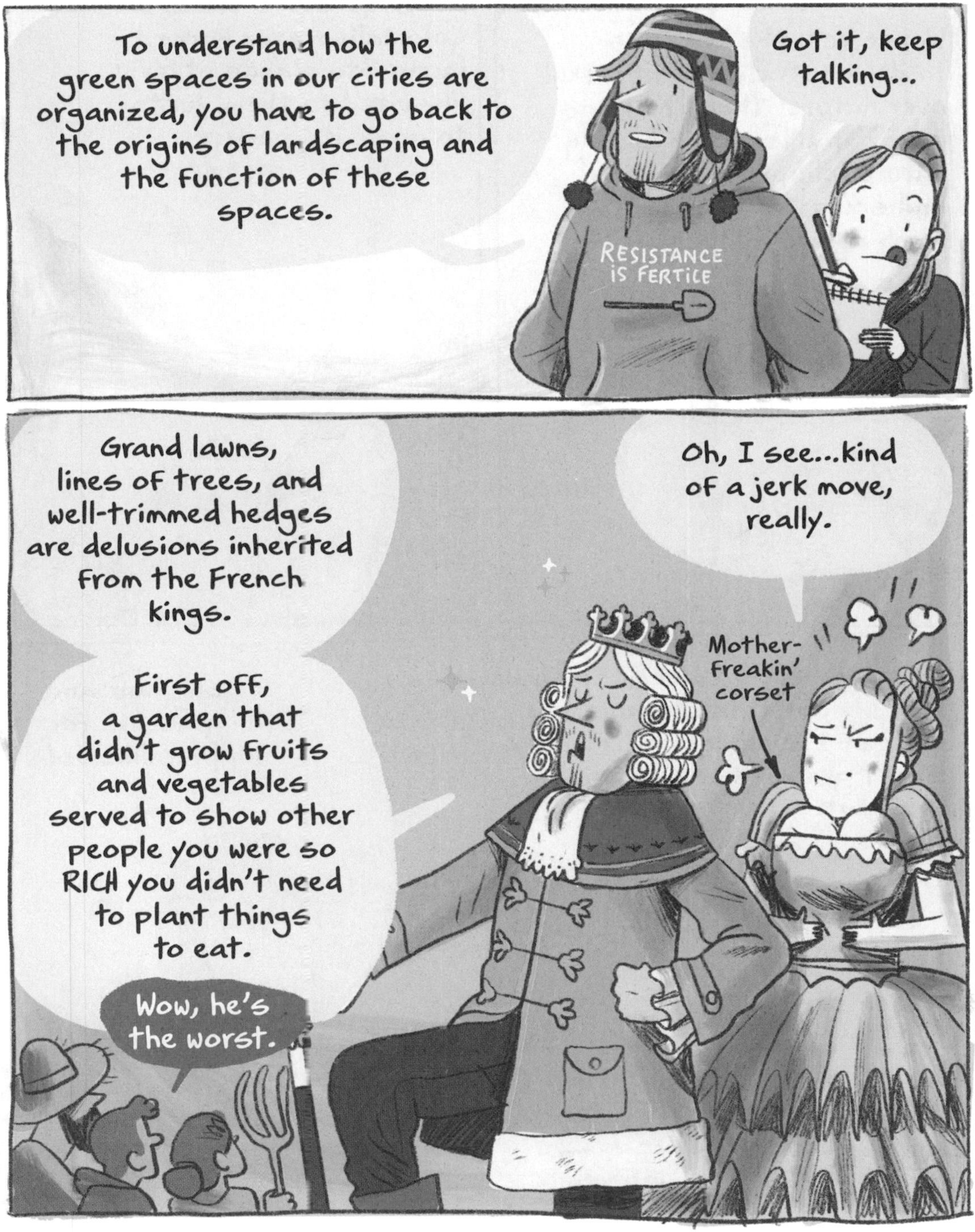
To understand how the green spaces in our cities are organized, you have to go back to the origins of landscaping and the function of these spaces.
Got it, keep talking...
RESISTANCE IS FERTILE
Grand lawns, lines of trees, and well-trimmed hedges are delusions inherited from the French kings.
First off, a garden that didn't grow fruits and vegetables served to show other people you were so RICH you didn't need to plant things to eat.
Oh, I see...kind of a jerk move, really.
Mother-Freakin' corset
Wow, he's the worst.

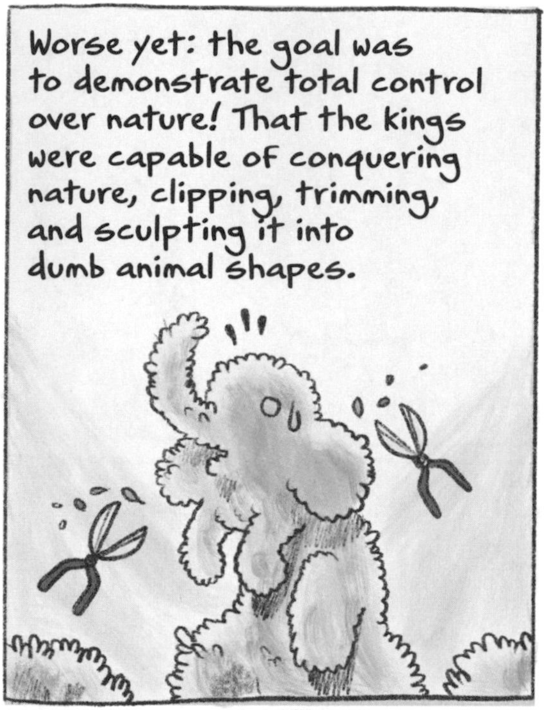
Worse yet: the goal was to demonstrate total control over nature! That the kings were capable of conquering nature, clipping, trimming, and sculpting it into dumb animal shapes.

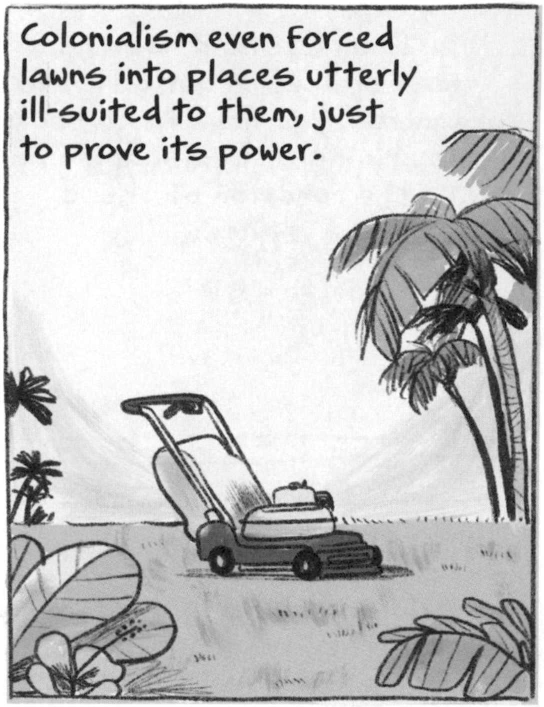
Colonialism even forced lawns into places utterly ill-suited to them, just to prove its power.

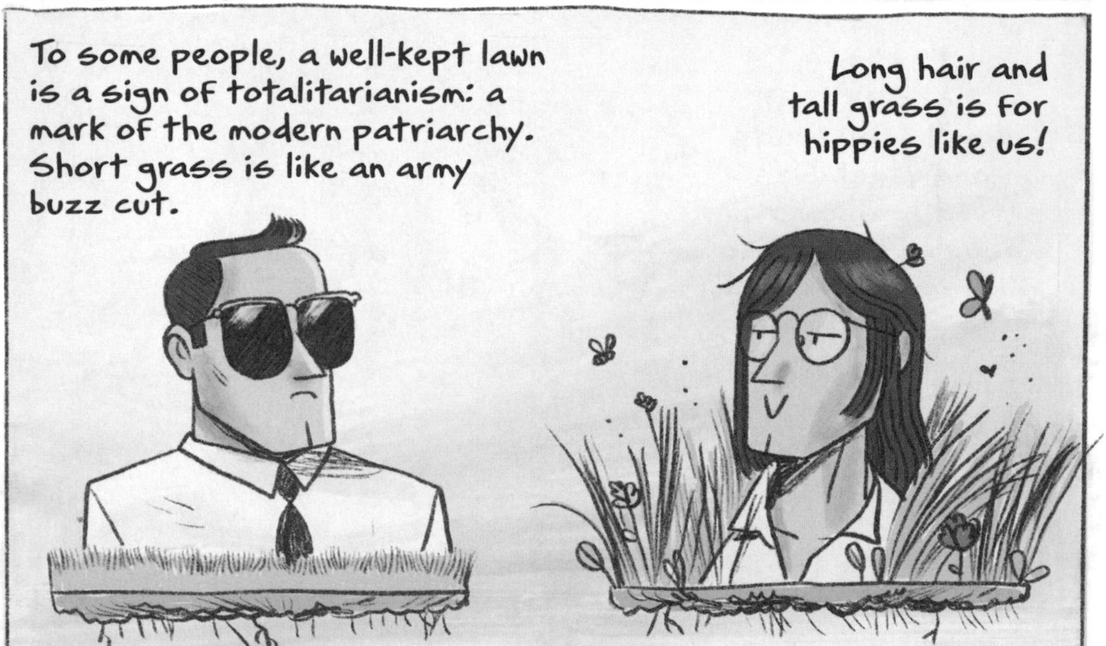
To some people, a well-kept lawn is a sign of totalitarianism: a mark of the modern patriarchy. Short grass is like an army buzz cut.
Long hair and tall grass is for hippies like us!

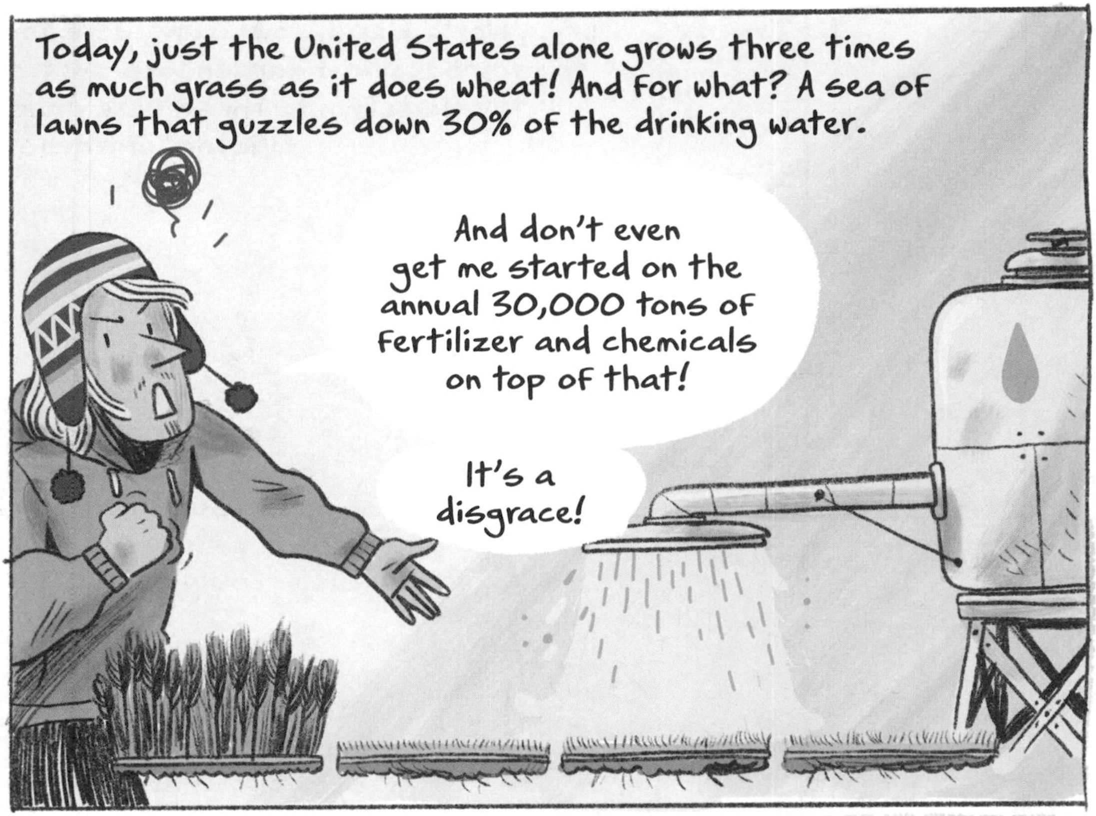
Today, just the United States alone grows three times as much grass as it does wheat! And for what? A sea of lawns that guzzles down 30% of the drinking water.
And don't even get me started on the annual 30,000 tons of fertilizer and chemicals on top of that!
It's a disgrace!

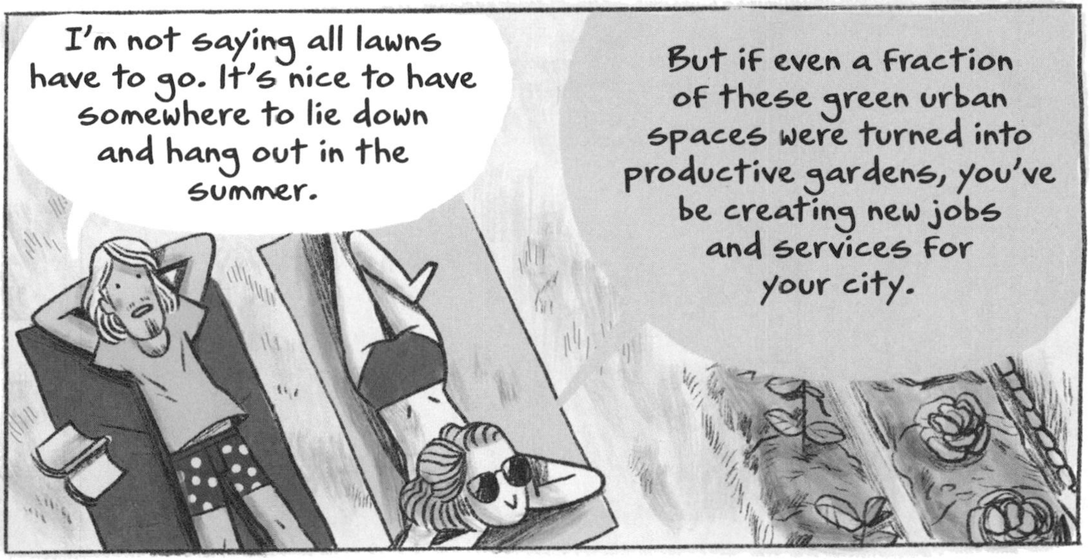
I'm not saying all lawns have to go. It's nice to have somewhere to lie down and hang out in the summer.
But if even a fraction of these green urban spaces were turned into productive gardens, you've be creating new jobs and services for your city.

For some good examples, look to the past. During World War II, Americans were told to grow backyard gardens as part of the war effort. These were called "Victory Gardens."
By the time the war ended, most households were self-sufficient. Can you imagine?
DIG ON FOR VICTORY
GROW YOUR OWN VEGETABLES
Then these gardens became a memory, a symbol of hard times and conflict.
As before, turning them into lawns was a display of luxury, showing that you didn't have to grow your own food anymore. Grampy and Grammy were sick of it!

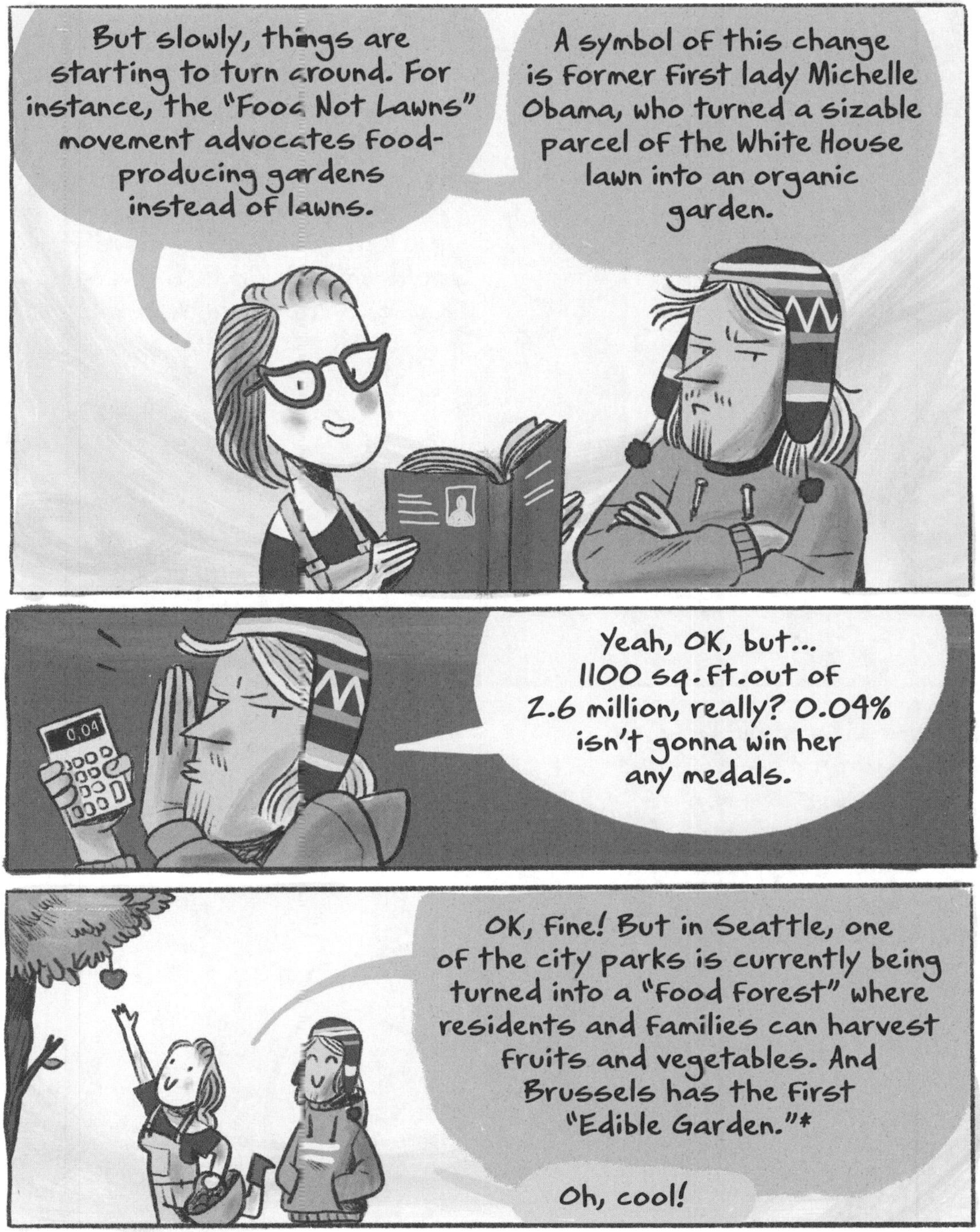
But slowly, things are starting to turn around. For instance, the "Food Not Lawns" movement advocates food-producing gardens instead of lawns.
A symbol of this change is former First lady Michelle Obama, who turned a sizable parcel of the White House lawn into an organic garden.
0,04
Yeah, OK, but... 1100 sq. ft. out of 2.6 million, really? 0.04% isn't gonna win her any medals.
OK, fine! But in Seattle, one of the city parks is currently being turned into a "Food Forest" where residents and families can harvest fruits and vegetables. And Brussels has the first "Edible Garden."*
Oh, cool!

*www.lifeinyourfood.be

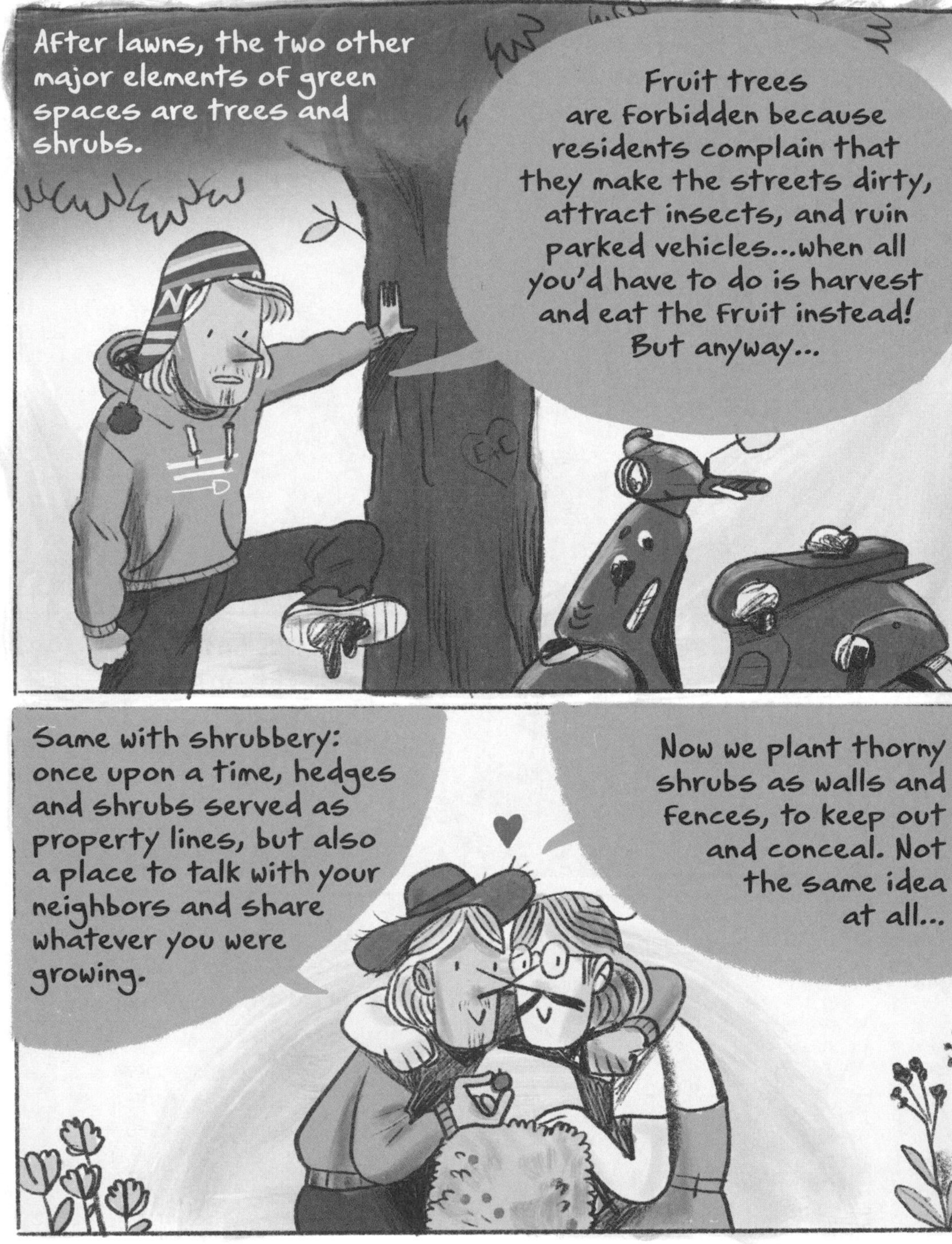
After lawns, the two other major elements of green spaces are trees and shrubs.
Fruit trees are forbidden because residents complain that they make the streets dirty, attract insects, and ruin parked vehicles...when all you'd have to do is harvest and eat the fruit instead! But anyway...
Same with shrubbery: once upon a time, hedges and shrubs served as property lines, but also a place to talk with your neighbors and share whatever you were growing.
Now we plant thorny shrubs as walls and fences, to keep out and conceal. Not the same idea at all...

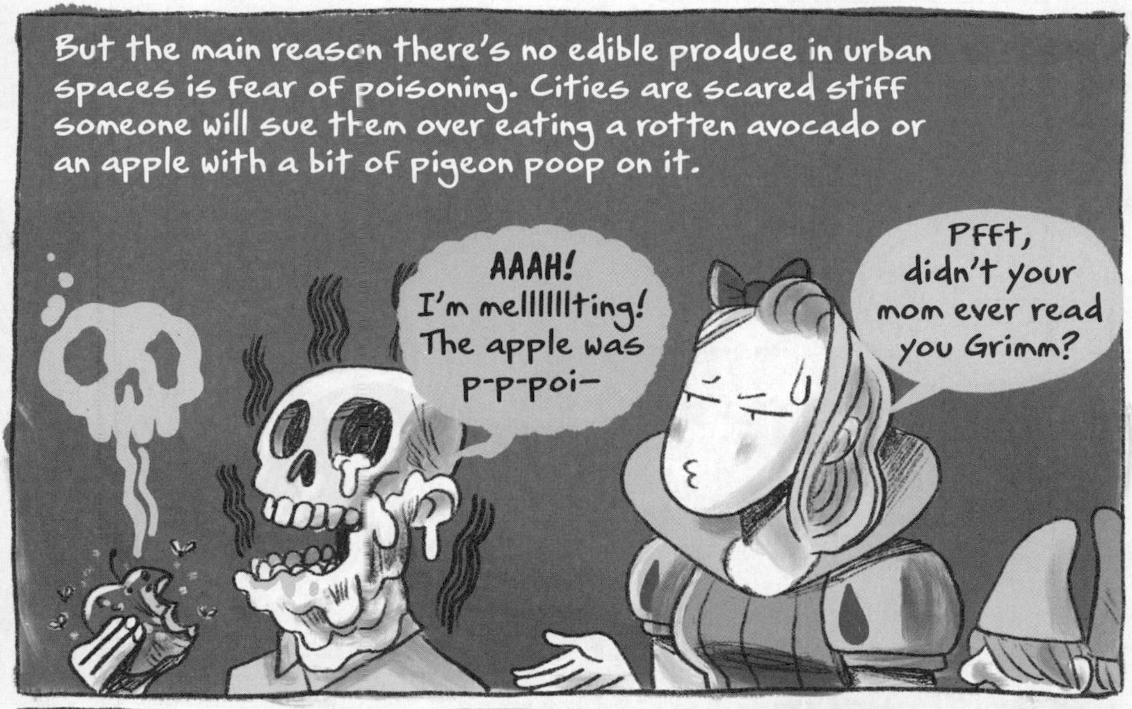
But the main reason there's no edible produce in urban spaces is fear of poisoning. Cities are scared stiff someone will sue them over eating a rotten avocado or an apple with a bit of pigeon poop on it.
AAAH! I'm mellllllting! The apple was p-p-poi–
Pfft, didn't your mom ever read you Grimm?

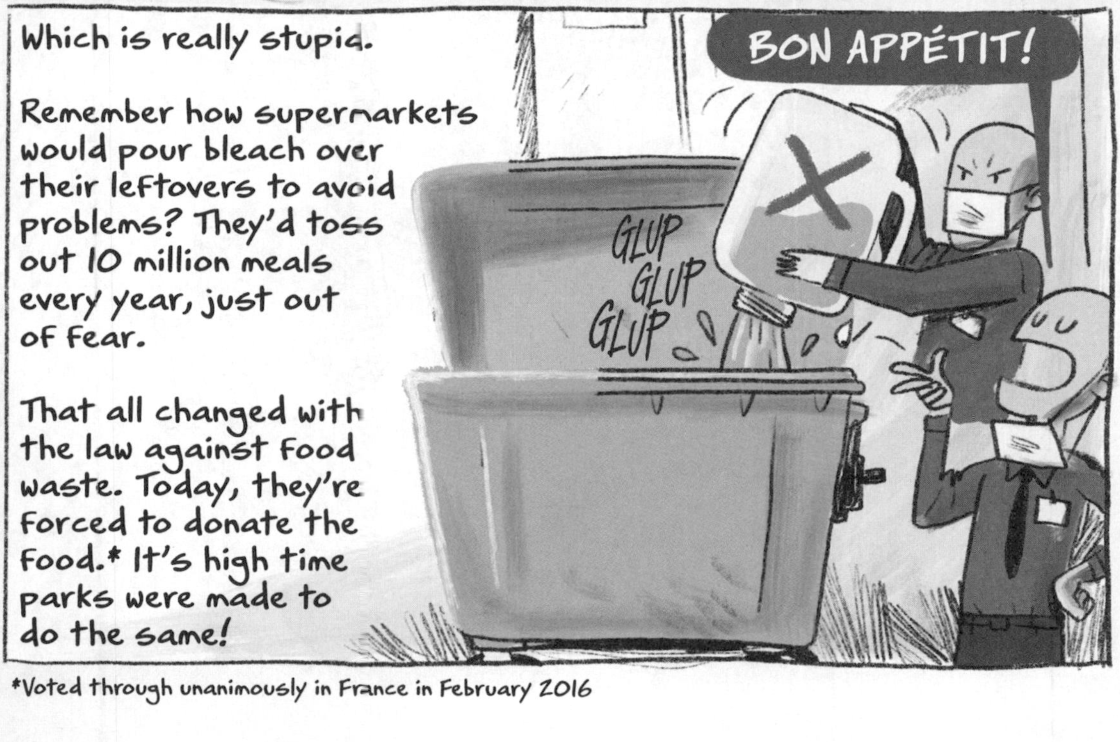
Which is really stupid.
Remember how supermarkets would pour bleach over their leftovers to avoid problems? They'd toss out 10 million meals every year, just out of fear.
That all changed with the law against food waste. Today, they're forced to donate the food.* It's high time parks were made to do the same!
BON APPÉTIT!
GLUP
GLUP
GLUP

*Voted through unanimously in France in February 2016

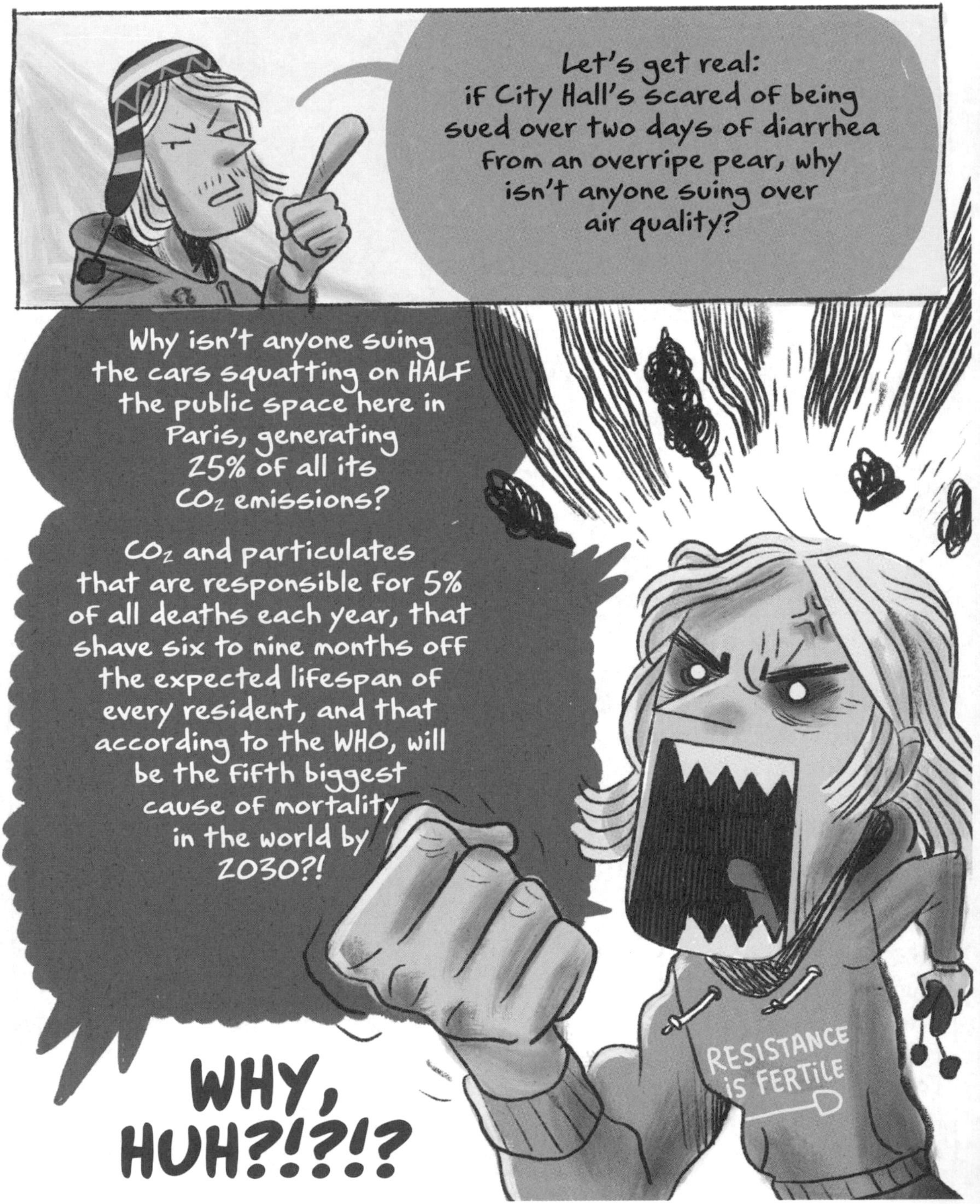

Let's get real: if City Hall's scared of being sued over two days of diarrhea from an overripe pear, why isn't anyone suing over air quality?
Why isn't anyone suing the cars squatting on HALF the public space here in Paris, generating 25% of all its CO_2 emissions?
CO_2 and particulates that are responsible for 5% of all deaths each year, that shave six to nine months off the expected lifespan of every resident, and that according to the WHO, will be the fifth biggest cause of mortality in the world by 2030?!
WHY, HUH?!?!?
RESISTANCE IS FERTILE

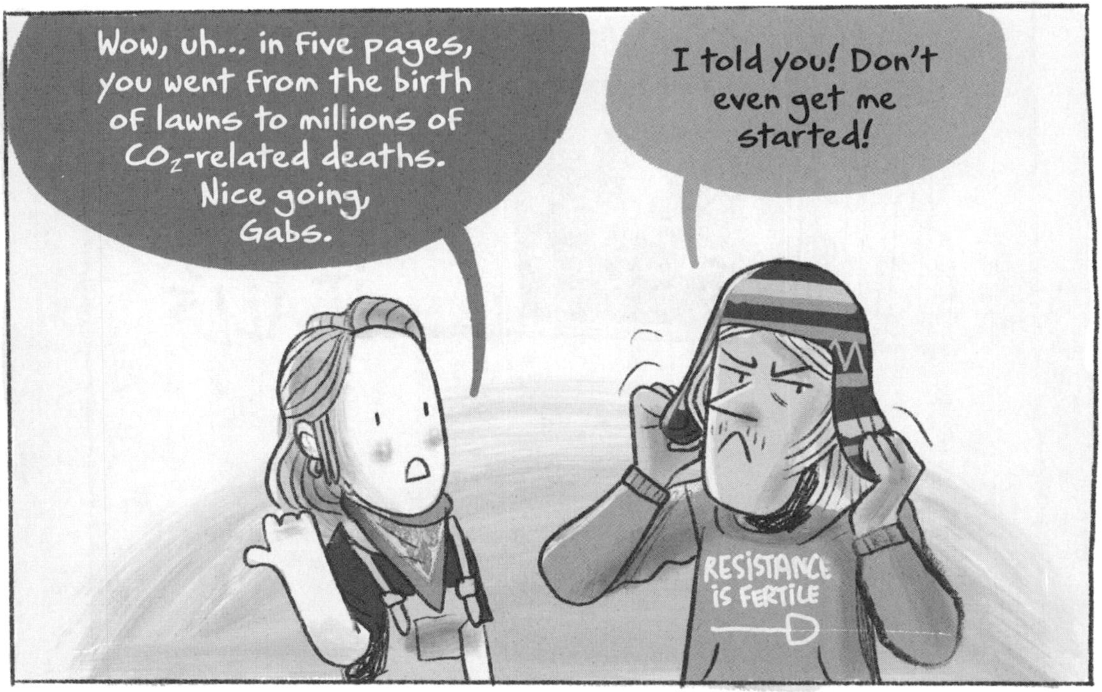
Wow, uh... in five pages, you went from the birth of lawns to millions of CO_2-related deaths. Nice going, Gabs.
I told you! Don't even get me started!
RESISTANCE IS FERTILE

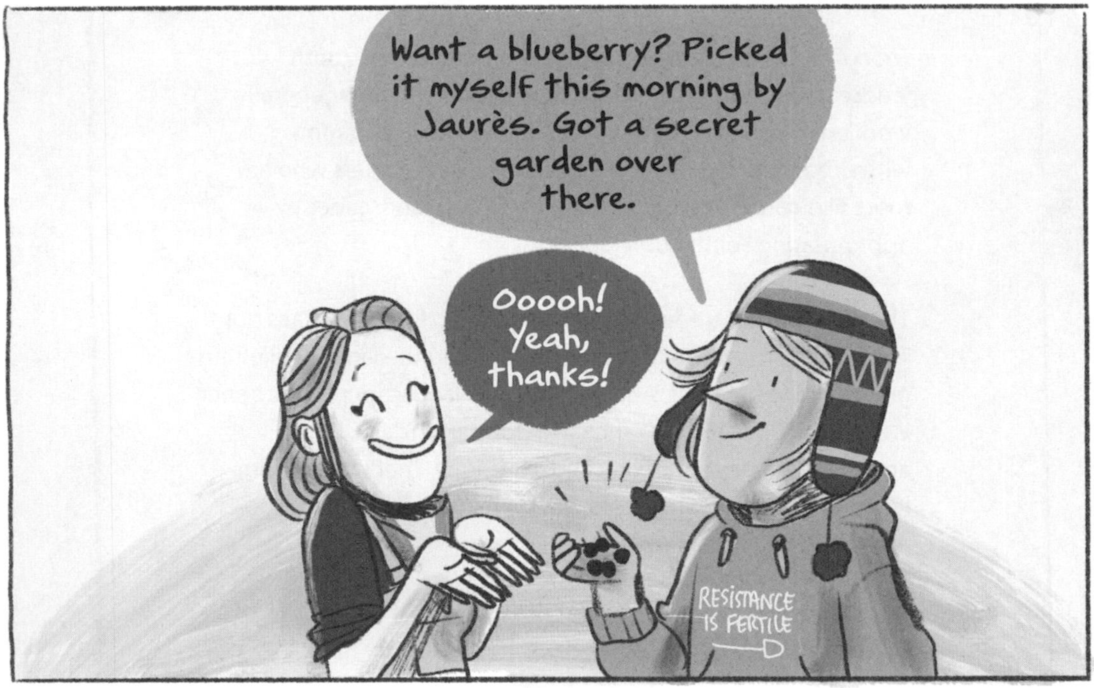
Want a blueberry? Picked it myself this morning by Jaurès. Got a secret garden over there.
Ooooh! Yeah, thanks!
RESISTANCE IS FERTILE

OPHÉLIE EXPLAINS IT ALL

LAWNS ARE FOR LOSERS

Ever notice how there's rarely anything edible growing in public parks? No apple trees, not even a solitary zucchini?

LANDSCAPING: WHAT'S IT ALL ABOUT?

First of all, landscaping is a profession that includes both landscape architects and landscape engineers, who generally work on much larger scales. They have more in common with urban planners. And then there are landscapers who are more like gardeners. Anyone can become a landscaper by appropriating some public space.

The most important landscapers of all are…farmers! That's right! They do the most when it comes to shaping the land by planting grains and vegetables. And yet the word landscaper, or gardener, is usually associated in France with formal gardens, highly artificial, with ties to nobility and ceremony. That's where big lawns in cities come from. No way were they planting potatoes and cabbage in the parks!

In the city, there are lots of places for growing things that are going unused. Members of Guerilla Gardening have claimed these spaces to grow food-producing plants (pear and apple trees, hops, etc…). In this way, they've made a visible garden near Point Éphémère here in Paris, along the banks of the Canal Saint-Martin a Paris.

THE PERFECT GEAR
FOR A GREEN GUERILLA

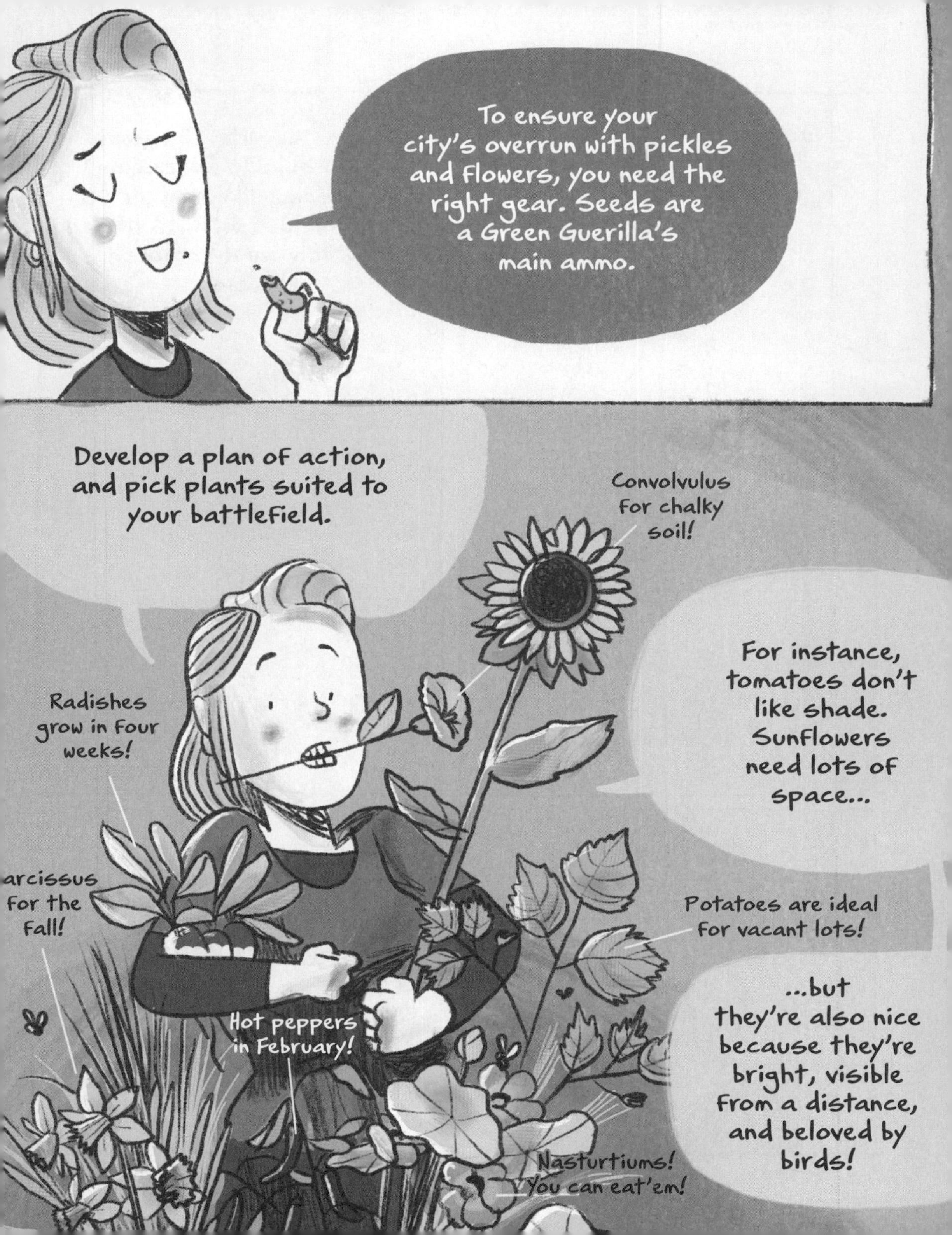
To ensure your city's overrun with pickles and flowers, you need the right gear. Seeds are a Green Guerilla's main ammo.
Develop a plan of action, and pick plants suited to your battlefield.
Convolvulus for chalky soil!
For instance, tomatoes don't like shade. Sunflowers need lots of space...
Radishes grow in four weeks!
arcissus for the fall!
Potatoes are ideal for vacant lots!
...but they're also nice because they're bright, visible from a distance, and beloved by birds!
Hot peppers in February!
Nasturtiums! You can eat'em!

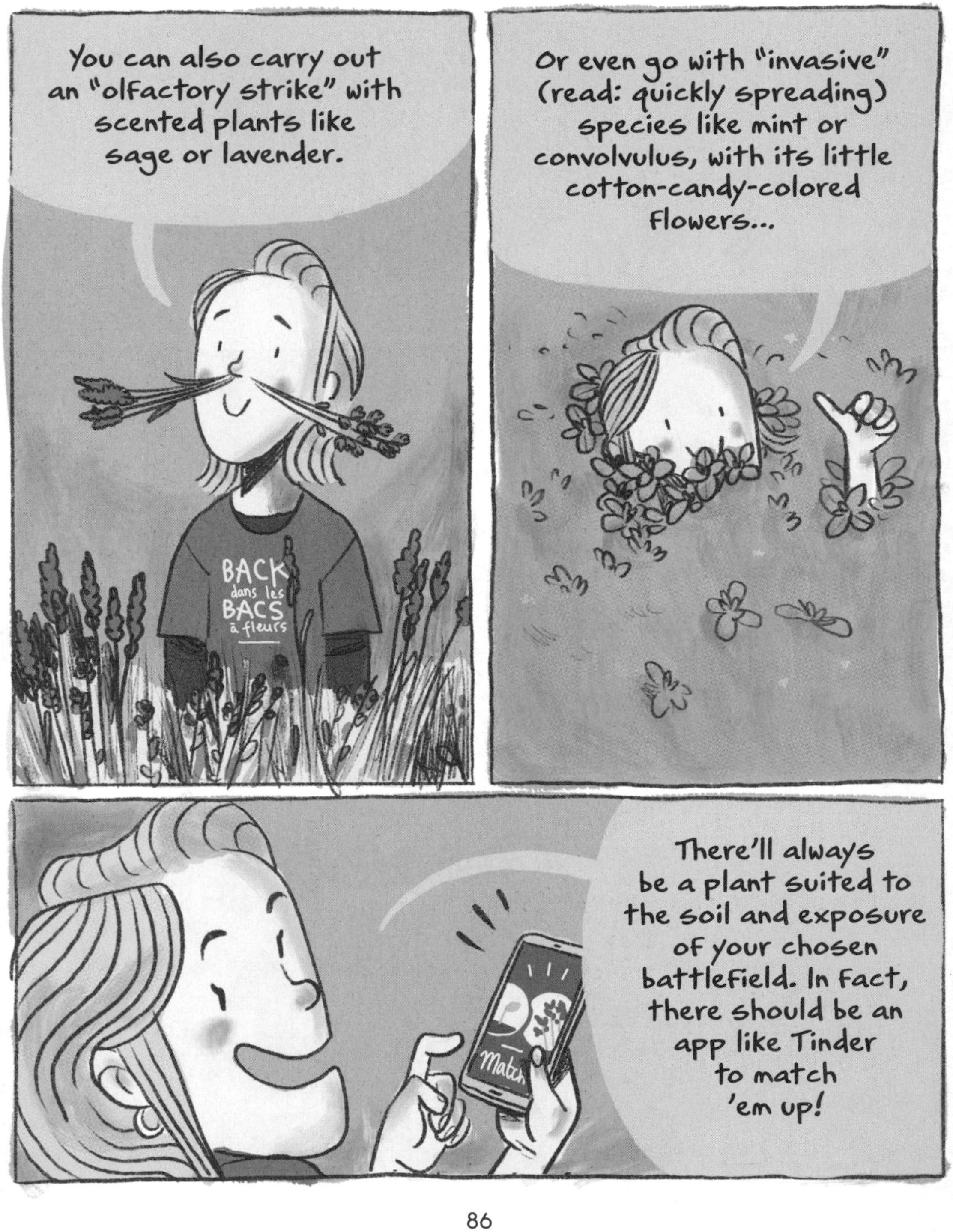
You can also carry out an "olfactory strike" with scented plants like sage or lavender.
BACK dans les BACS à fleurs
Or even go with "invasive" (read: quickly spreading) species like mint or convolvulus, with its little cotton-candy-colored flowers...
Match
There'll always be a plant suited to the soil and exposure of your chosen battlefield. In fact, there should be an app like Tinder to match 'em up!

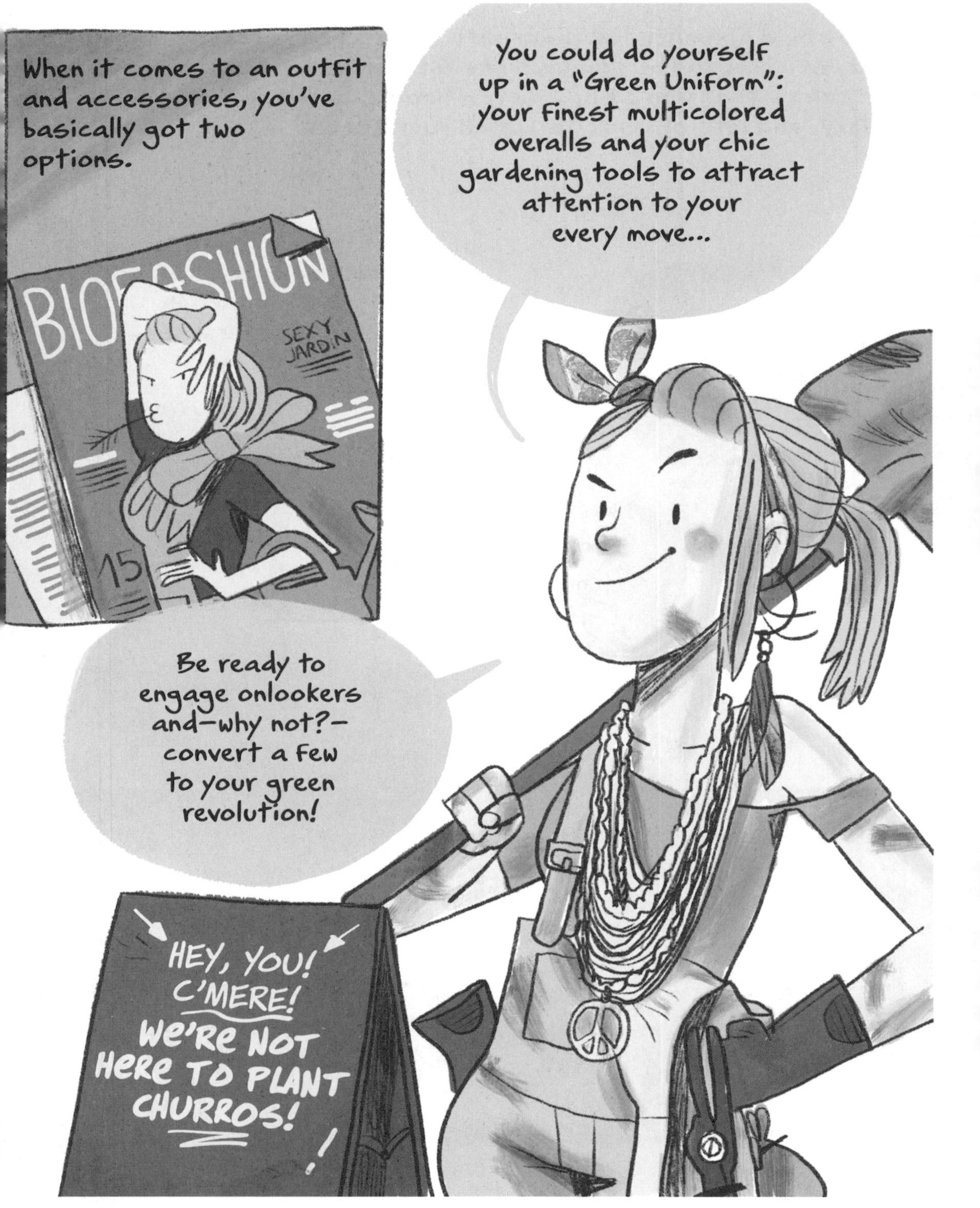

When it comes to an outfit and accessories, you've basically got two options.
BIOFASHION
SEXY JARDIN
15
You could do yourself up in a "Green Uniform": your finest multicolored overalls and your chic gardening tools to attract attention to your every move...
Be ready to engage onlookers and—why not?—convert a few to your green revolution!
HEY, YOU! C'MERE! WE'RE NOT HERE TO PLANT CHURROS!

Or you could go under the radar with a "Green Undercover" theme, sticking to the shadows like Batman with a hoe. Dark colors that won't show dirt, a hoodie, an air of mystery, and lots of pockets for all your seeds.

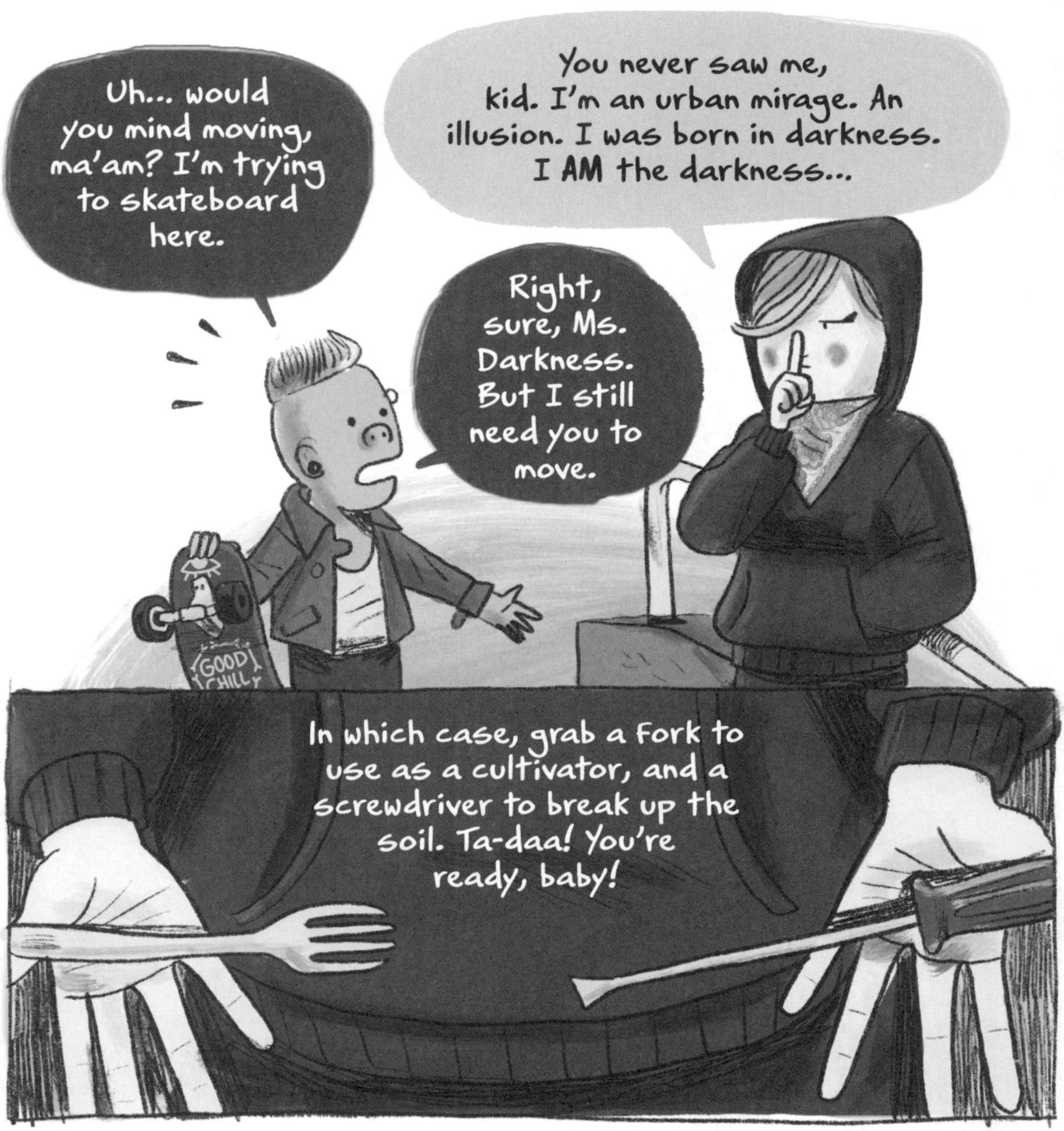
Uh... would you mind moving, ma'am? I'm trying to skateboard here.
You never saw me, kid. I'm an urban mirage. An illusion. I was born in darkness. I AM the darkness...
Right, sure, Ms. Darkness. But I still need you to move.
In which case, grab a fork to use as a cultivator, and a screwdriver to break up the soil. Ta-daa! You're ready, baby!

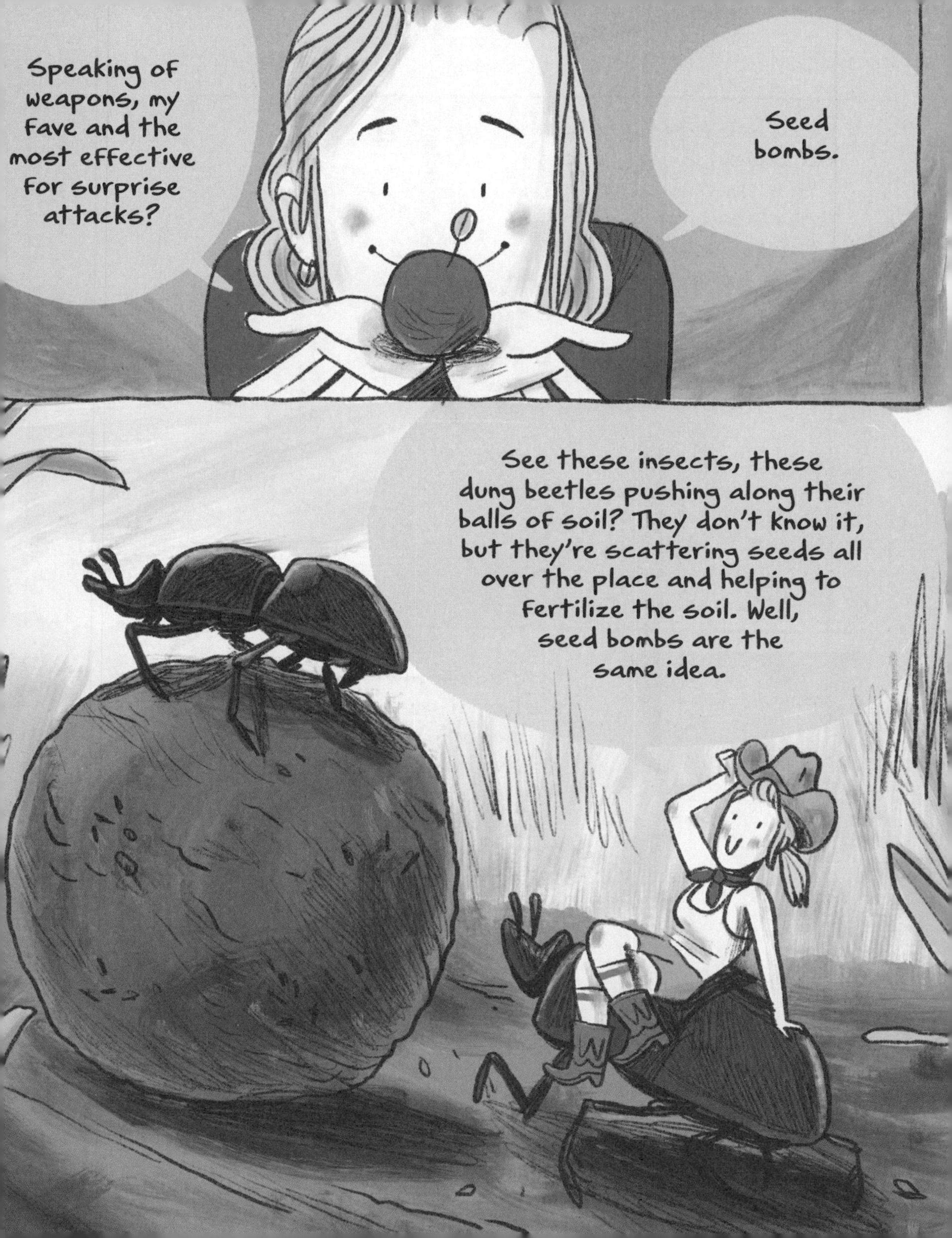
Speaking of weapons, my fave and the most effective for surprise attacks?
Seed bombs.
See these insects, these dung beetles pushing along their balls of soil? They don't know it, but they're scattering seeds all over the place and helping to fertilize the soil. Well, seed bombs are the same idea.

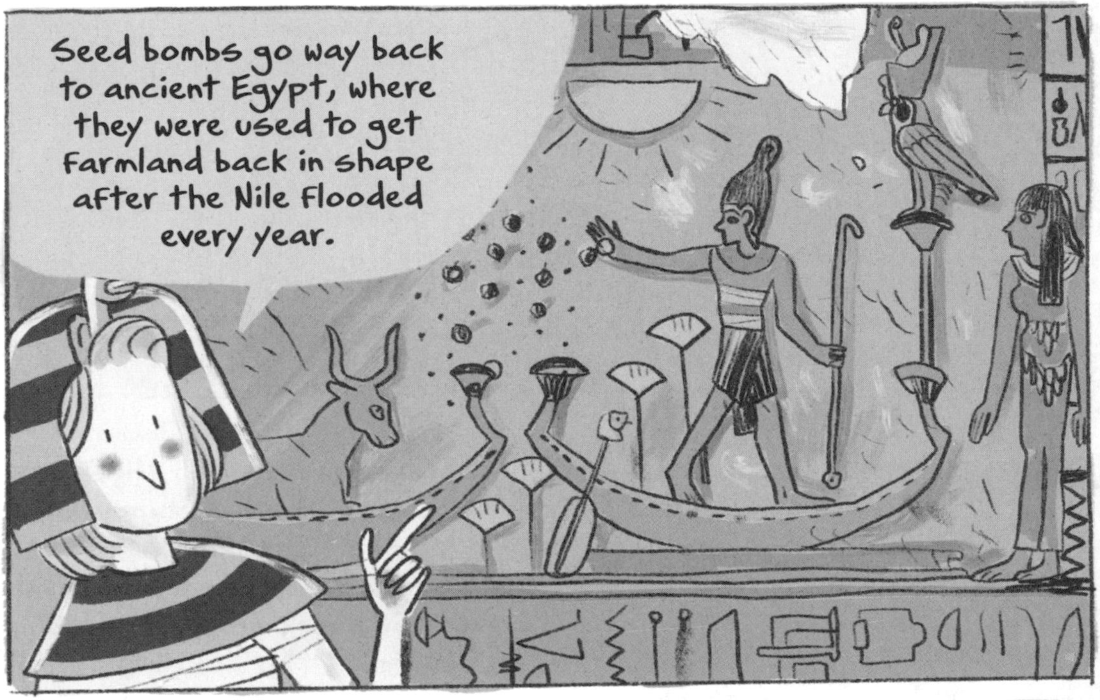
Seed bombs go way back to ancient Egypt, where they were used to get farmland back in shape after the Nile flooded every year.

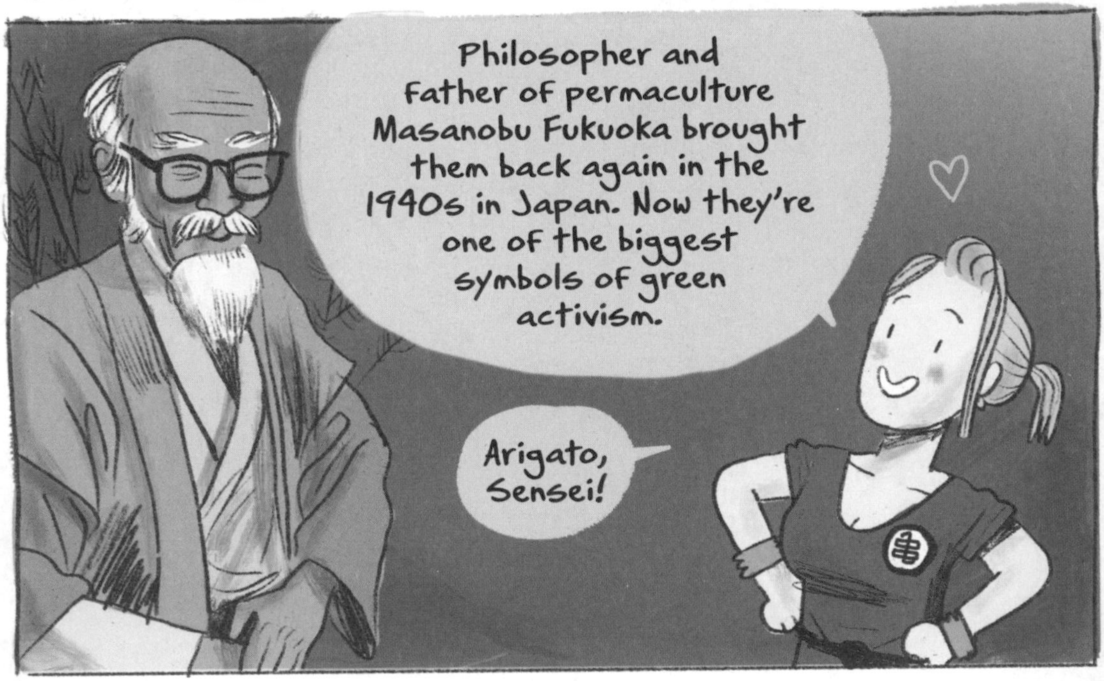
Philosopher and father of permaculture Masanobu Fukuoka brought them back again in the 1940s in Japan. Now they're one of the biggest symbols of green activism.
Arigato, Sensei!

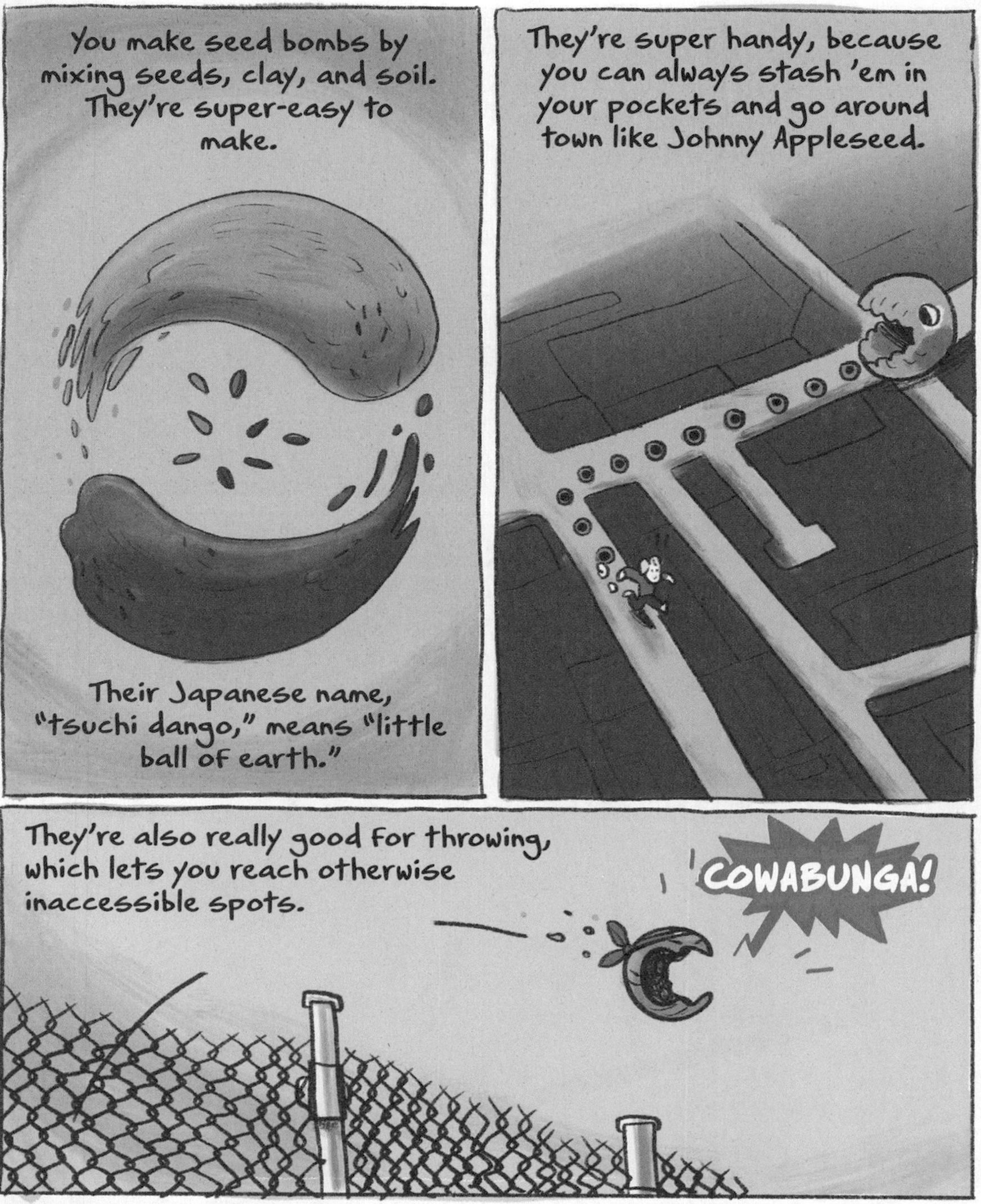
You make seed bombs by mixing seeds, clay, and soil. They're super-easy to make.
Their Japanese name, "tsuchi dango," means "little ball of earth."
They're super handy, because you can always stash 'em in your pockets and go around town like Johnny Appleseed.
They're also really good for throwing, which lets you reach otherwise inaccessible spots.
COWABUNGA!

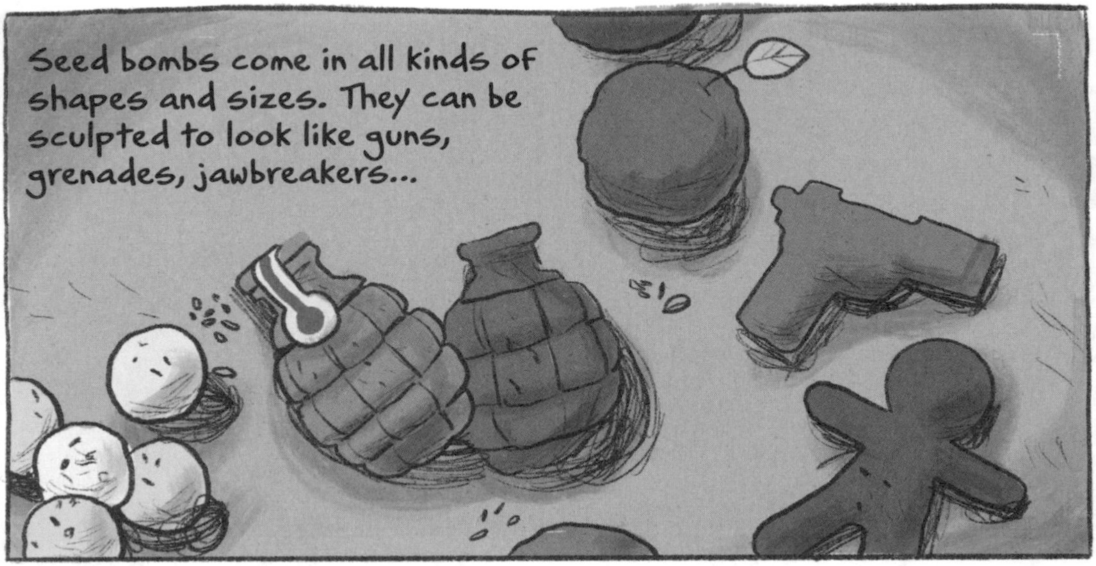
Seed bombs come in all kinds of shapes and sizes. They can be sculpted to look like guns, grenades, jawbreakers...

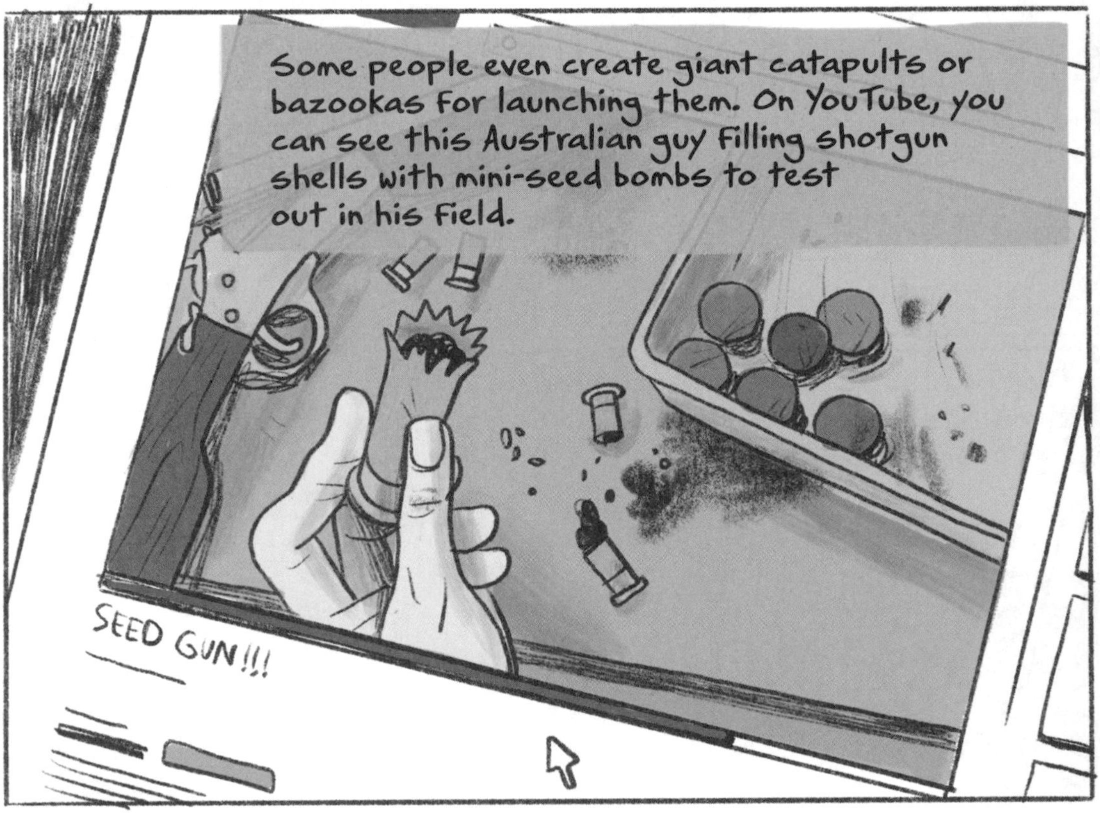
Some people even create giant catapults or bazookas for launching them. On YouTube, you can see this Australian guy filling shotgun shells with mini-seed bombs to test out in his field.
SEED GUN!!!

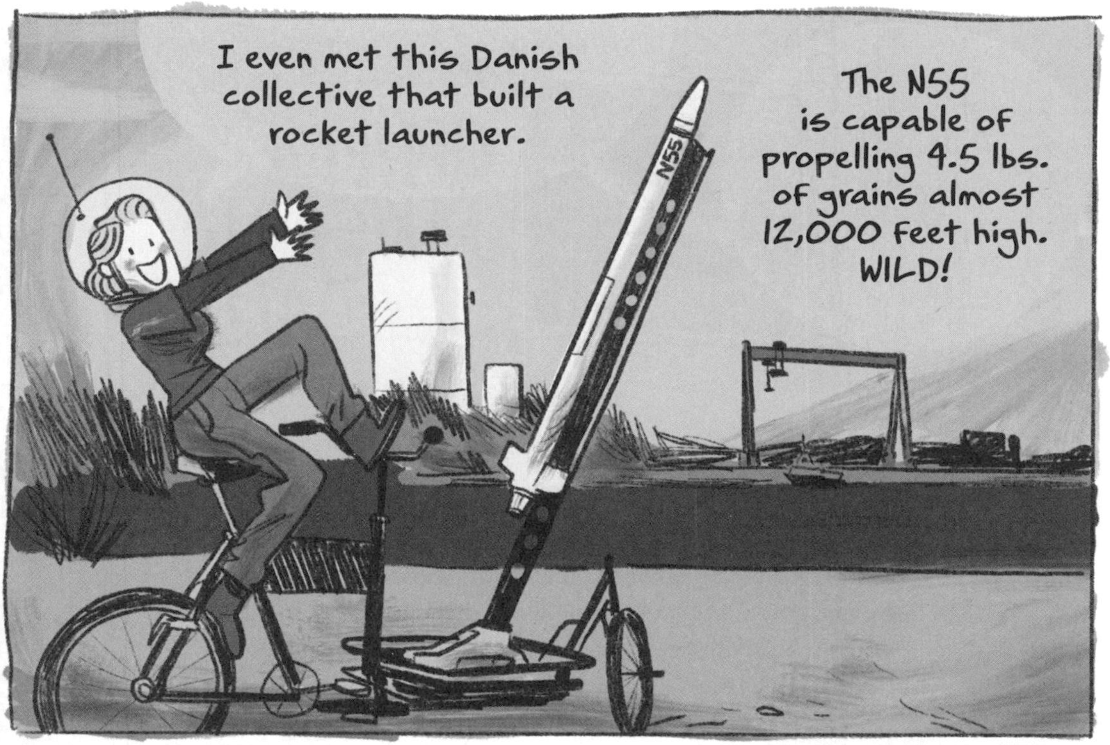
I even met this Danish collective that built a rocket launcher.
N55
The N55 is capable of propelling 4.5 lbs. of grains almost 12,000 feet high. WILD!

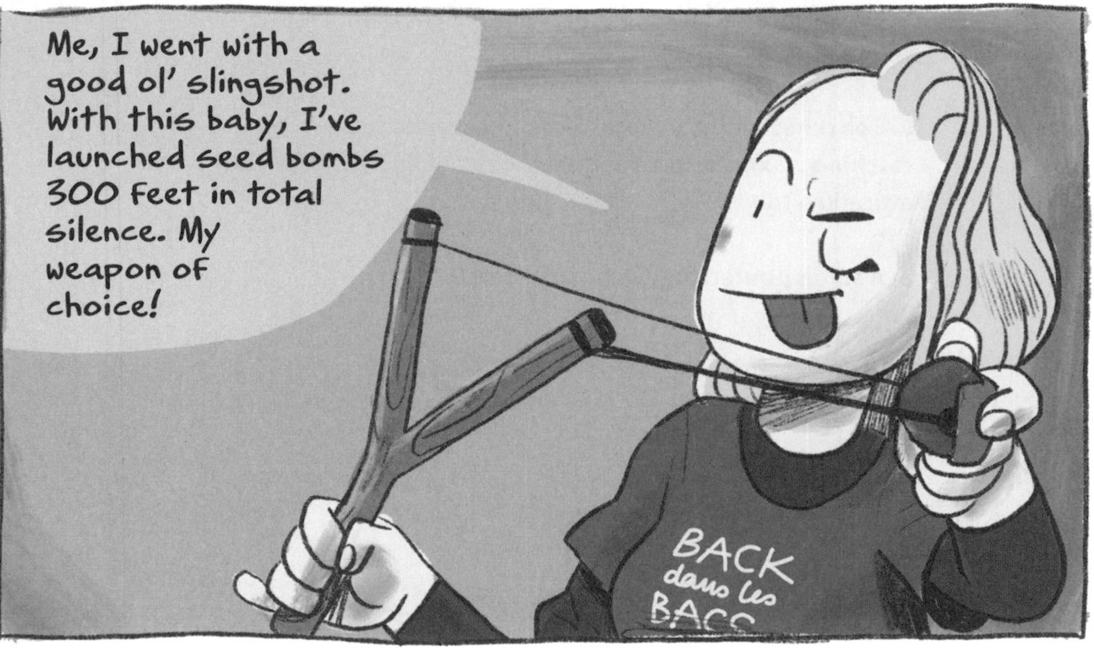
Me, I went with a good ol' slingshot. With this baby, I've launched seed bombs 300 feet in total silence. My weapon of choice!
BACK
dans les
BACS

OPHÉLIE EXPLAINS IT ALL

THE PERFECT GEAR FOR A GREEN GUERILLA

In Montreuil, I met Juliette, who uses the Instagram account @plantplantzineplant to disseminate fanzines about how to get free plants. Her subscribers can download her guides for free and print them out. With her advice, you'll be able to trick yourself out with all the necessary gear to be a good Green Guerilla!

1. Plastic bottles for seedlings: a few balls of clay, soil, and you've got your own tiny greenhouse!

2. Bobeches (glass or metal discs, like candle saucers, for catching wax): use these as dishes to get things to sprout, like avocado pits.

3. A sugar pourer: for sowing small seeds.

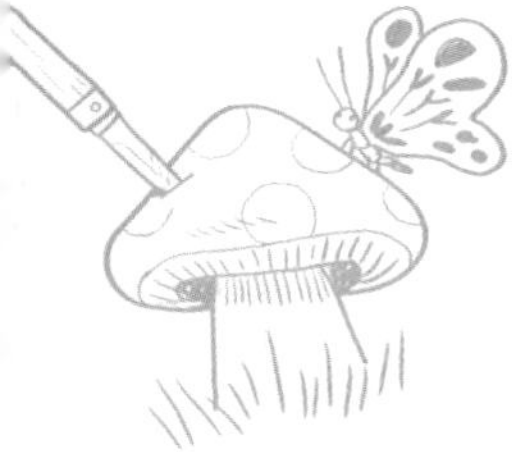

4. Seed bombs (and a slingshot!): 1/3 natural clay + 2/3 compost or soil. Make a ball and put a few seeds inside (preferably ones that sprout easily). Then just go and toss 'em somewhere in town!

5. An oya: a porous clay vessel that you plant in your garden. Pour water in, and it will seep through the walls to irrigate the soil. Plug the top so the water doesn't evaporate.

6. And of course, tools: spade, hoe, shovel, etc.

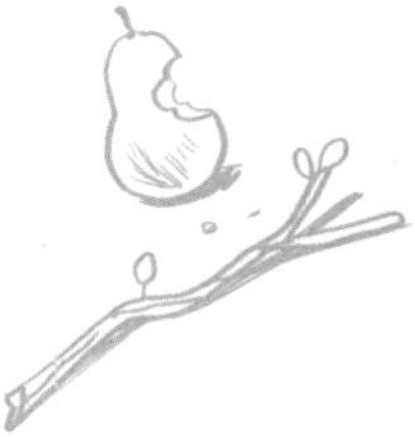

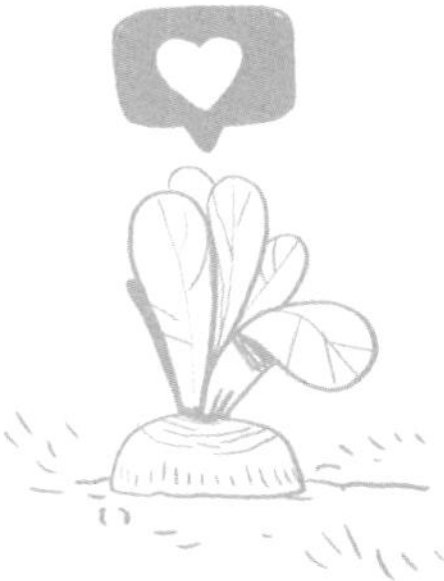

GARDENING
AND HEALING

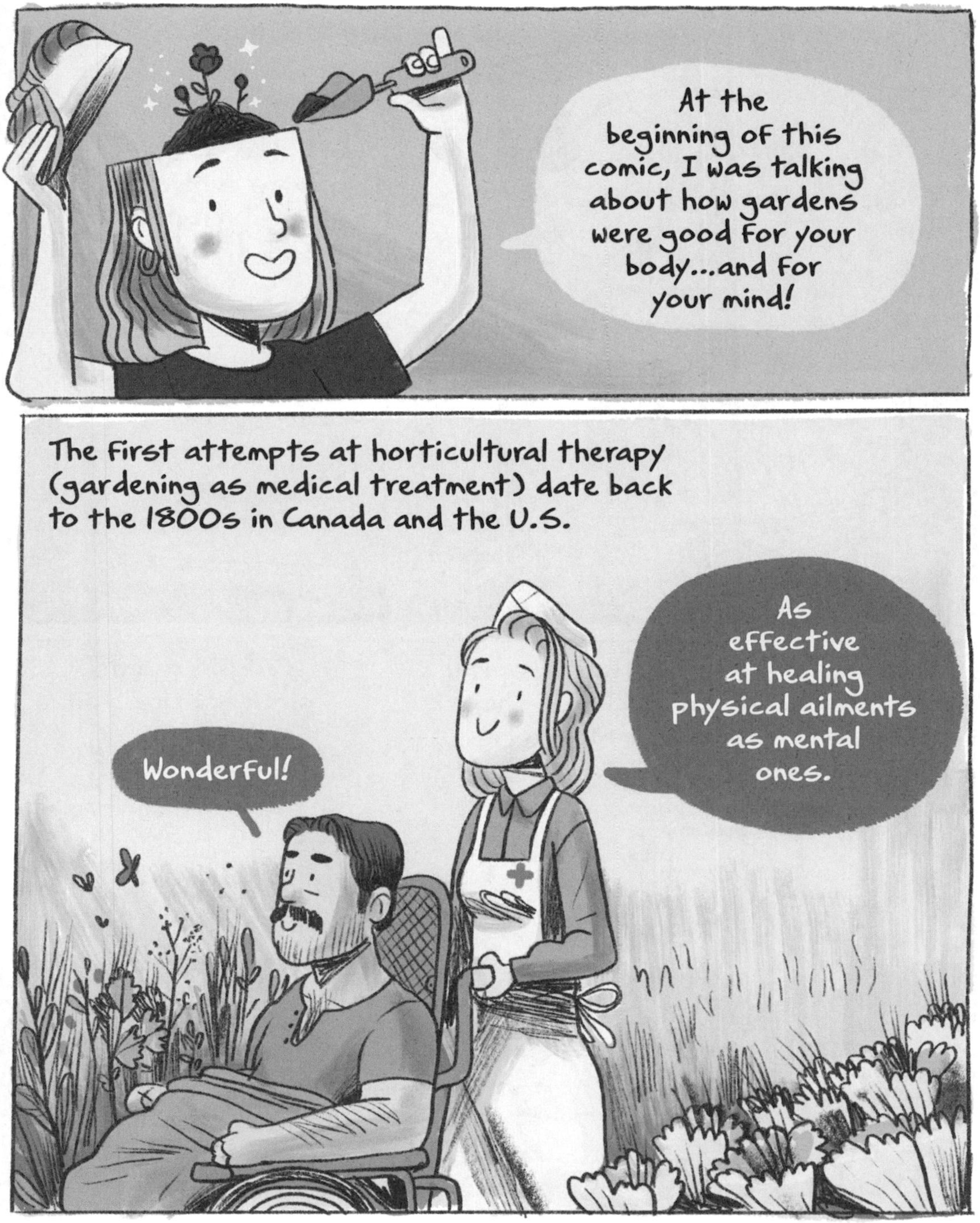
At the beginning of this comic, I was talking about how gardens were good for your body...and for your mind!
The first attempts at horticultural therapy (gardening as medical treatment) date back to the 1800s in Canada and the U.S.
Wonderful!
As effective at healing physical ailments as mental ones.

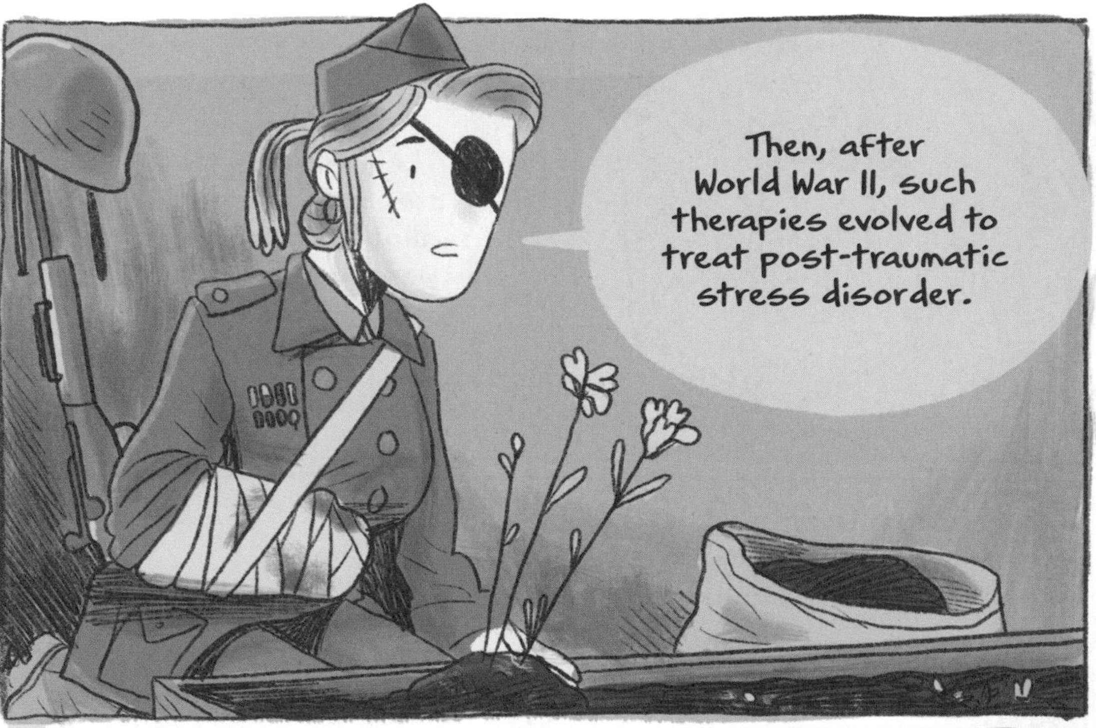
Then, after World War II, such therapies evolved to treat post-traumatic stress disorder.

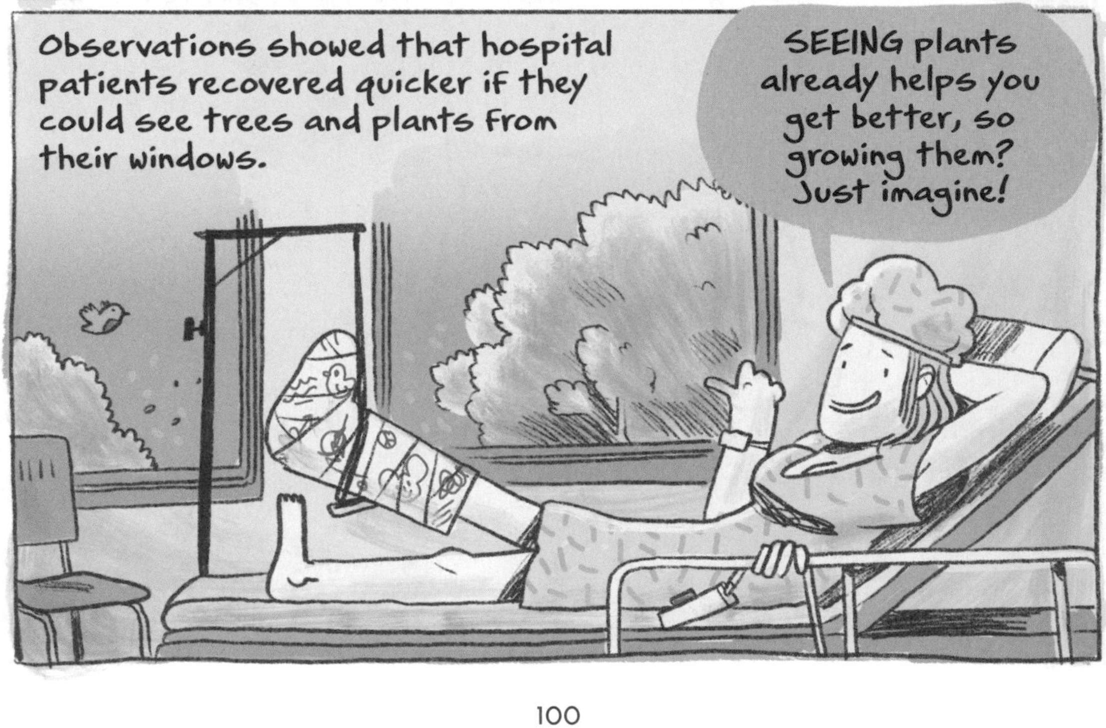
Observations showed that hospital patients recovered quicker if they could see trees and plants from their windows.
SEEING plants already helps you get better, so growing them? Just imagine!

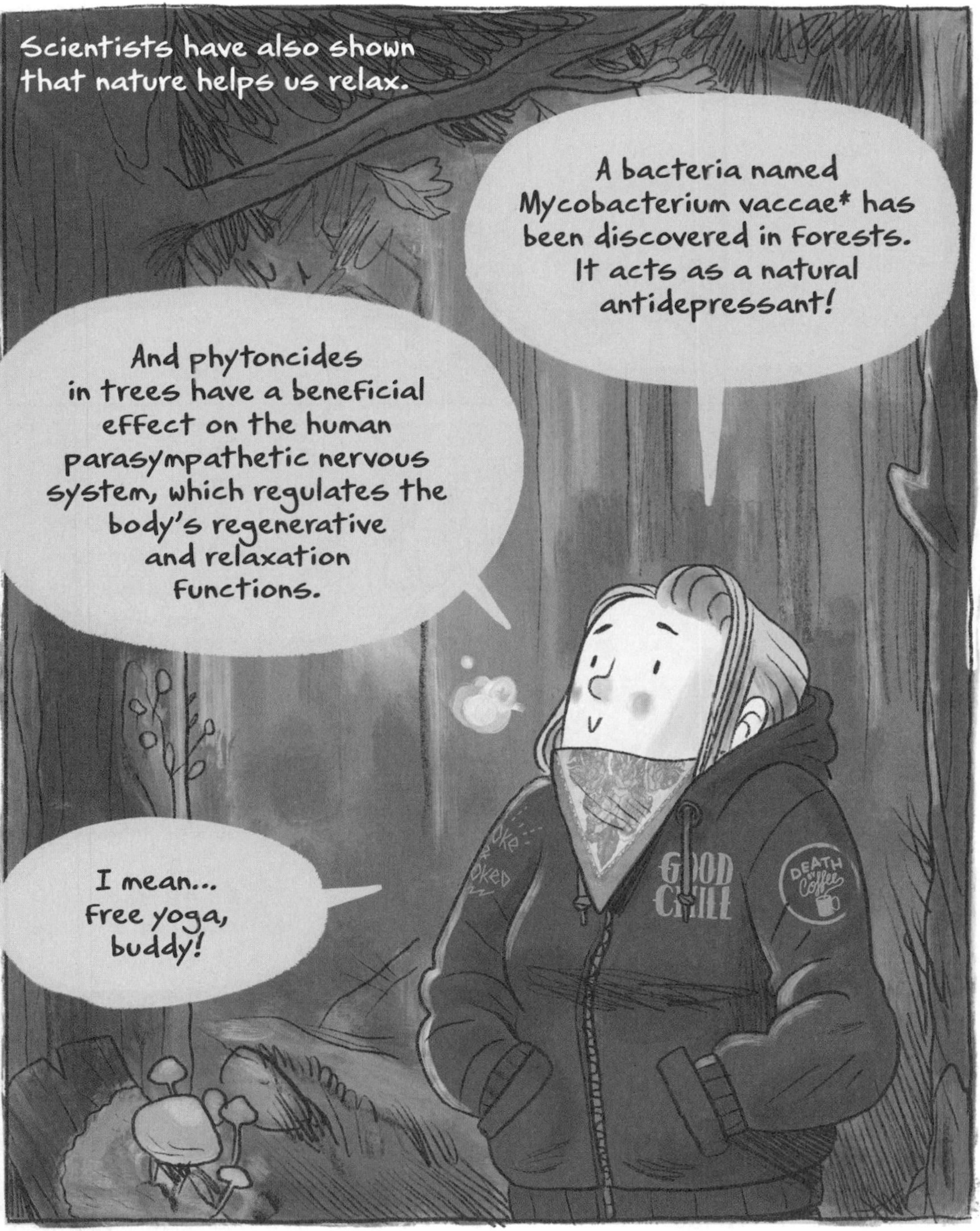
Scientists have also shown that nature helps us relax.
A bacteria named Mycobacterium vaccae* has been discovered in forests. It acts as a natural antidepressant!
And phytoncides in trees have a beneficial effect on the human parasympathetic nervous system, which regulates the body's regenerative and relaxation functions.
I mean... Free yoga, buddy!
GOOD CHILL

*Bristol University (2007)

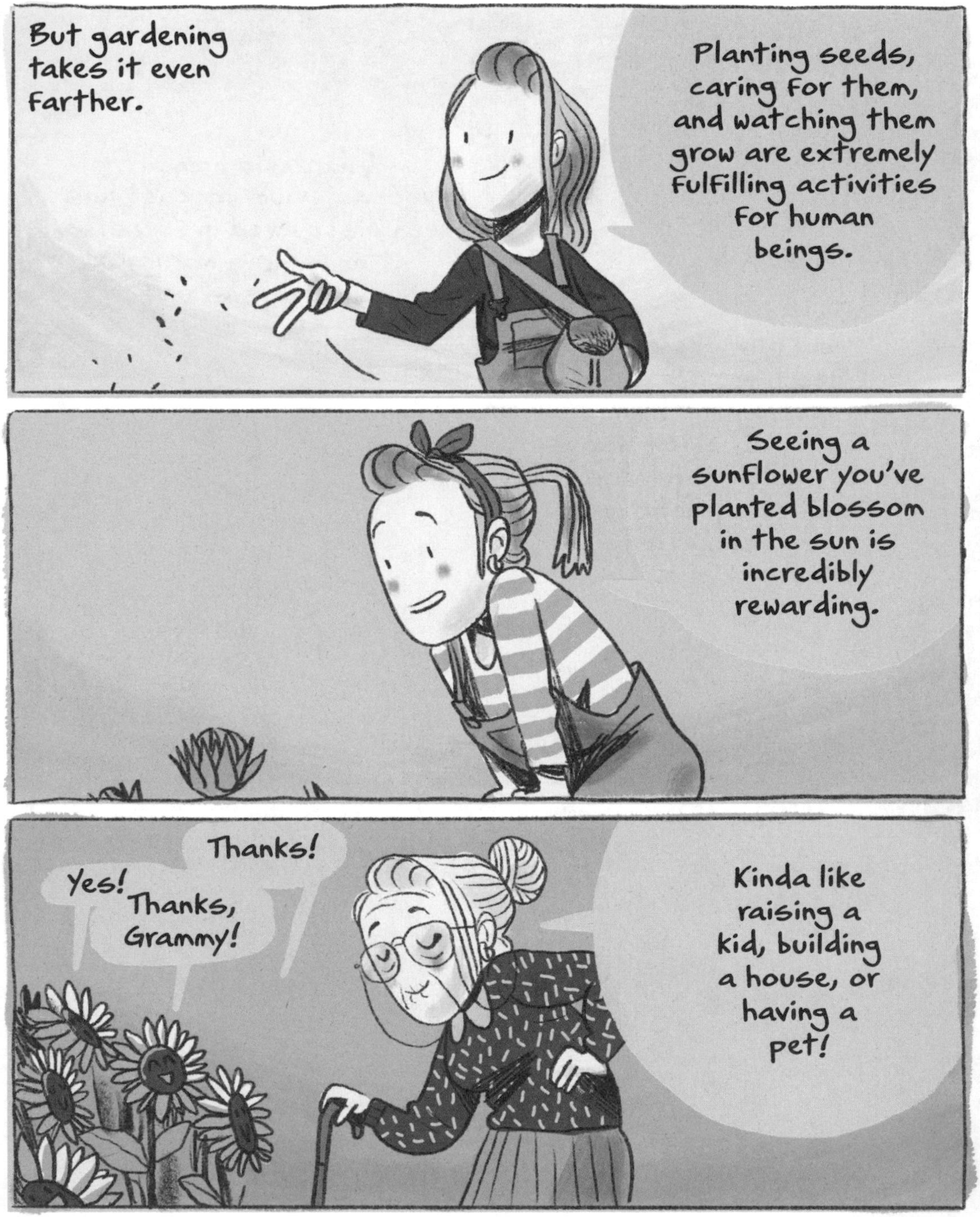
But gardening takes it even farther.
Planting seeds, caring for them, and watching them grow are extremely fulfilling activities for human beings.
Seeing a sunflower you've planted blossom in the sun is incredibly rewarding.
Yes!
Thanks!
Thanks, Grammy!
Kinda like raising a kid, building a house, or having a pet!

These days, we're hooked on instant but fleeting gratifications.
TU-DUM!
BZZZ
PING!
BZZ!
('Fess up, you check your Instagram 73 times a day!)
BZZZ!
TU-DUM
GLING!
MATCH!
Personal growth over the long term is essential to our well-being, honey! It soothes us and gives us tangible goals, a reason to get up in the morning.
TA MÈRE MATURE
PING!
(No way, Oprah's following me!)

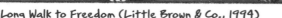

That's why gardening is a vital activity in penal environments.

In two of the three prisons where he was held, Nelson Mandela managed to convince the guards to slip him some empty cans to use as flowerpots, and a few gardening tools.

In his autobiography*, Mandela writes that he had 900 plants in his mini-farm, and shared his harvests with the guards. His gardens helped him hold on for all those years.

You kept yourself busy!

*Long Walk to Freedom (Little Brown & Co., 1994)

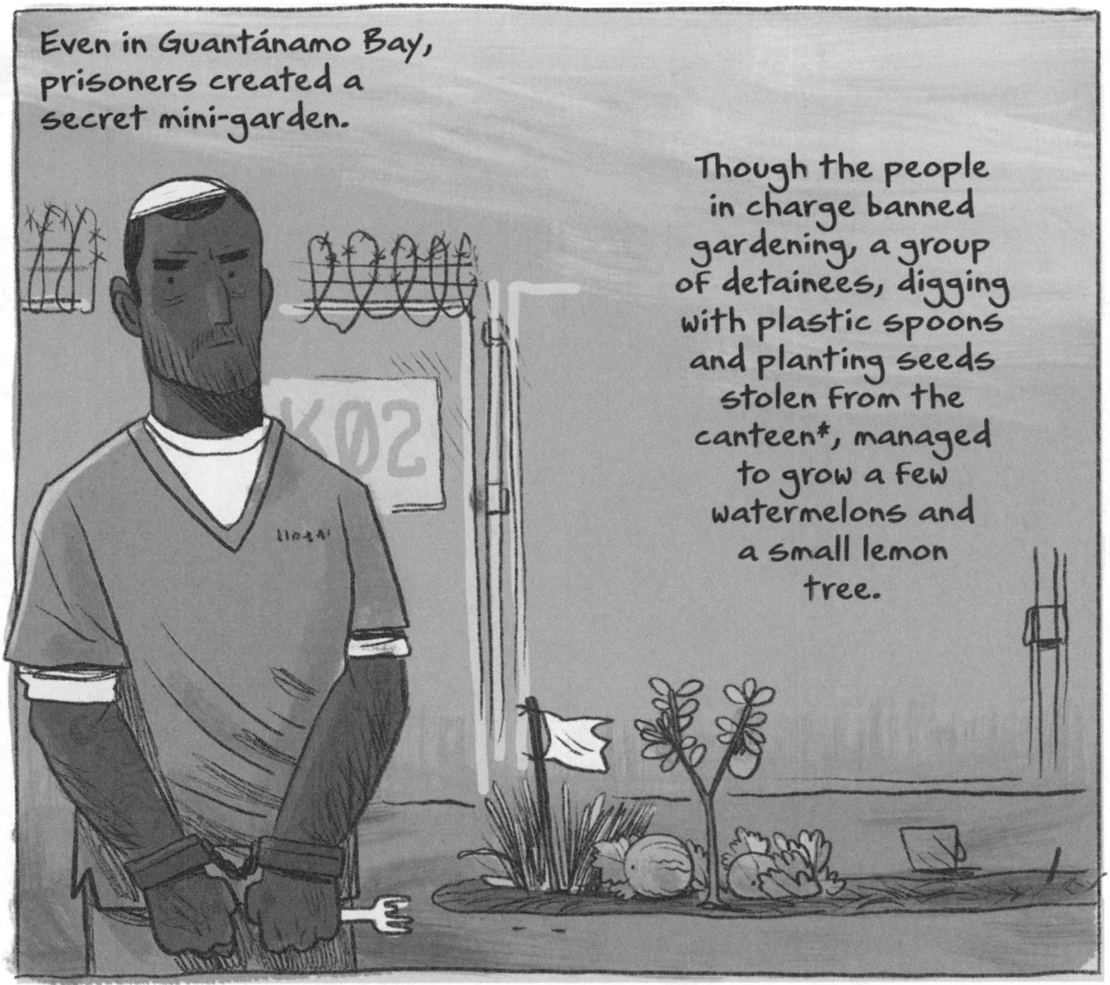
Even in Guantánamo Bay, prisoners created a secret mini-garden.
Though the people in charge banned gardening, a group of detainees, digging with plastic spoons and planting seeds stolen from the canteen*, managed to grow a few watermelons and a small lemon tree.
K02

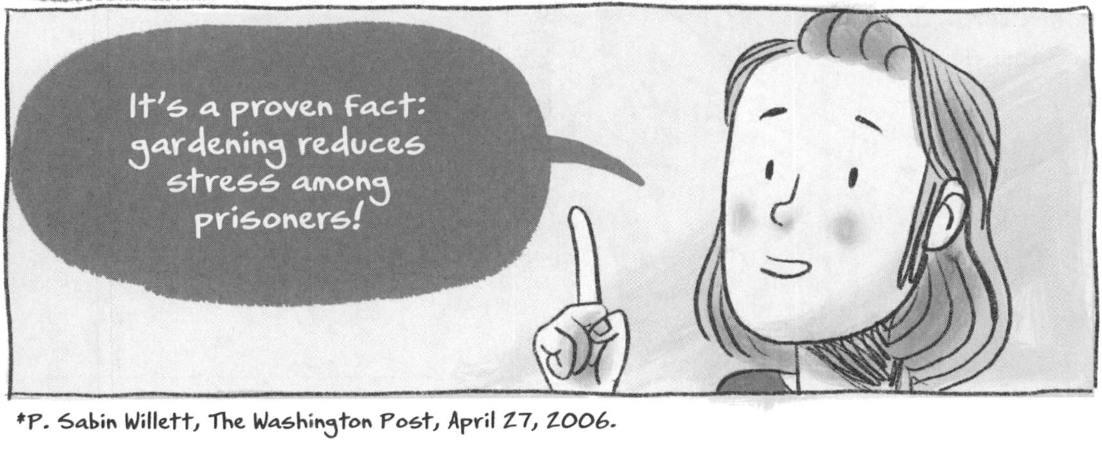
It's a proven fact: gardening reduces stress among prisoners!

*P. Sabin Willett, The Washington Post, April 27, 2006.

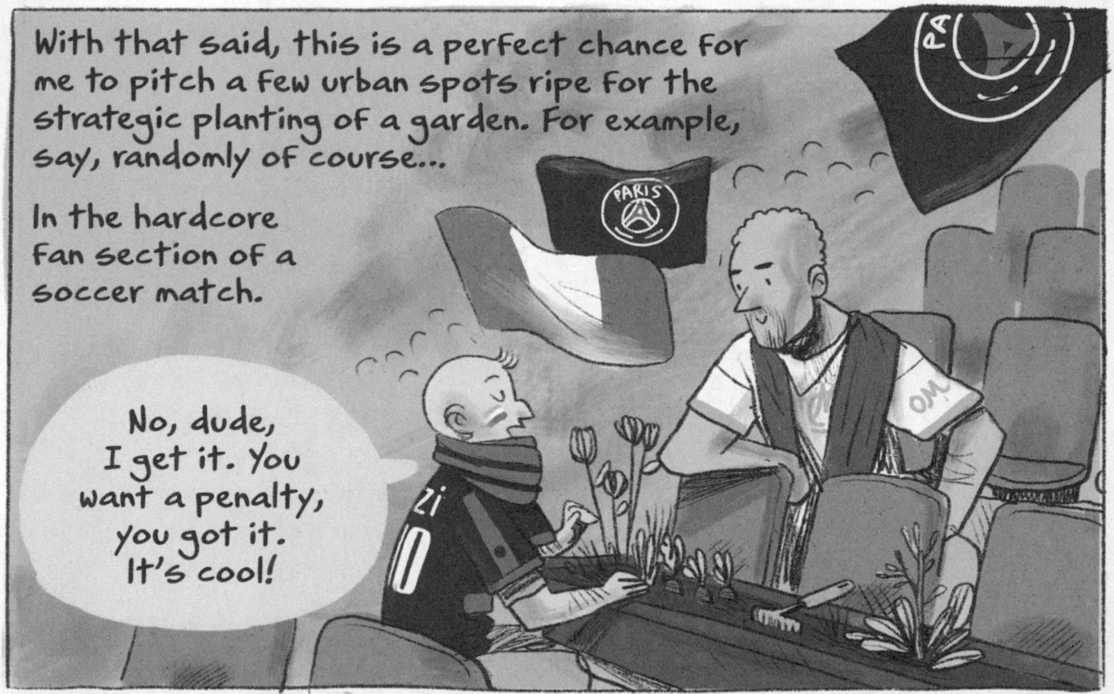
With that said, this is a perfect chance for me to pitch a few urban spots ripe for the strategic planting of a garden. For example, say, randomly of course...
In the hardcore fan section of a soccer match.
No, dude, I get it. You want a penalty, you got it. It's cool!

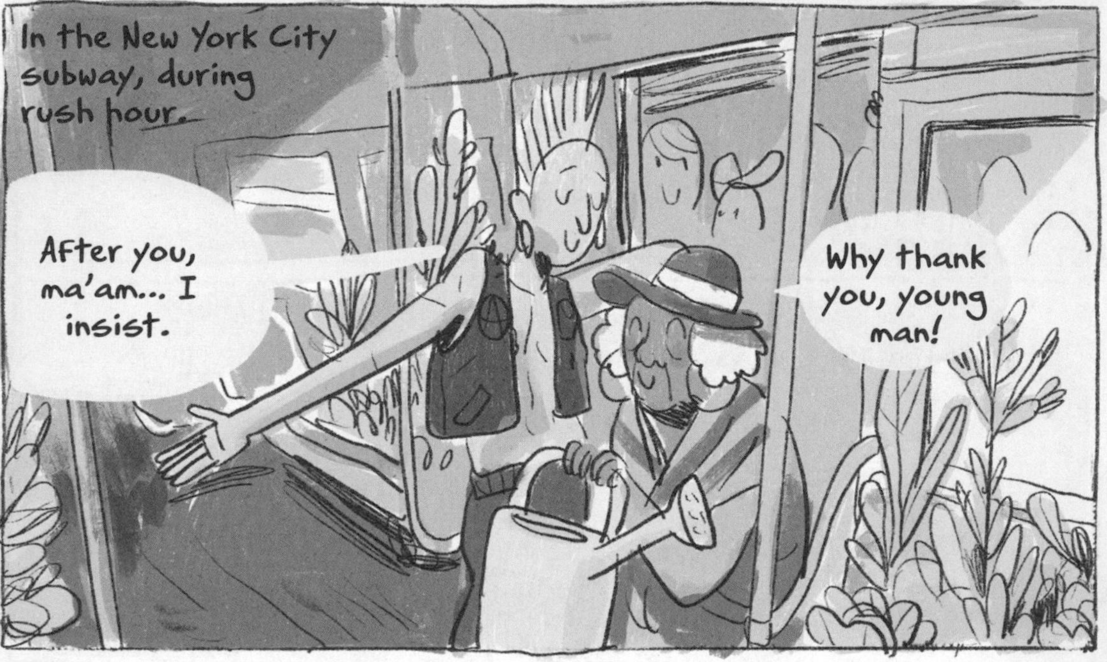
In the New York City subway, during rush hour.
After you, ma'am... I insist.
Why thank you, young man!

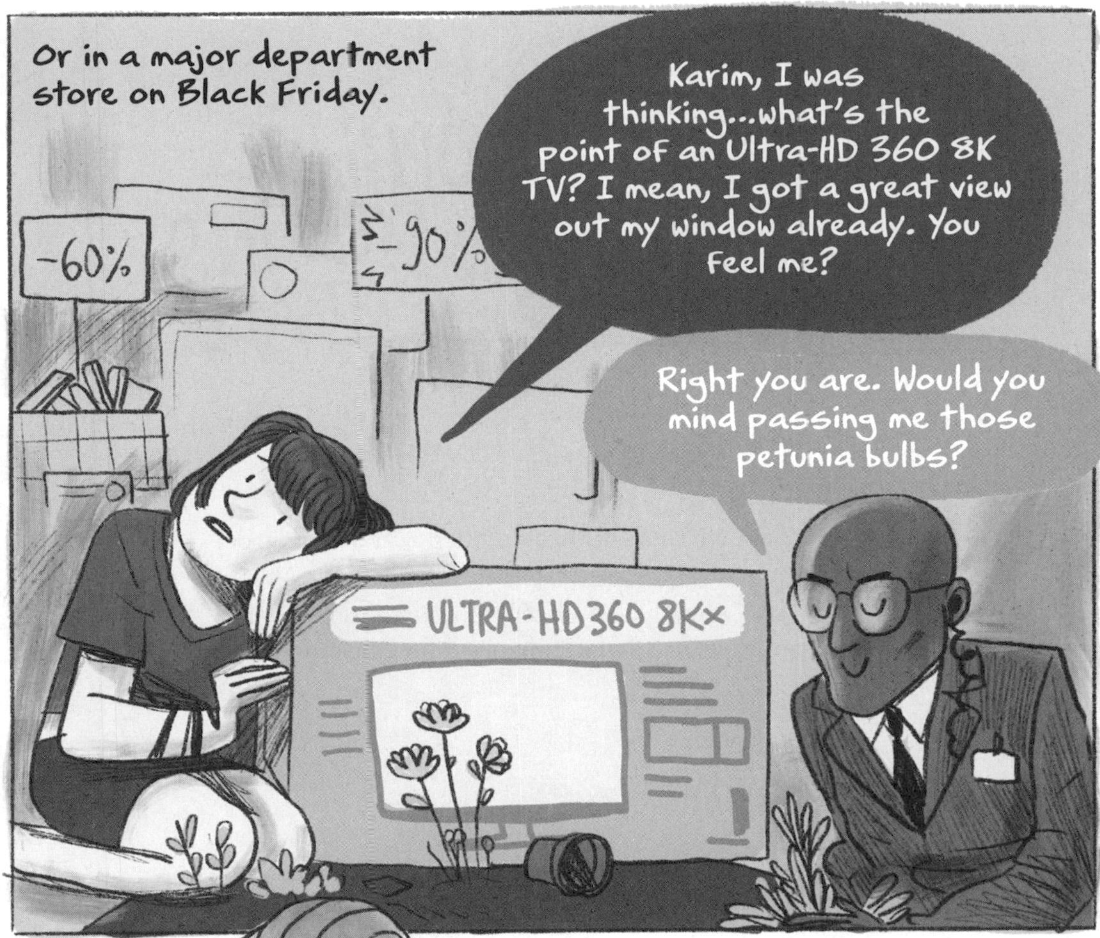
Or in a major department store on Black Friday.
Karim, I was thinking...what's the point of an Ultra-HD 360 8K TV? I mean, I got a great view out my window already. You Feel me?
Right you are. Would you mind passing me those petunia bulbs?
-60%
ULTRA-HD360 8Kx
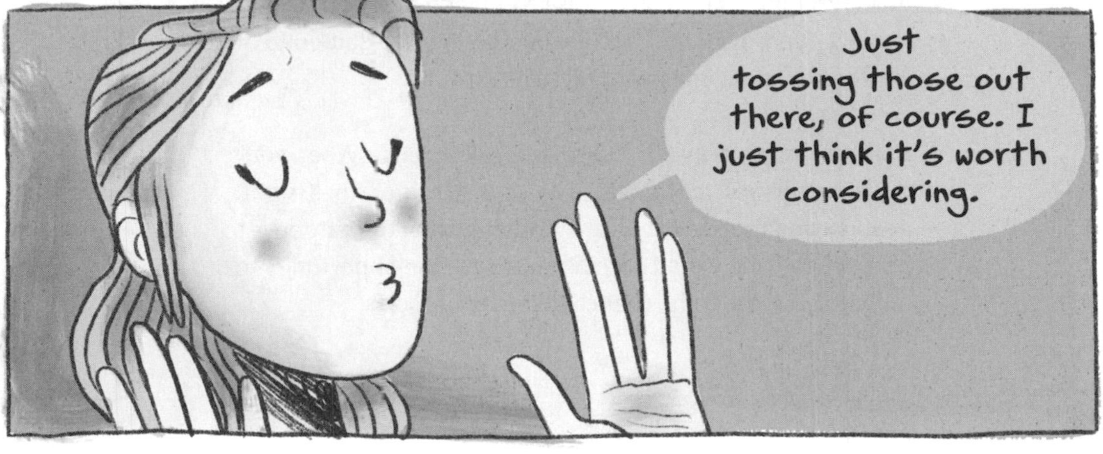
Just tossing those out there, of course. I just think it's worth considering.

OPHÉLIE EXPLAINS IT ALL

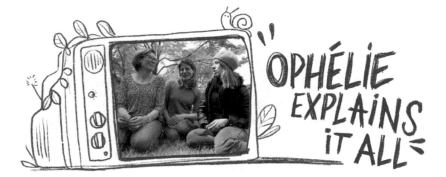

GARDENING AND HEALING

I met Stéphanie and Laure of Projet Terr'Happy at the Jardin des Possibles [Garden of Possibilities] on the grounds of the Abbey of de Maubuisson, which has now been turned into contemporary art site. There, I spoke to them about plants and their therapeutic properties.

HORTICULTURAL THERAPY

Terr'Happy tends its Garden of Possibilities on a parcel of the abbey grounds that began as a kitchen garden grown by medieval nuns. They bring in disadvantaged groups (the ill, handicapped, or cut off) and encourage them to garden to help improve their mental and physical health.

Horticultural therapy is a very sensory experience. When you're out in nature, you're stimulated by your senses of smell, sight, hearing, and touch all at once. Another goal of the garden is to give people who would normally not have the opportunity to run into each other the chance to meet outdoors.

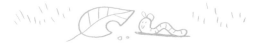

Horticultural therapy isn't widely recognized in France as a healing practice, unlike in other countries such as the U.S., the cradle of modern horticultural therapy.

One of the founding figures of the movement, Benjamin Rush, was a physician who noticed that patients with psychiatric issues did much better when they were gardening.

Today, scientific studies have proven that nature has a real impact on health and well-being. For instance, one study showed that patients in hospital rooms with a view of trees checked out of the hospital earlier, requested fewer pain medications, and had better relationships with their caregivers.

Whenever you go walking in the woods, the trees, which are full of water, release countless molecules into the air (in a process called evapotranspiration) that we then inhale. In so doing, we increase the number of natural killer cells in our bodies, which then go on to consume cancer cells. A two-hour walk is enough to give your immune system a boost!

Thanks, nature!

GREEN GUERILLAS
AROUND THE WORLD

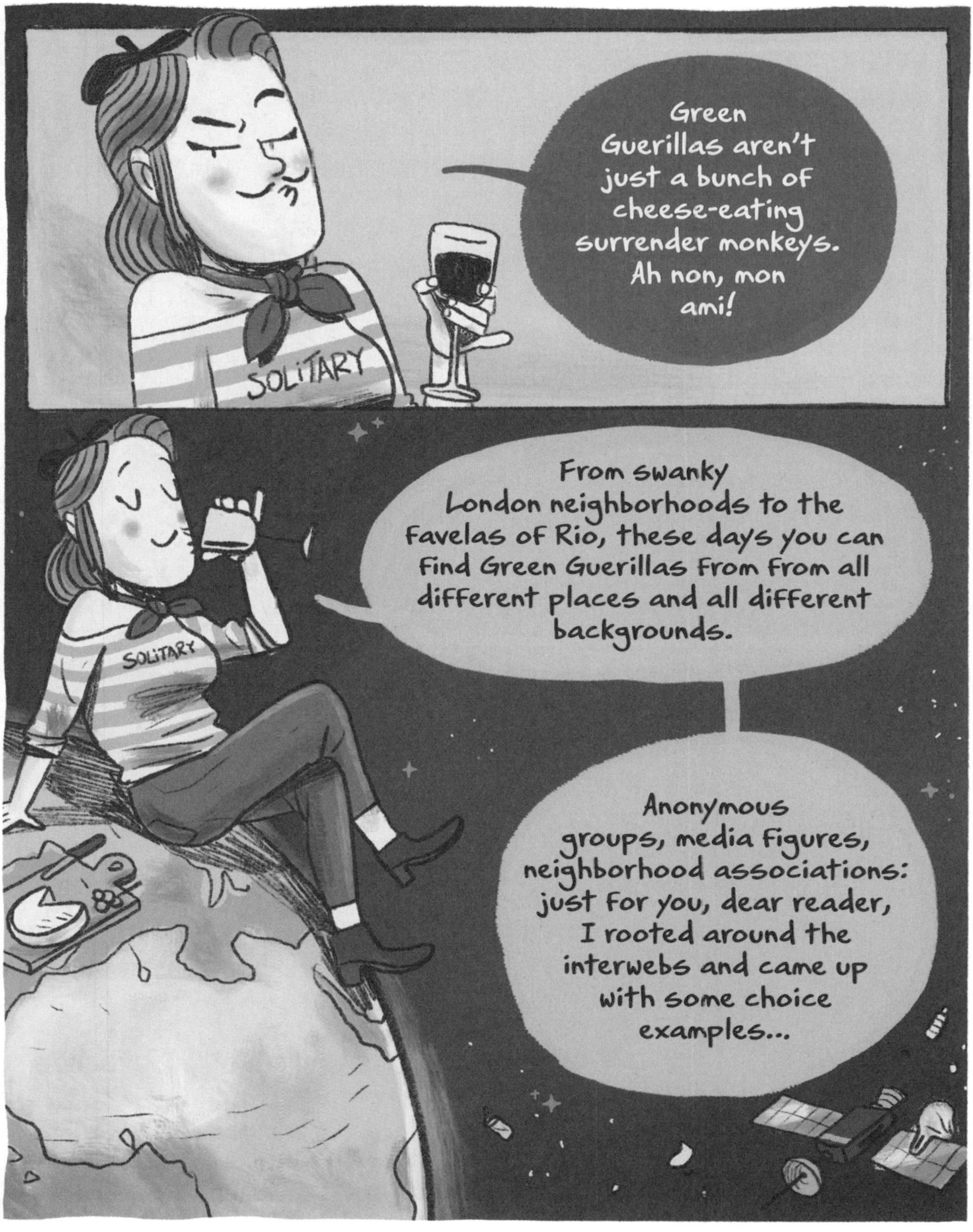

Green Guerillas aren't just a bunch of cheese-eating surrender monkeys. Ah non, mon ami!
SOLITARY
From swanky London neighborhoods to the Favelas of Rio, these days you can find Green Guerillas from from all different places and all different backgrounds.
SOLITARY
Anonymous groups, media figures, neighborhood associations: just for you, dear reader, I rooted around the interwebs and came up with some choice examples...

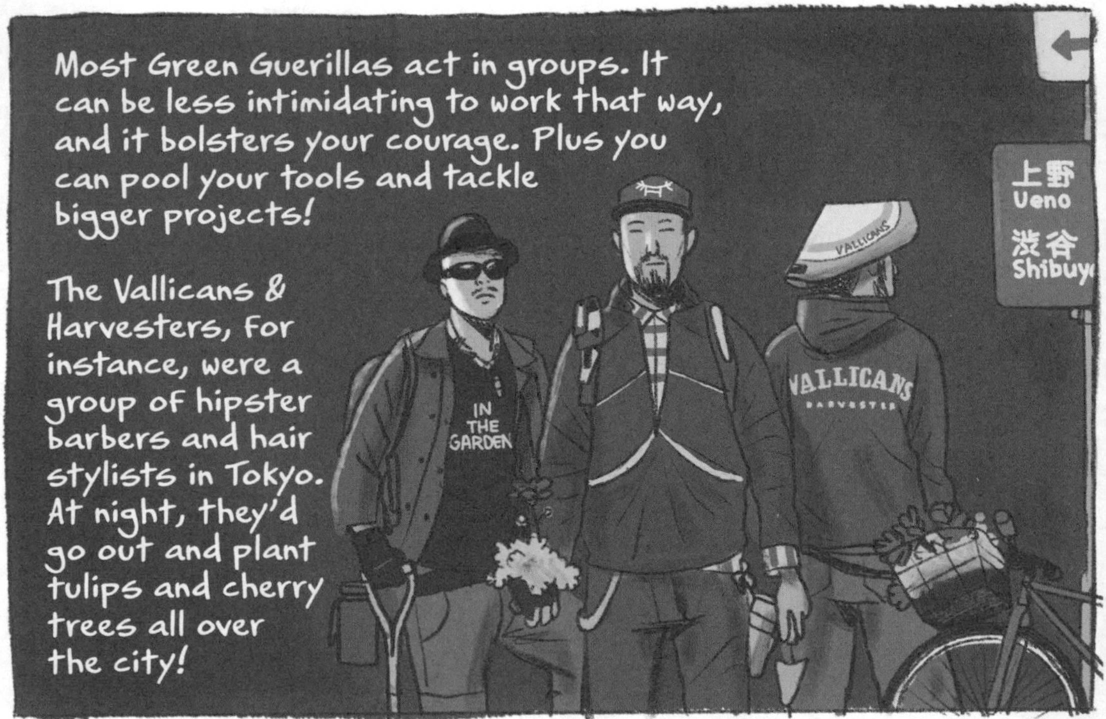
Most Green Guerillas act in groups. It can be less intimidating to work that way, and it bolsters your courage. Plus you can pool your tools and tackle bigger projects!
The Vallicans & Harvesters, for instance, were a group of hipster barbers and hair stylists in Tokyo. At night, they'd go out and plant tulips and cherry trees all over the city!
IN THE GARDEN
VALLICANS
VALLICANS
上野
Ueno
渋谷
Shibuy

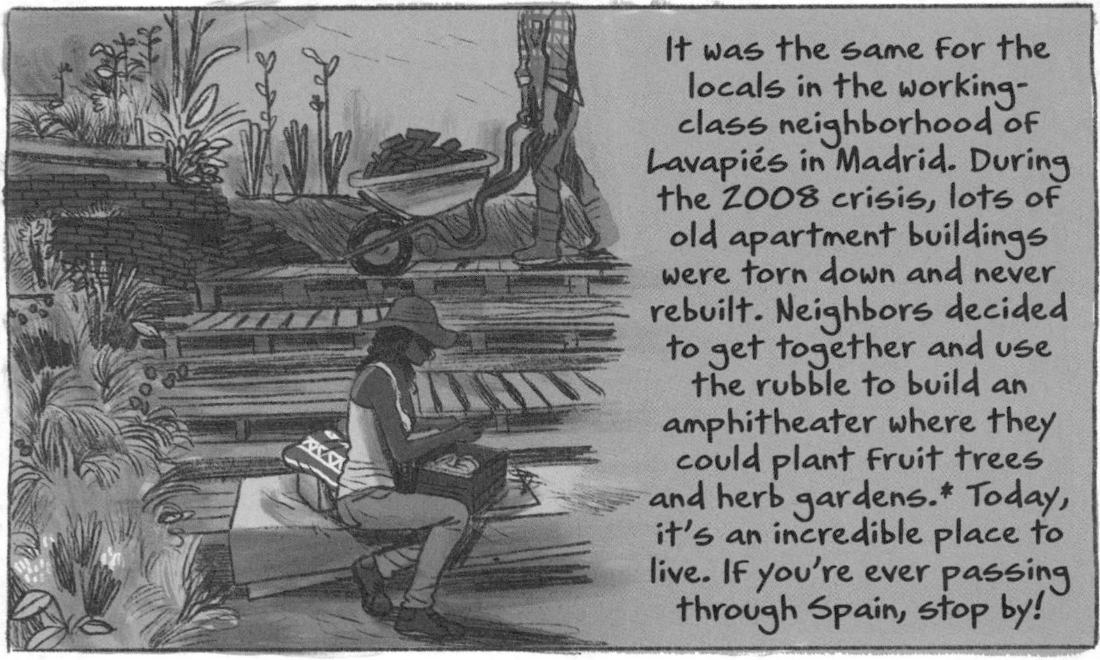
It was the same for the locals in the working-class neighborhood of Lavapiés in Madrid. During the 2008 crisis, lots of old apartment buildings were torn down and never rebuilt. Neighbors decided to get together and use the rubble to build an amphitheater where they could plant fruit trees and herb gardens.* Today, it's an incredible place to live. If you're ever passing through Spain, stop by!

*www.estaesunaplaza.blogspot.com

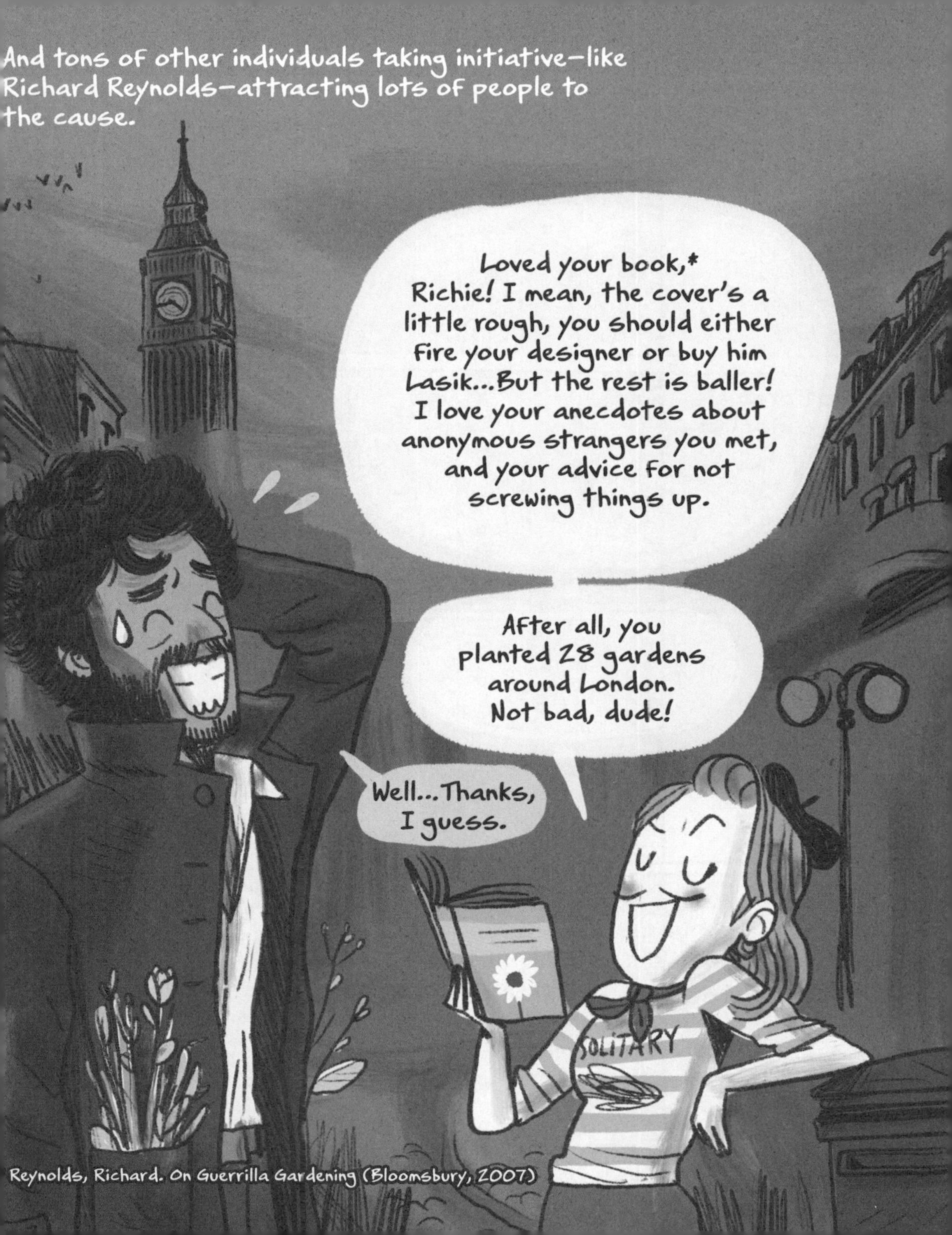
And tons of other individuals taking initiative—like Richard Reynolds—attracting lots of people to the cause.
Loved your book,* Richie! I mean, the cover's a little rough, you should either fire your designer or buy him Lasik...But the rest is baller! I love your anecdotes about anonymous strangers you met, and your advice for not screwing things up.
After all, you planted 28 gardens around London. Not bad, dude!
Well...Thanks, I guess.
SOLITARY
Reynolds, Richard. On Guerrilla Gardening (Bloomsbury, 2007)

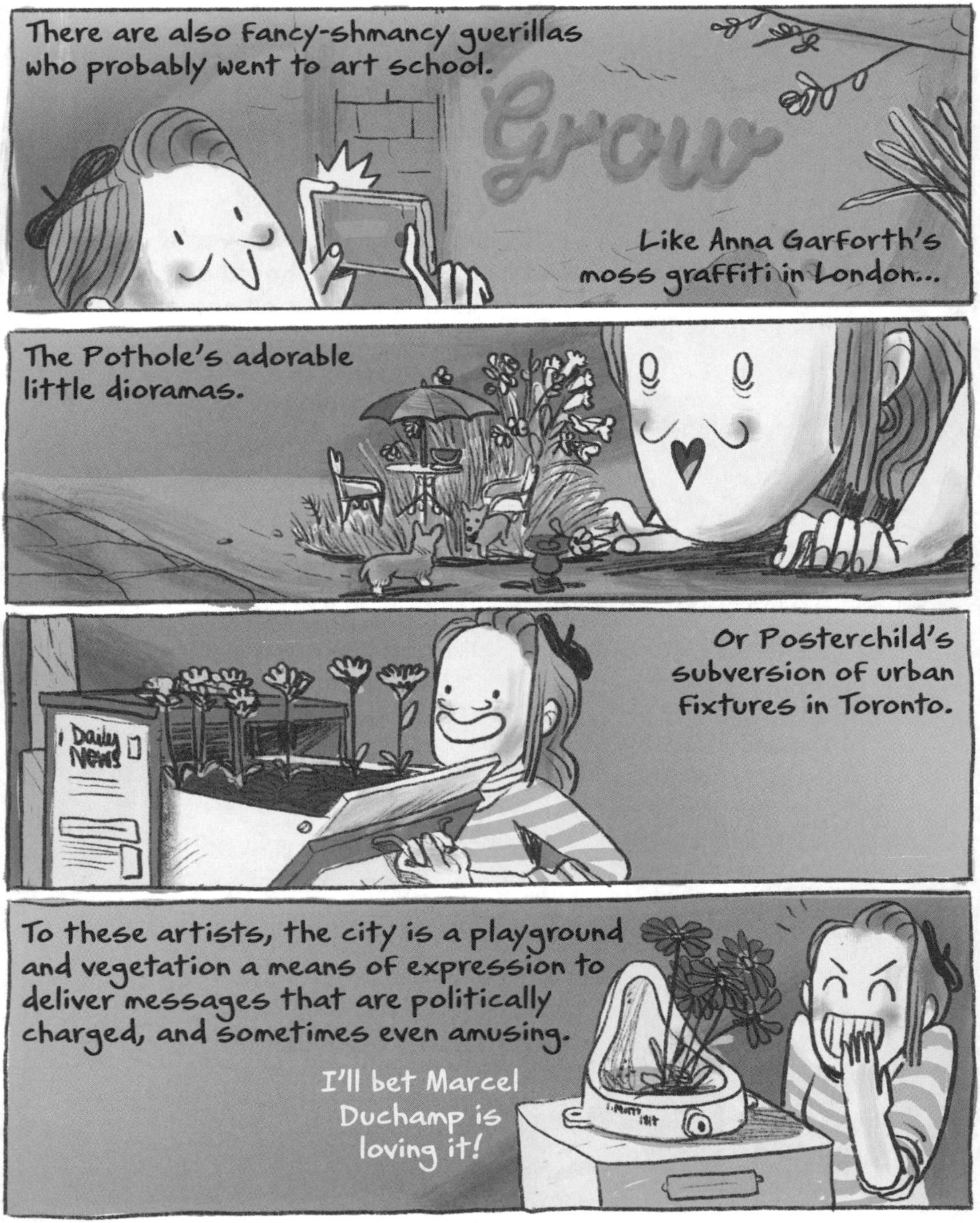
There are also fancy-shmancy guerillas who probably went to art school.
Grow
Like Anna Garforth's moss graffiti in London...
The Pothole's adorable little dioramas.
Or Posterchild's subversion of urban fixtures in Toronto.
Daily News
To these artists, the city is a playground and vegetation a means of expression to deliver messages that are politically charged, and sometimes even amusing.
I'll bet Marcel Duchamp is loving it!

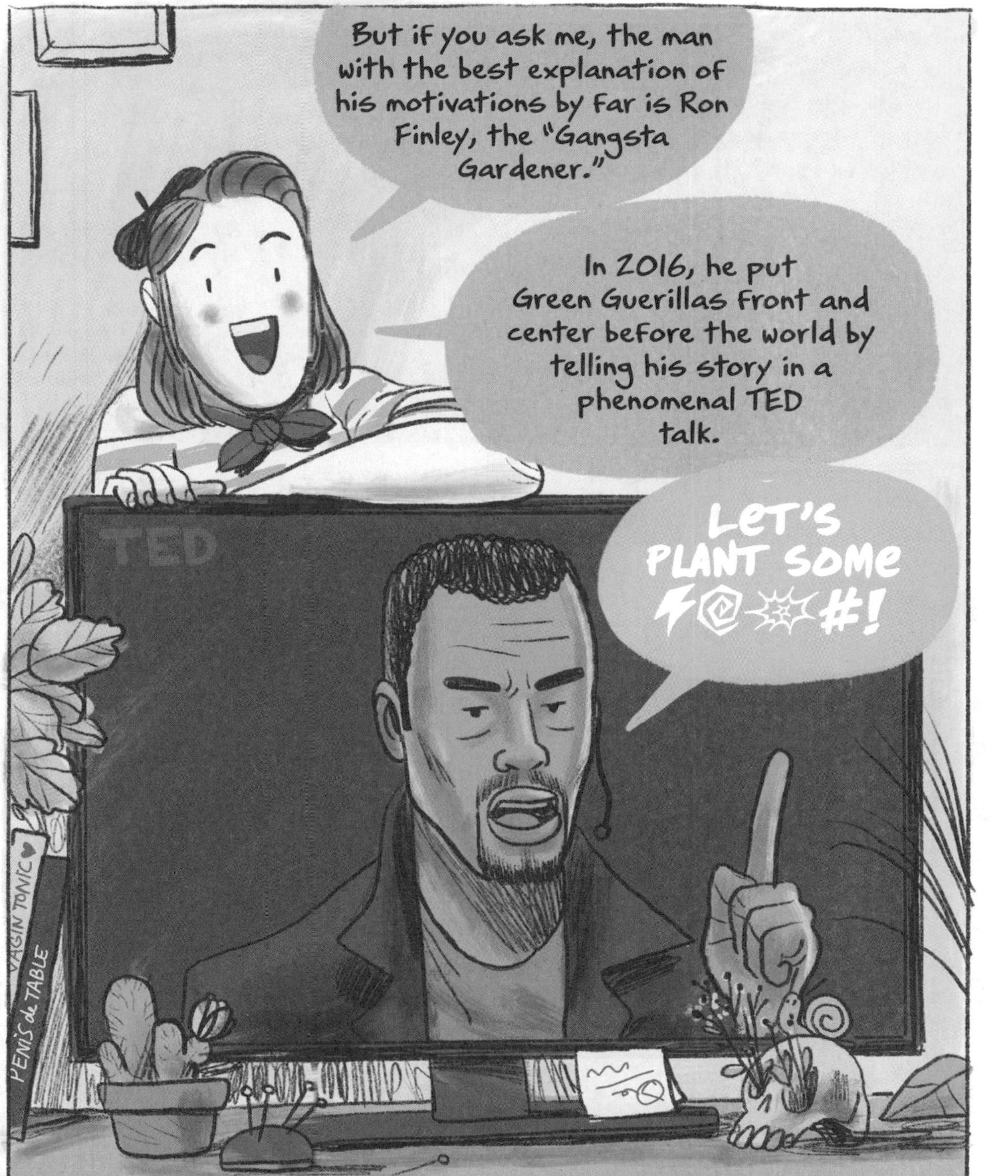
But if you ask me, the man with the best explanation of his motivations by far is Ron Finley, the "Gangsta Gardener."
In 2016, he put Green Guerillas front and center before the world by telling his story in a phenomenal TED talk.
TED
LET'S PLANT SOME
#!
VAGIN TONIC
PENIS de TABLE

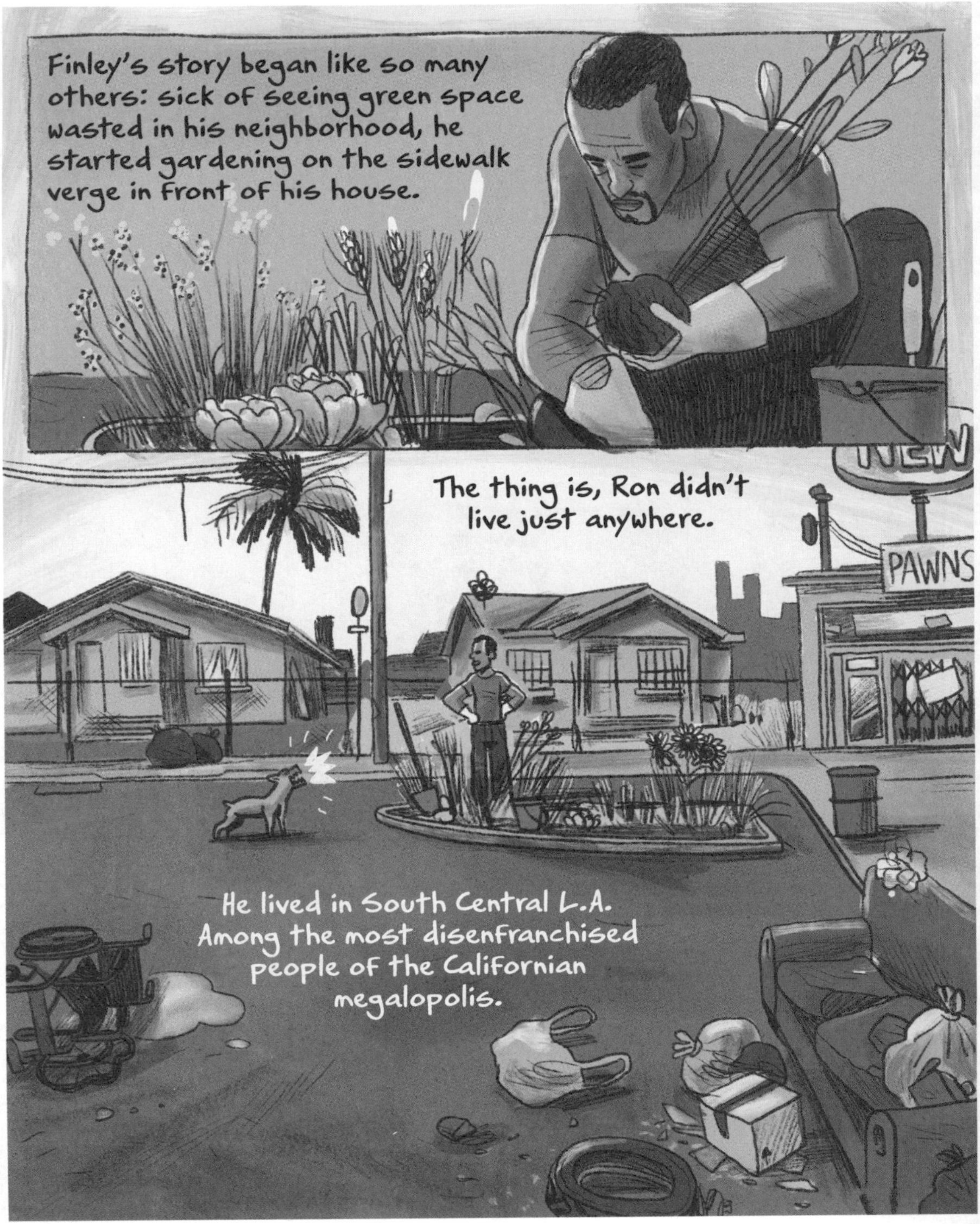
Finley's story began like so many others: sick of seeing green space wasted in his neighborhood, he started gardening on the sidewalk verge in front of his house.
The thing is, Ron didn't live just anywhere.
PAWNS
He lived in South Central L.A. Among the most disenfranchised people of the Californian megalopolis.

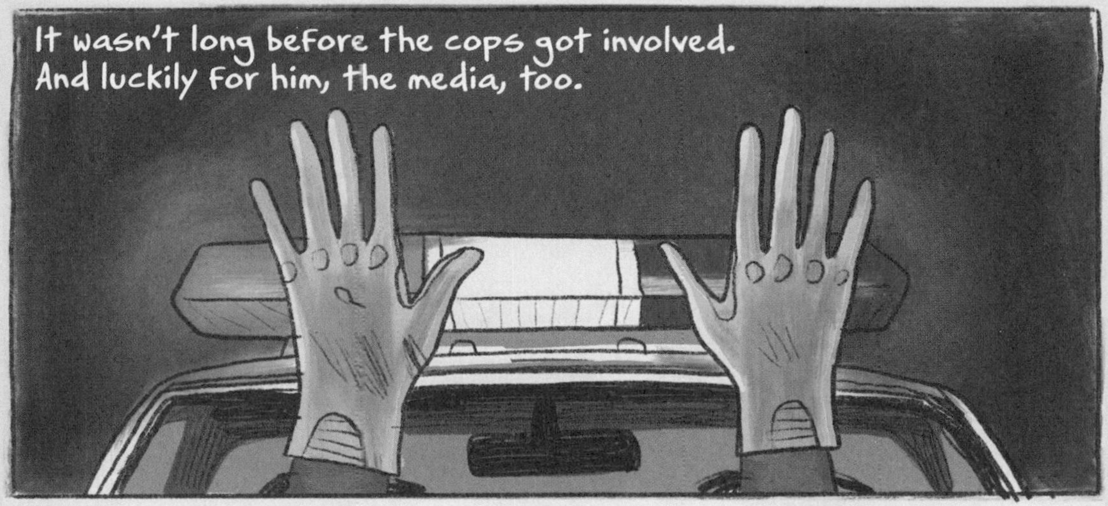
It wasn't long before the cops got involved.
And luckily for him, the media, too.

What Finley championed was access to a healthy, balanced diet for one and all. In an area ravaged by poverty, low education, and obesity, Finley denounced American-style "food deserts."* To get fresh veggies, he had to drive 25 minutes from his house. The only food for miles around was from fast food and gas stations.

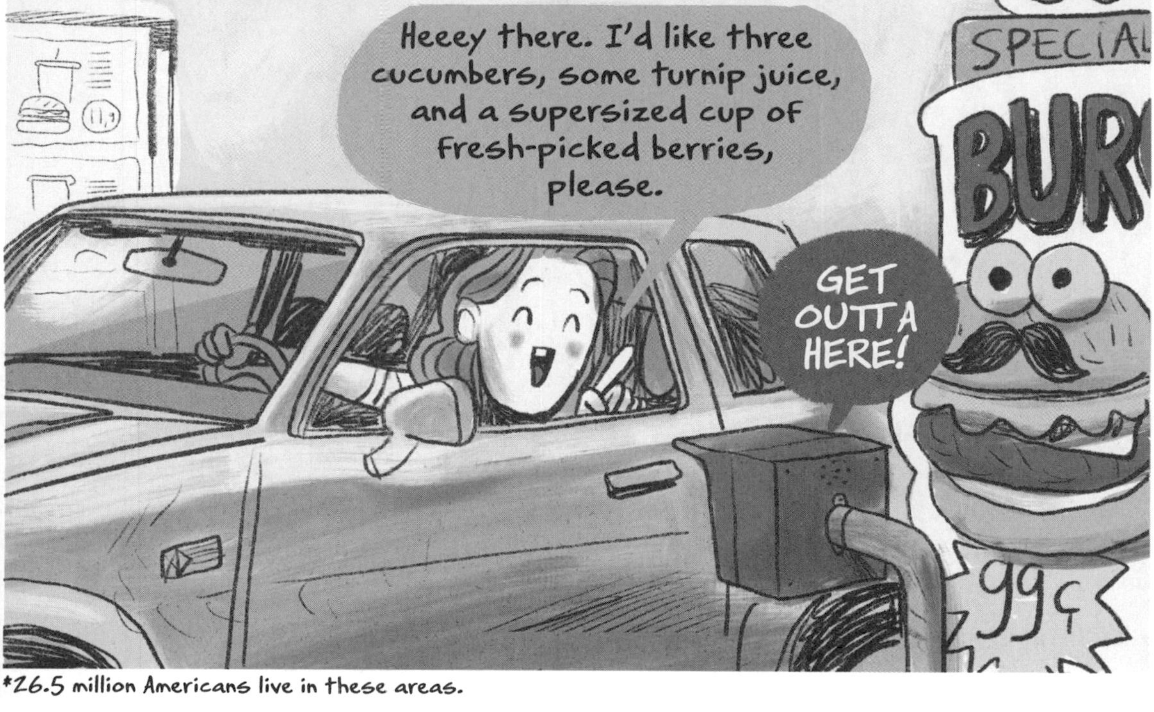
Heeey there. I'd like three cucumbers, some turnip juice, and a supersized cup of fresh-picked berries, please.
GET OUTTA HERE!
99¢

*26.5 million Americans live in these areas.

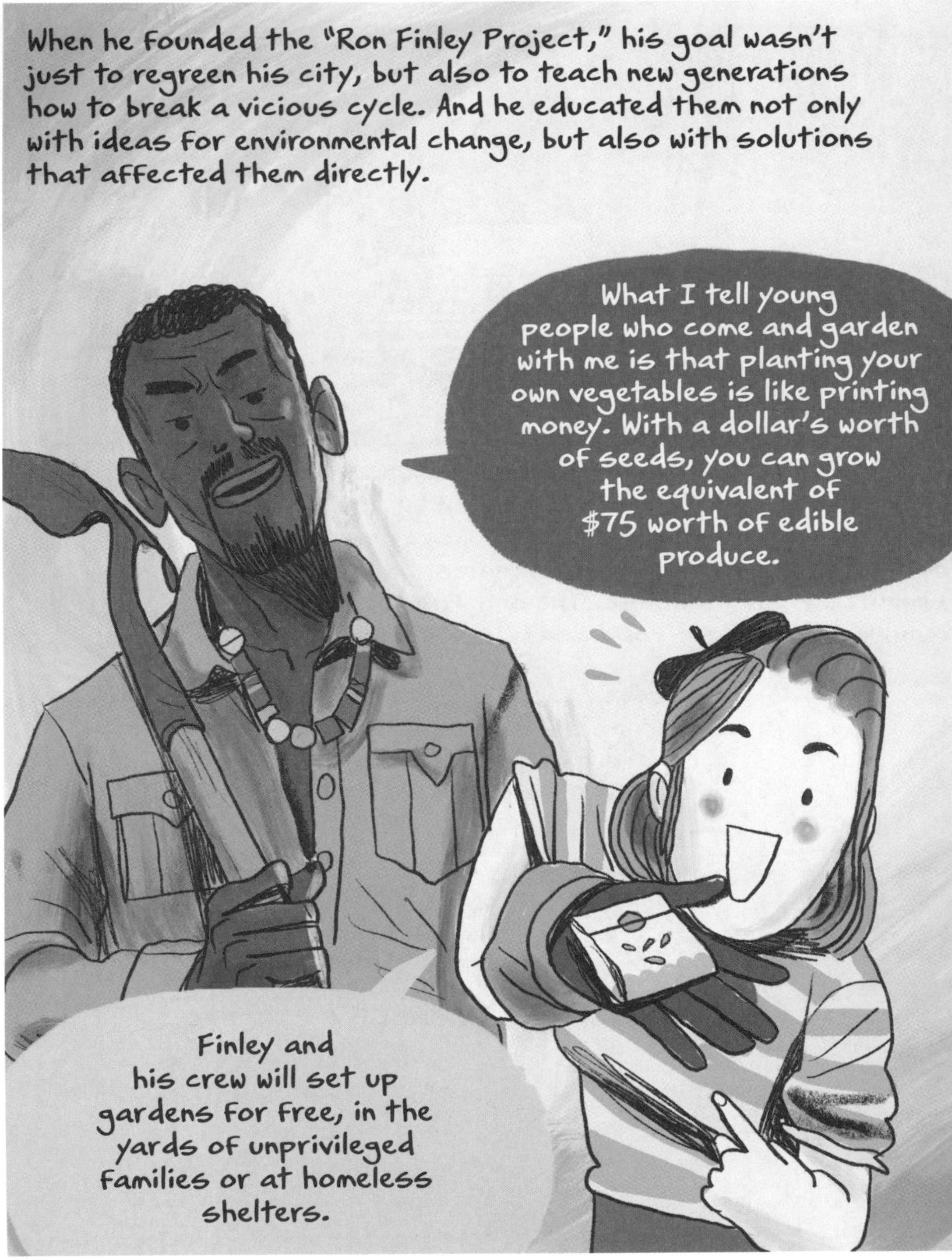
When he founded the "Ron Finley Project," his goal wasn't just to regreen his city, but also to teach new generations how to break a vicious cycle. And he educated them not only with ideas for environmental change, but also with solutions that affected them directly.
What I tell young people who come and garden with me is that planting your own vegetables is like printing money. With a dollar's worth of seeds, you can grow the equivalent of $75 worth of edible produce.
Finley and his crew will set up gardens for free, in the yards of unprivileged families or at homeless shelters.

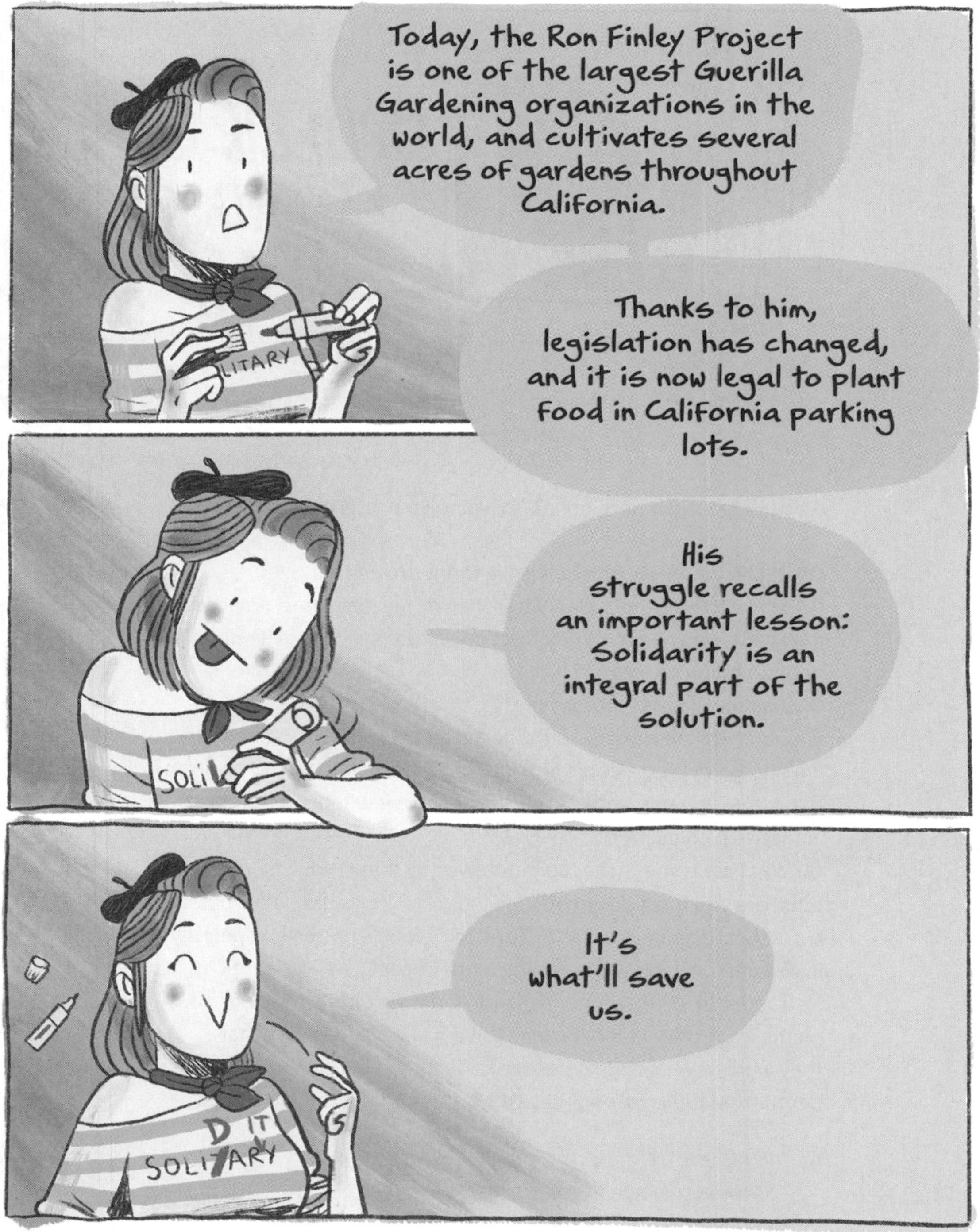
Today, the Ron Finley Project is one of the largest Guerilla Gardening organizations in the world, and cultivates several acres of gardens throughout California.
Thanks to him, legislation has changed, and it is now legal to plant food in California parking lots.
His struggle recalls an important lesson: Solidarity is an integral part of the solution.
It's what'll save us.

"OPHÉLIE EXPLAINS IT ALL"

GREEN GUERILLAS HERE IN PARIS
WHAT HAVE WE ACCOMPLISHED?

Gaby, the founder of Guerilla Gardening France, is here to fill us in…

OPHÉLIE: When was this collective formed?
GABY: In 2009, in Paris. I launched it all by my lonesome, and soon a few others joined me. The group goes from five to twenty people, depending on the season.
O.: Do most activists fit a profile?
G.: Oh, there are all kinds! Still, the average age is over 30, and most are into gardening. People looking for a career change, people from IT, people who miss the countryside…and a few more full-time activists, of course!
O.: What are some of the more noteworthy things you've done? What are you most proud of?
G.: Our participation in ZAD ["Zone to Defend"] protests, especially in Montesson. I feel like we made a real impact, that we were instrumental in protecting the land. And if we didn't, well, we planted a Virginia creeper over a town hall placard saying that they were never going to be able to get anything done due to people's lack of courtesy. These days, the sign is often covered in

ivy, which makes for a double victory--functional and visual--for reappropriation from the city, all while being an activist protest.

O.: How often do you take action?

G.: Once or twice a month.

O.: Ever been arrested? C'mon, spill!

G.: We've gotten off with police warnings. Usually for things we do at night. We're told that gardening is cool, and we can keep going with permission from the property owner (but so long as the landlord doesn't say a thing, in theory the police can't do anything to us either). Sometimes we get told to leave the property, but we just come back ten minutes later. If we ever get arrested for gardening, there ll be a scandal. The anti-crime squad stopped us once during a protest on the Paris Accords, but nothing ever really nasty.

O.: How can people get involved?

G.: Just write us and say you want to join in when we do something, or show up at a protest we've publicly announced online. Afterwards, if everything goes well and you decide you really want to commit, we'll put you in the loop for the next secret meet-ups. Otherwise, you don't have to join us just to be part of the movement!

For more info, go to **http://guerrillagardening.org/**

SAVING
BIODIVERSITY

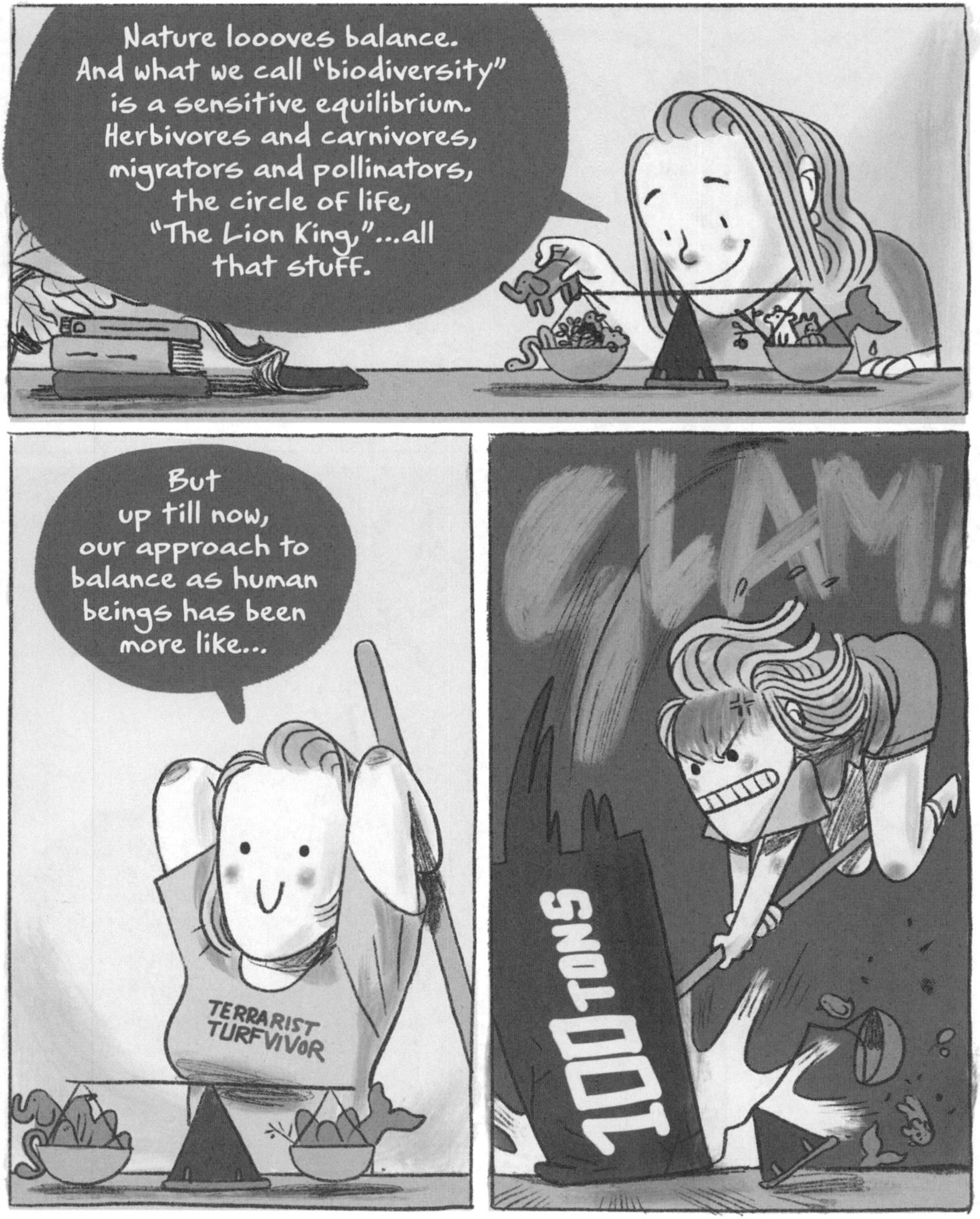
Nature loooves balance. And what we call "biodiversity" is a sensitive equilibrium. Herbivores and carnivores, migrators and pollinators, the circle of life, "The Lion King,"...all that stuff.
But up till now, our approach to balance as human beings has been more like...
TERRARIST TURFVIVOR
CLAM!
100 TONS

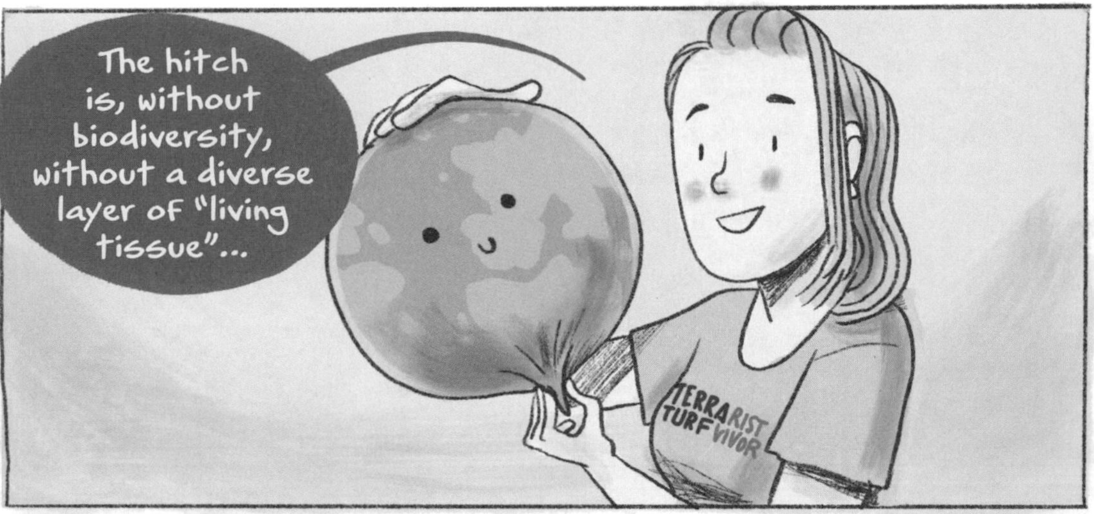
The hitch is, without biodiversity, without a diverse layer of "living tissue"...
TERRARIST TURFVIVOR

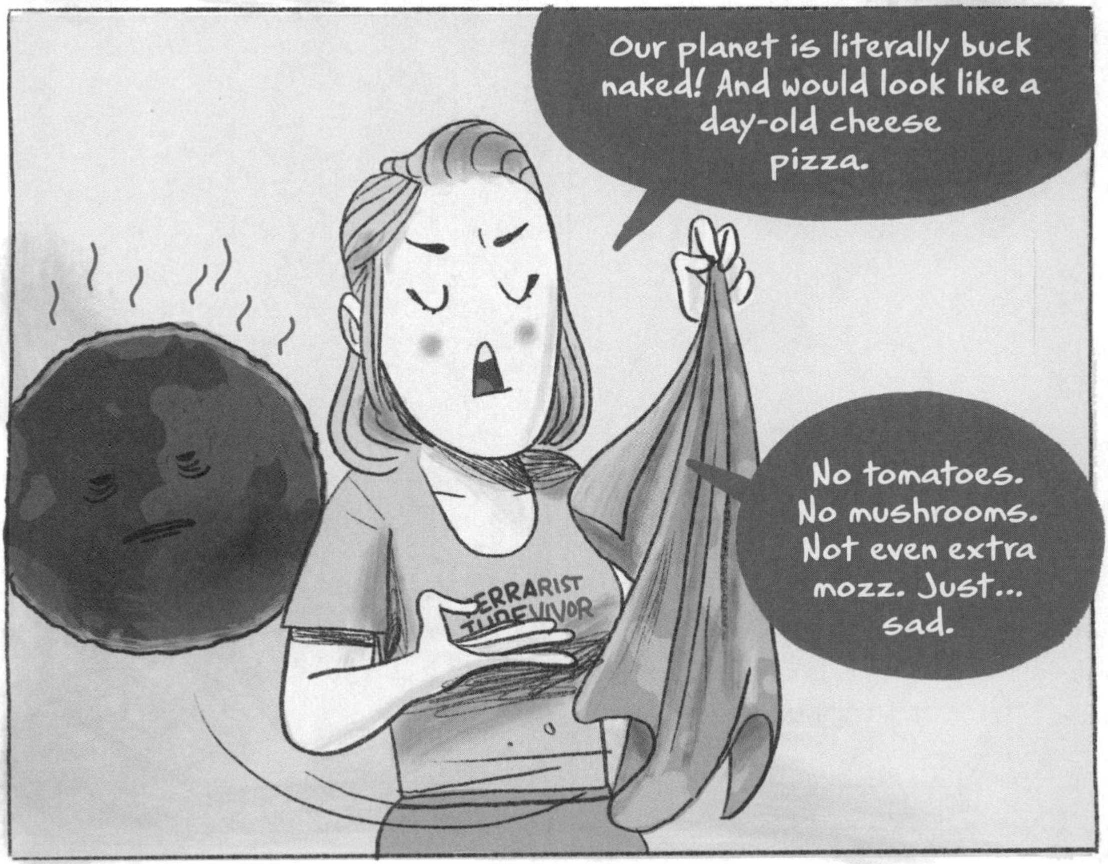
Our planet is literally buck naked! And would look like a day-old cheese pizza.
No tomatoes. No mushrooms. Not even extra mozz. Just... sad.
TERRARIST TURFVIVOR

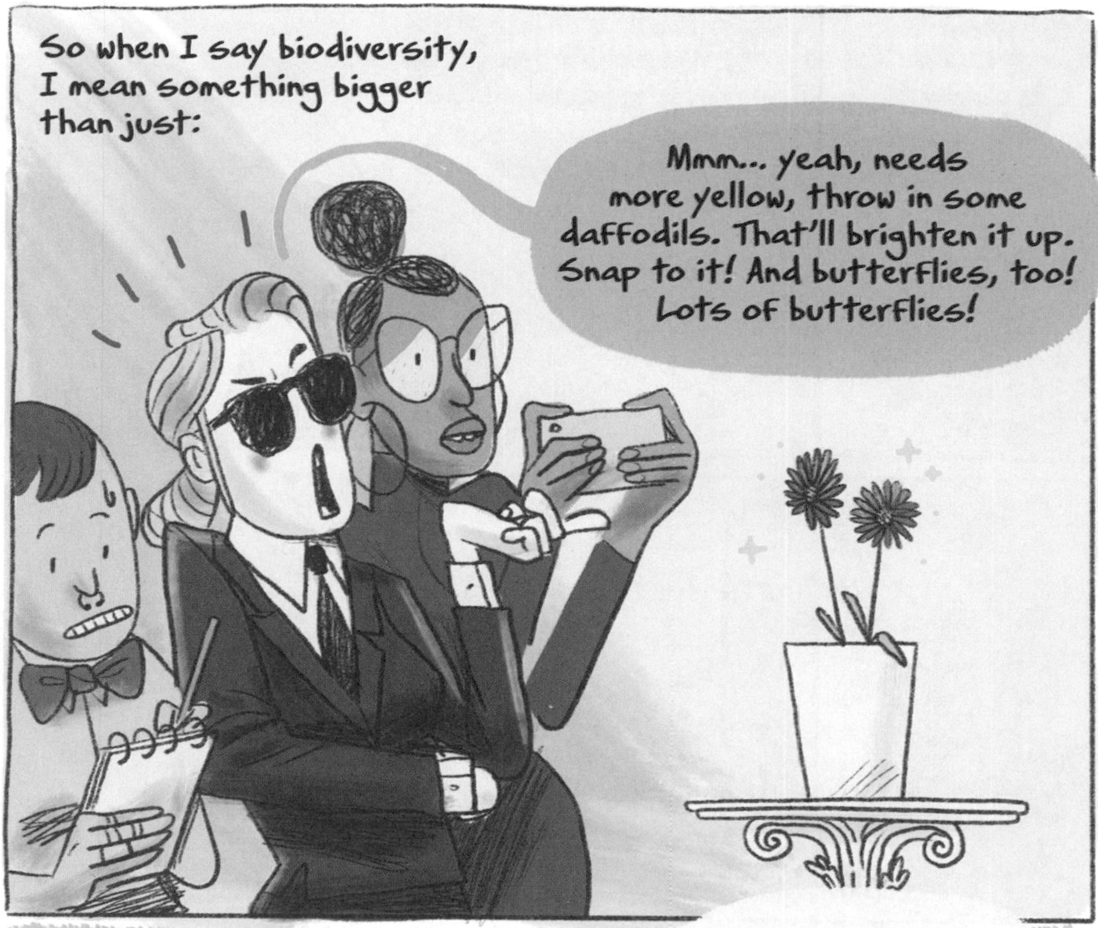
So when I say biodiversity, I mean something bigger than just:
Mmm... yeah, needs more yellow, throw in some daffodils. That'll brighten it up. Snap to it! And butterflies, too! Lots of butterflies!

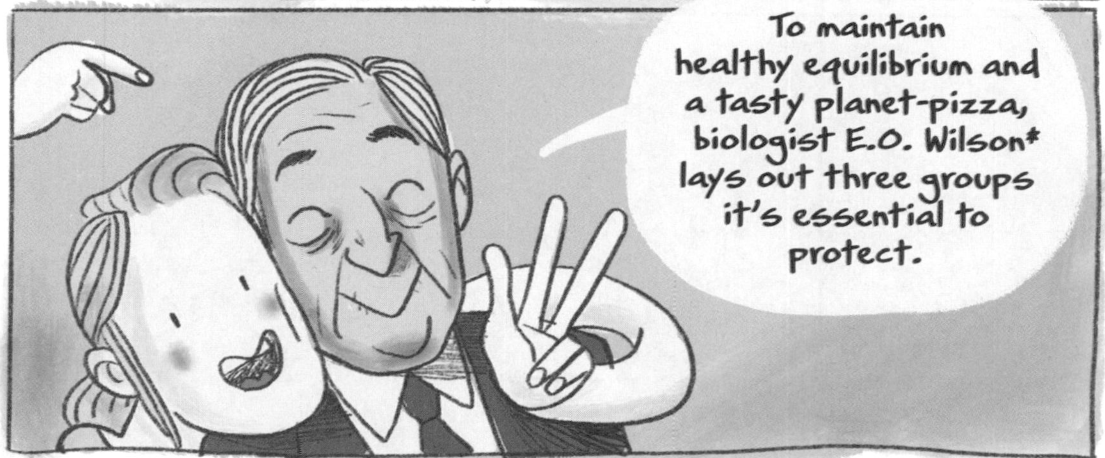
To maintain healthy equilibrium and a tasty planet-pizza, biologist E.O. Wilson* lays out three groups it's essential to protect.

*Winner of the 1979 Pulitzer Prize for *On Human Nature*

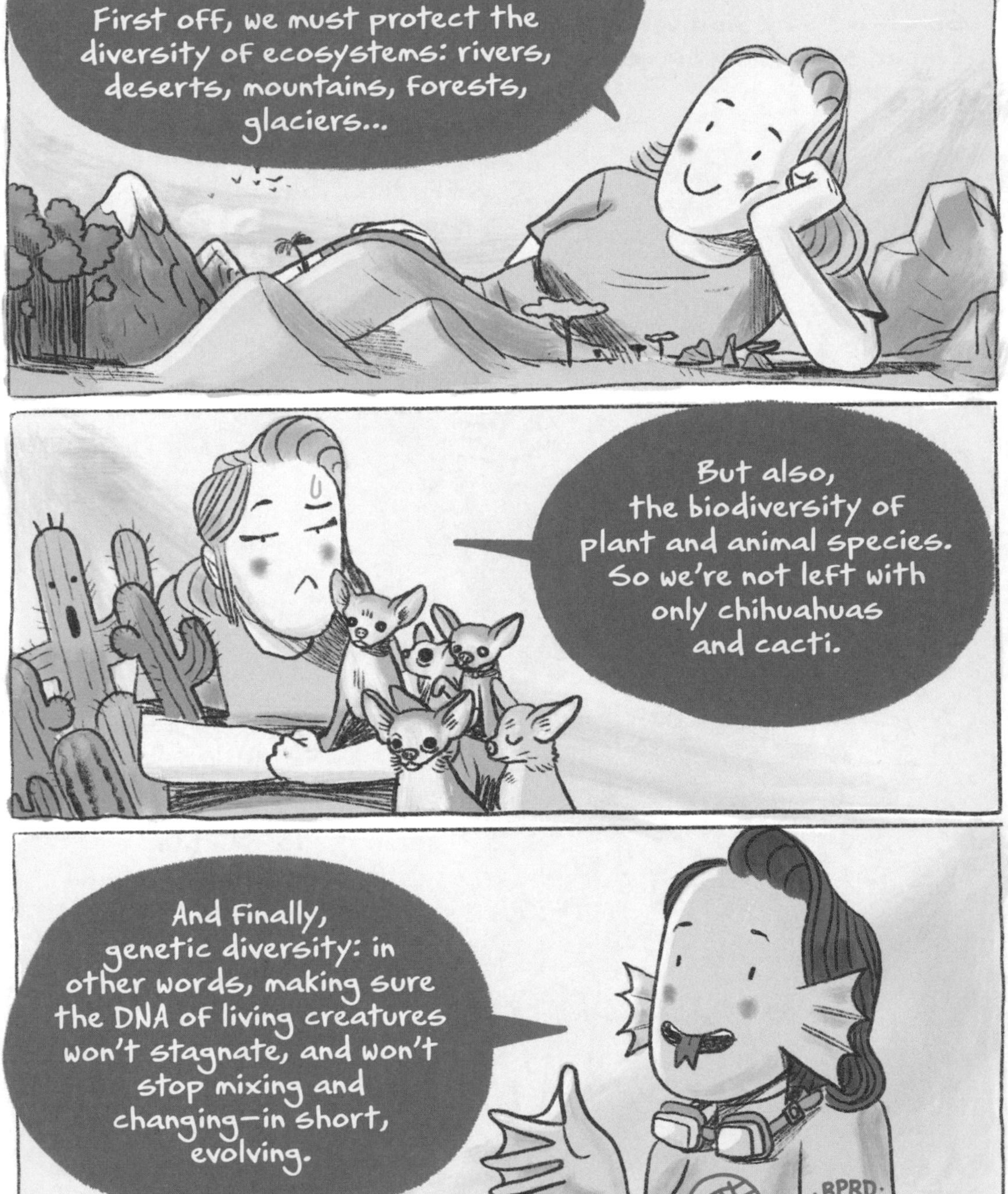
First off, we must protect the diversity of ecosystems: rivers, deserts, mountains, forests, glaciers...
But also, the biodiversity of plant and animal species. So we're not left with only chihuahuas and cacti.
And finally, genetic diversity: in other words, making sure the DNA of living creatures won't stagnate, and won't stop mixing and changing—in short, evolving.
·BPRD·

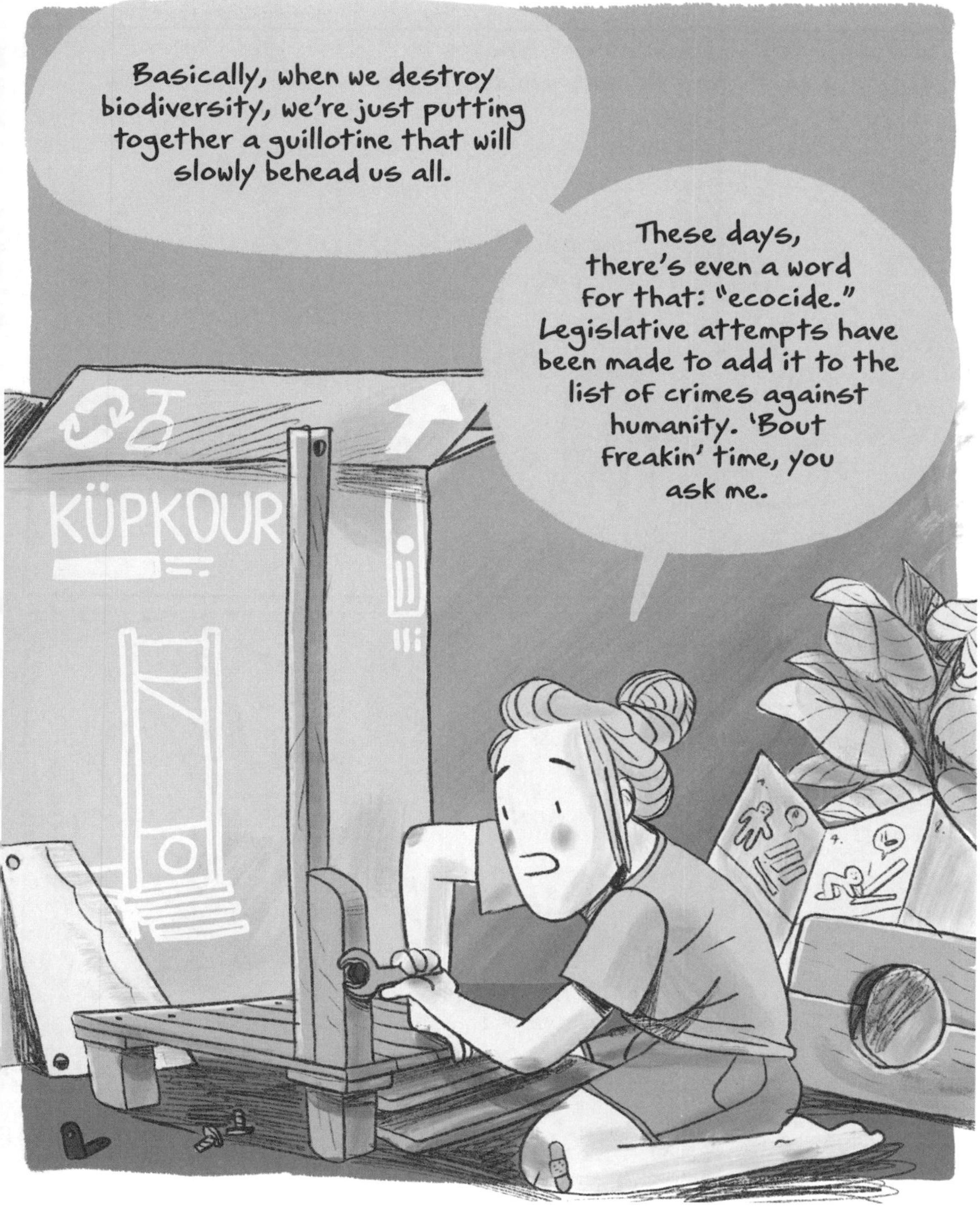
Basically, when we destroy biodiversity, we're just putting together a guillotine that will slowly behead us all.
These days, there's even a word for that: "ecocide." Legislative attempts have been made to add it to the list of crimes against humanity. 'Bout freakin' time, you ask me.
KÜPKOUR

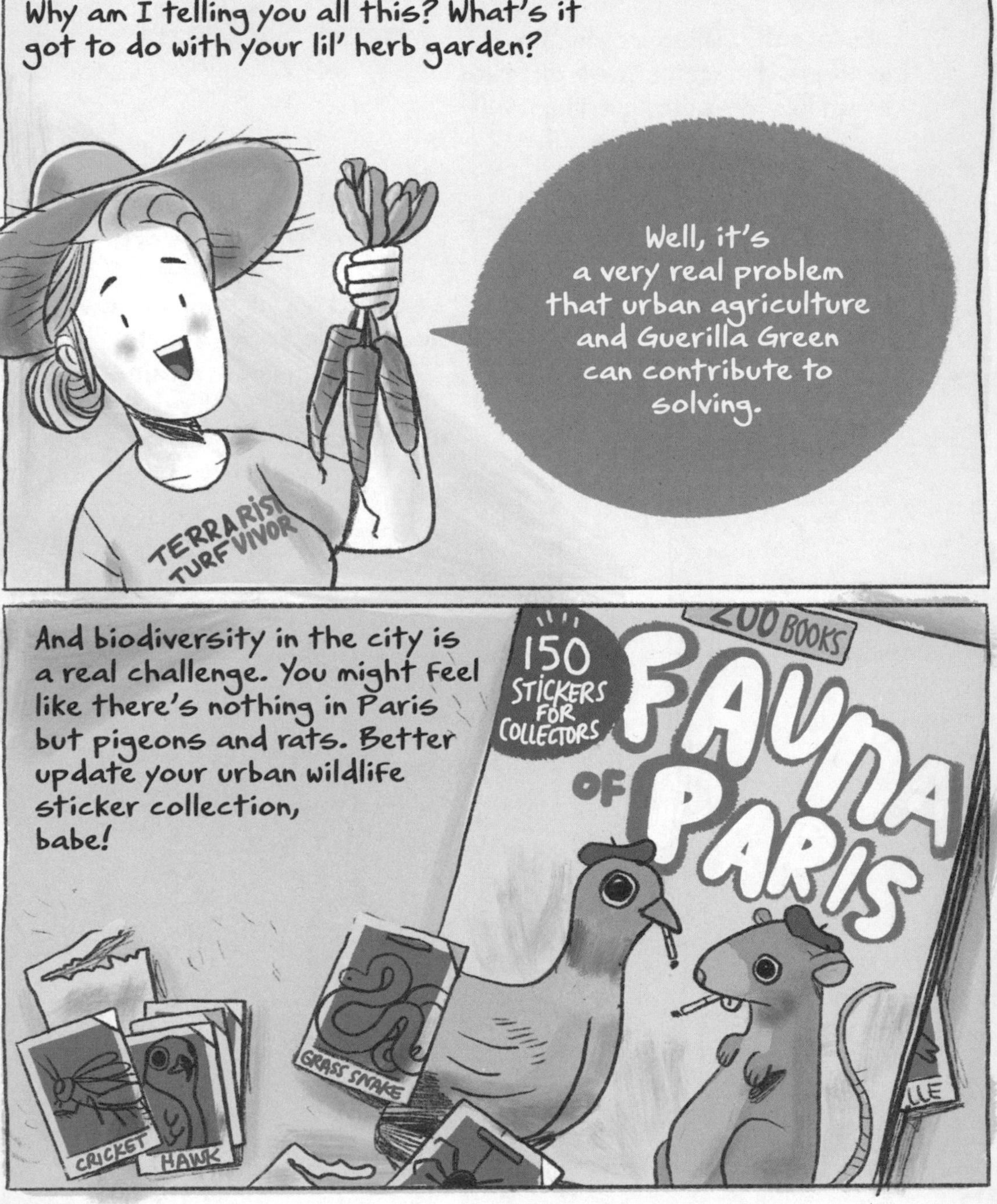
Why am I telling you all this? What's it got to do with your lil' herb garden?
Well, it's a very real problem that urban agriculture and Guerilla Green can contribute to solving.
TERRARIST
TURFVIVOR
And biodiversity in the city is a real challenge. You might feel like there's nothing in Paris but pigeons and rats. Better update your urban wildlife sticker collection, babe!
200 BOOKS
150 STICKERS FOR COLLECTORS
FAUNA OF PARIS
GRASS SNAKE
CRICKET
HAWK

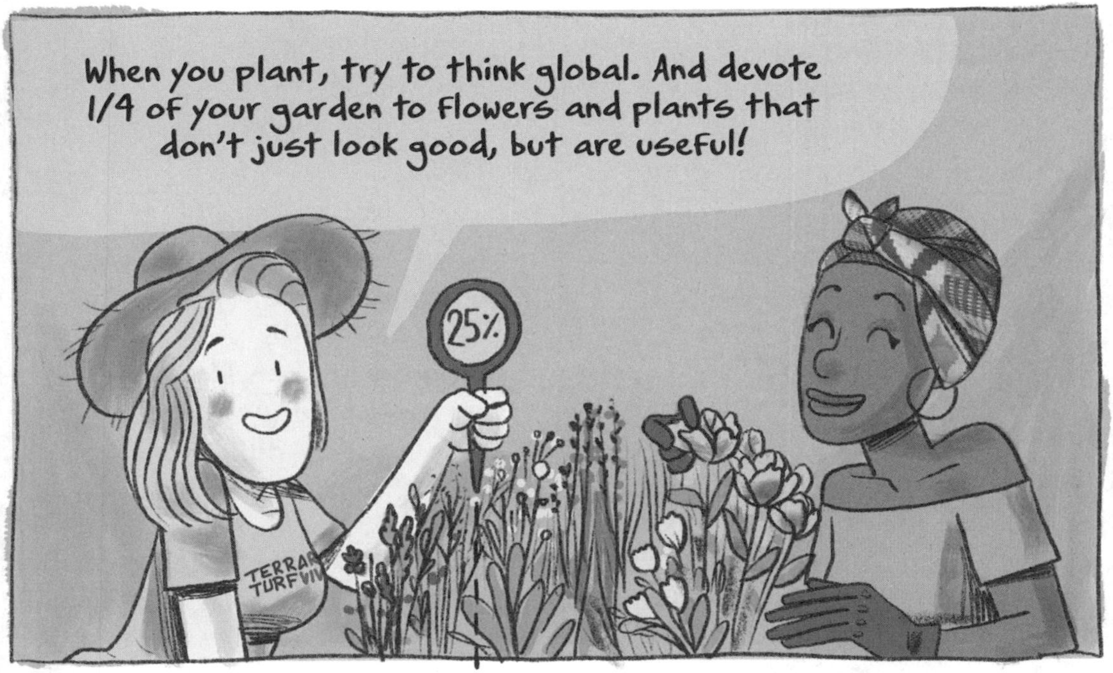
When you plant, try to think global. And devote 1/4 of your garden to flowers and plants that don't just look good, but are useful!
25%
TERRA TURF VIV

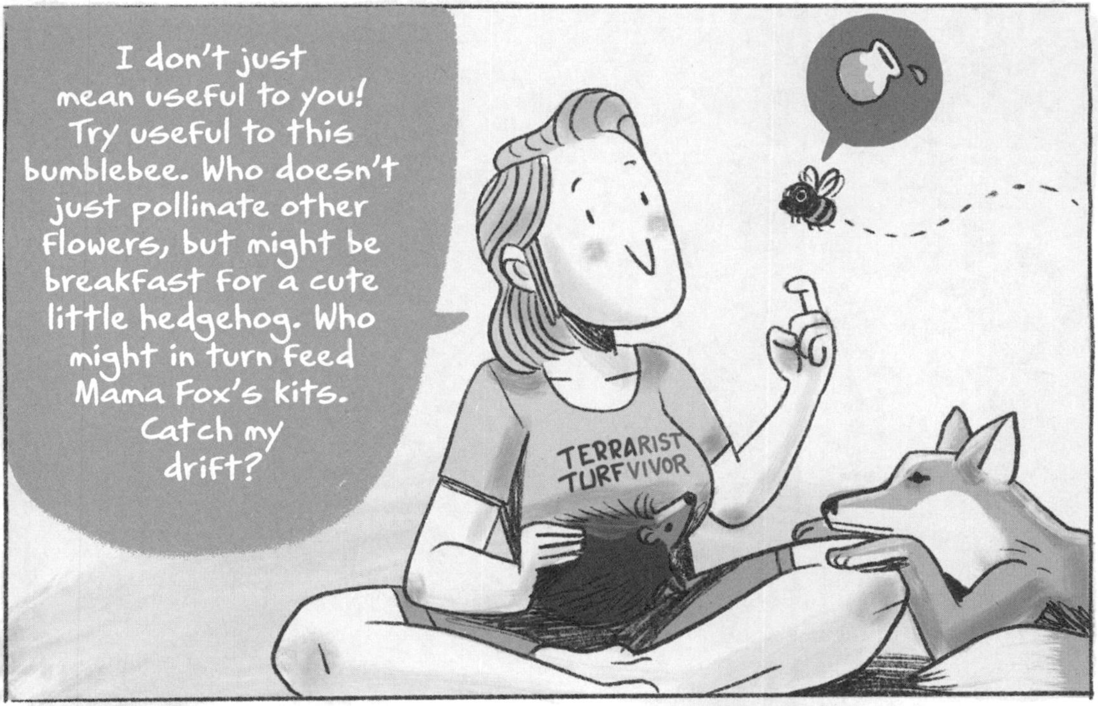
I don't just mean useful to you! Try useful to this bumblebee. Who doesn't just pollinate other flowers, but might be breakfast for a cute little hedgehog. Who might in turn feed Mama Fox's kits. Catch my drift?
TERRARIST TURFVIVOR

The other big behavioral change we need to make is to stop wiping out all the urban animals just for the petty sake of our comfort.

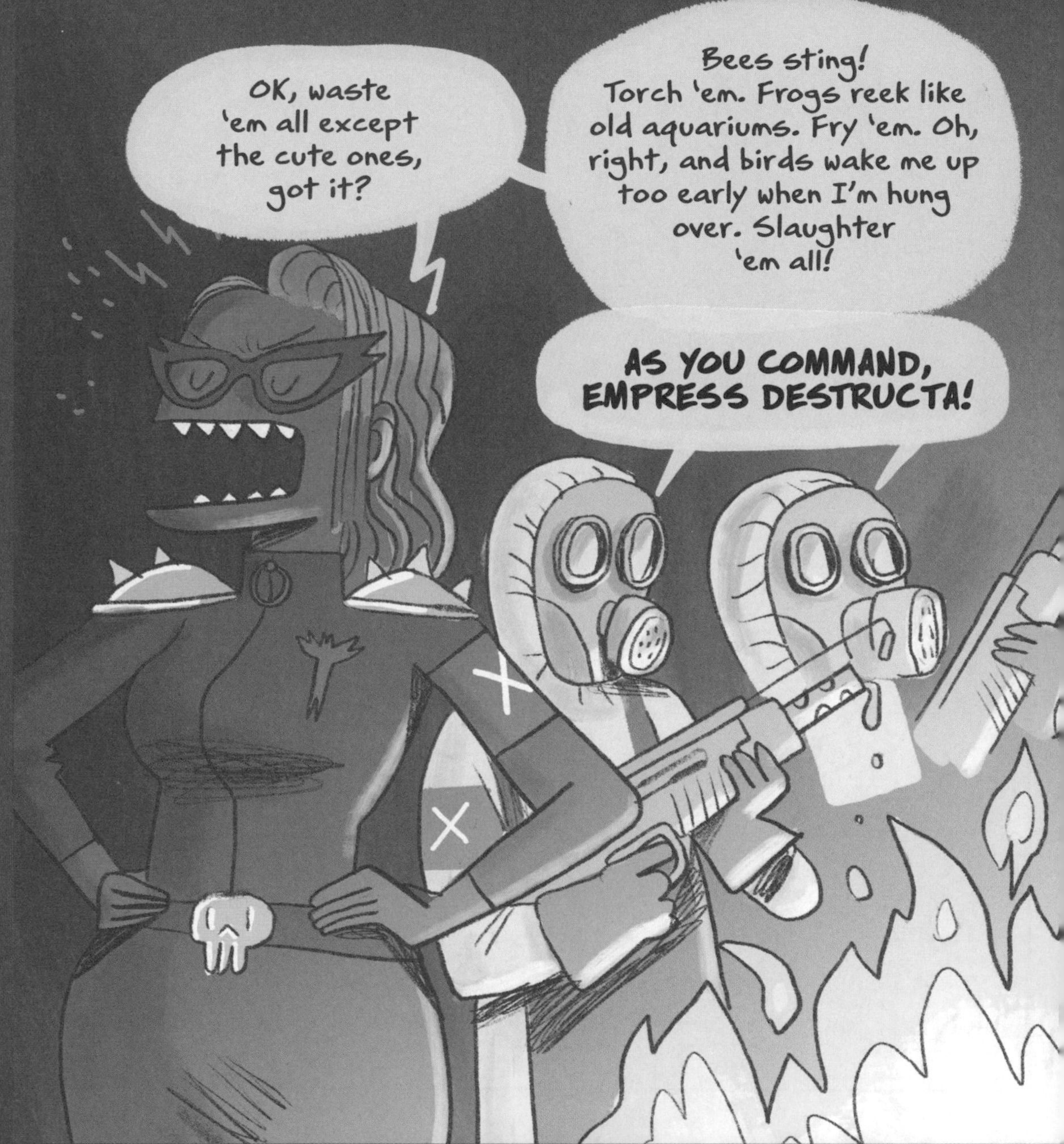
OK, waste 'em all except the cute ones, got it?
Bees sting! Torch 'em. Frogs reek like old aquariums. Fry 'em. Oh, right, and birds wake me up too early when I'm hung over. Slaughter 'em all!
AS YOU COMMAND, EMPRESS DESTRUCTA!

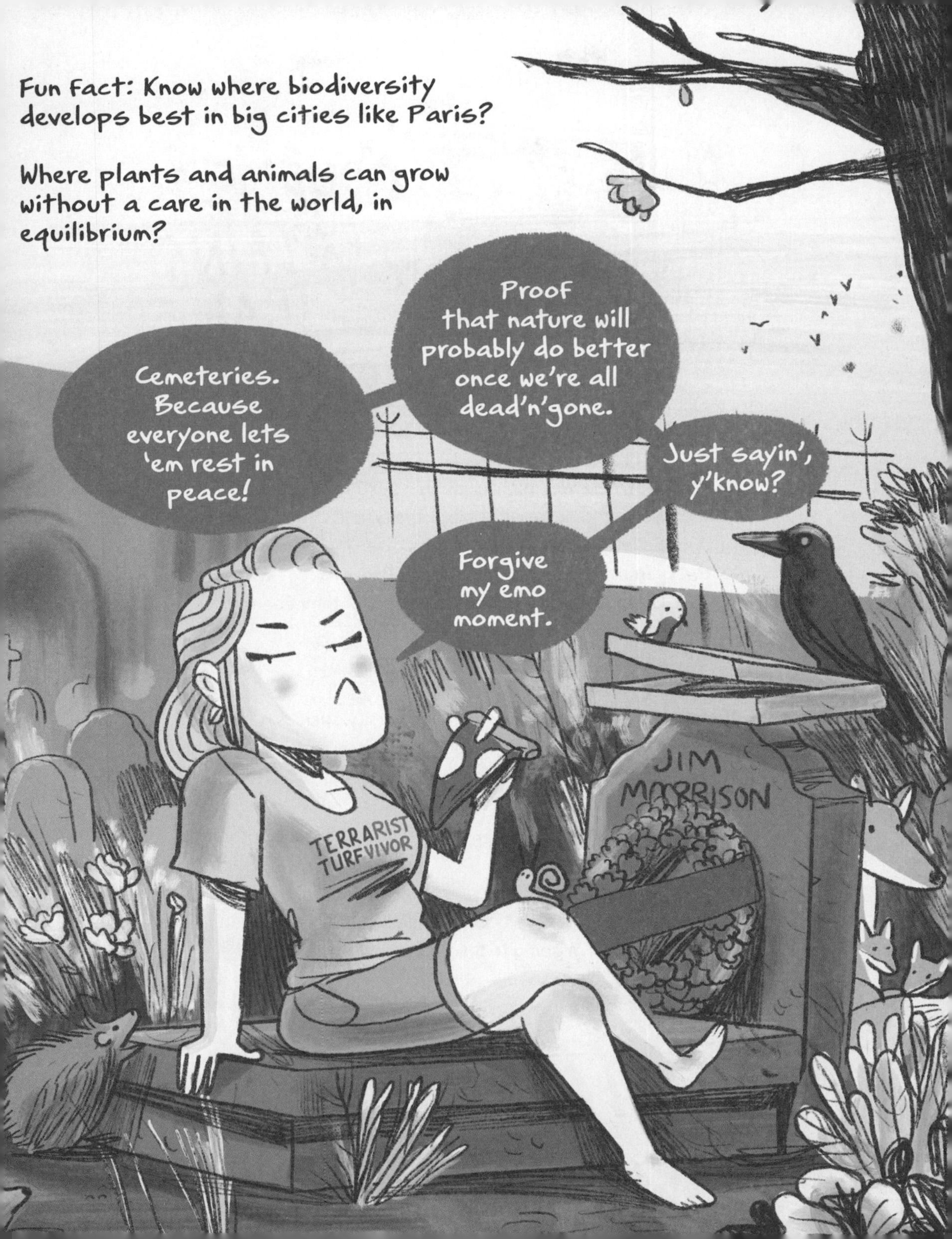
Fun Fact: Know where biodiversity develops best in big cities like Paris?
Where plants and animals can grow without a care in the world, in equilibrium?
Cemeteries. Because everyone lets 'em rest in peace!
Proof that nature will probably do better once we're all dead'n'gone.
Just sayin', y'know?
Forgive my emo moment.
TERRARIST TURFVIVOR
JIM MORRISON

OPHÉLIE EXPLAINS IT ALL

SAVING BIODIVERSITY

Ready or not, here we go: the sixth mass extinction event is underway. A rapid decrease in biodiversity, and whose fault is it? Ours! So let's stop the carnage. If biodiversity goes, we'll all follow! Even the conservative magazine *Paris Match** says so!

- "Over 2 billion people depend on wood for their energy"
- "4 billion use natural remedies"
- "75% of crops need insects for pollination"

There are lots of ways to preserve biodiversity, such as not lifting a finger…when it comes to your yard. That is, letting it grow wild so animals can make their homes and babies there.

If you're a citydweller without a yard, there are also tons of things you can do, like build shelters.

Sparrow populations have been in freefall in major European cities. That's why I'm going to teach you how to make a little sparrow B&B.

* United Nations report: "One million species risk extinction due to humans" (April 23, 2019)

HOW TO MAKE A SPARROW B&B FOR THREE

(from the website of Paris' City Hall)

You'll need

A plank of wood (40" x 27"), a pencil, a set square, a saw, a drill, a file, screws, a screwdriver, hinges, a brush, linseed oil.

The sides

- Bottom: 5"x20" - Roof: 8.25"x22"
- Back: 10.5"x22" - 8.25"x22" + hole (1.25"-1.5")
- Inner wall: 9.5"x5.25"x7.5"- Side walls (x2) : 10"x5.25"x8.25" (1.25"-1.5")

Assembly

- Plan where you're going to put the hole
- Drill the hole
- Make the opening bigger with a file
- Assemble your house
- Screw on the hinges
- Weatherproof the wood with linseed oil

Recommendations

- Hang your birdhouse over ten feet up, facing south/southwest
- Put it somewhere quiet (courtyard, graveyard, shared garden, etc.)
- Whatever you do, don't paint it!

PERMACULTURE
ALL THE THINGS!

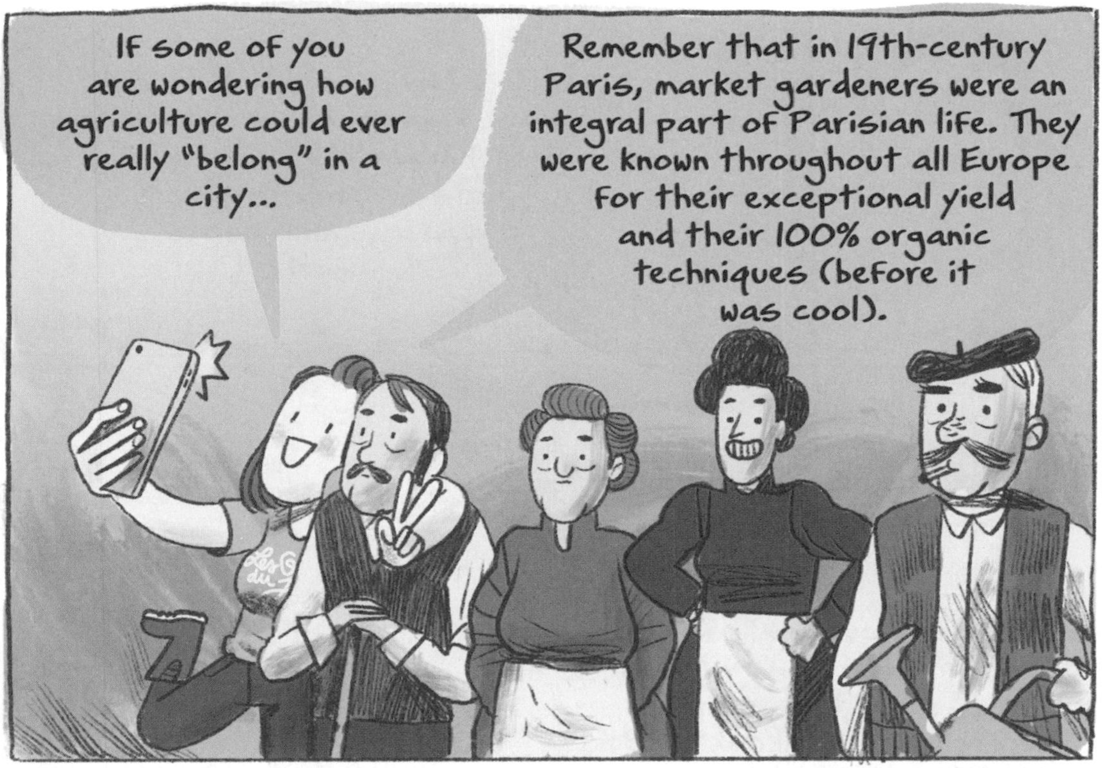
If some of you are wondering how agriculture could ever really "belong" in a city...
Remember that in 19th-century Paris, market gardeners were an integral part of Parisian life. They were known throughout all Europe for their exceptional yield and their 100% organic techniques (before it was cool).

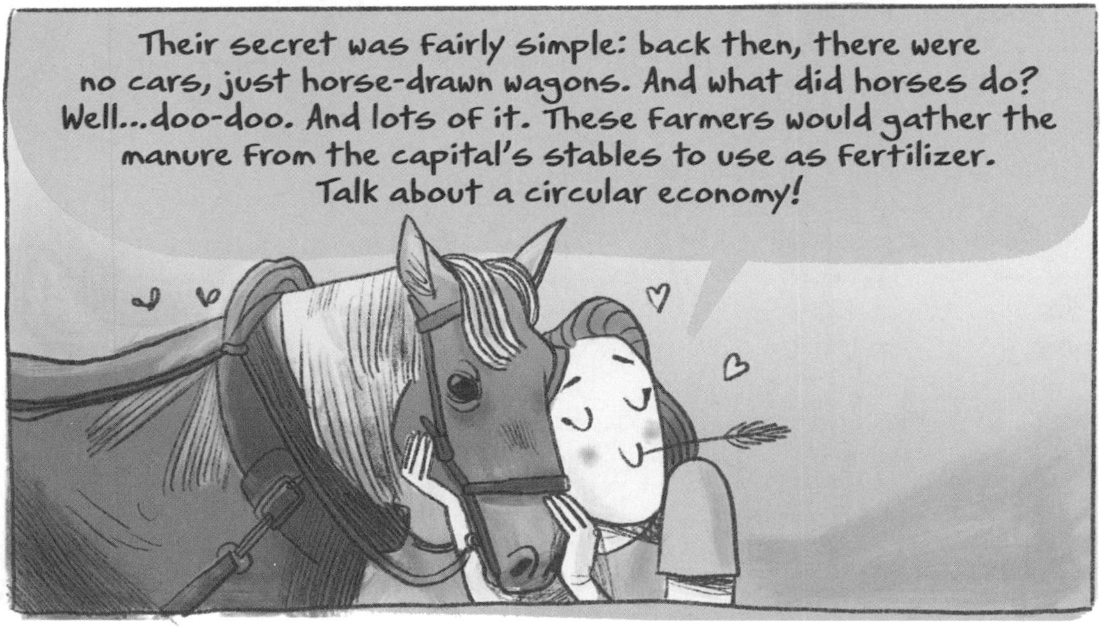
Their secret was fairly simple: back then, there were no cars, just horse-drawn wagons. And what did horses do? Well...doo-doo. And lots of it. These farmers would gather the manure from the capital's stables to use as fertilizer. Talk about a circular economy!

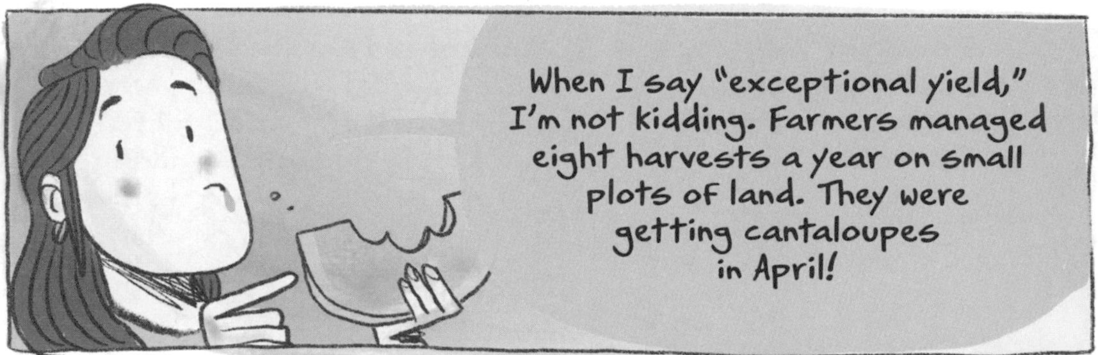
When I say "exceptional yield," I'm not kidding. Farmers managed eight harvests a year on small plots of land. They were getting cantaloupes in April!

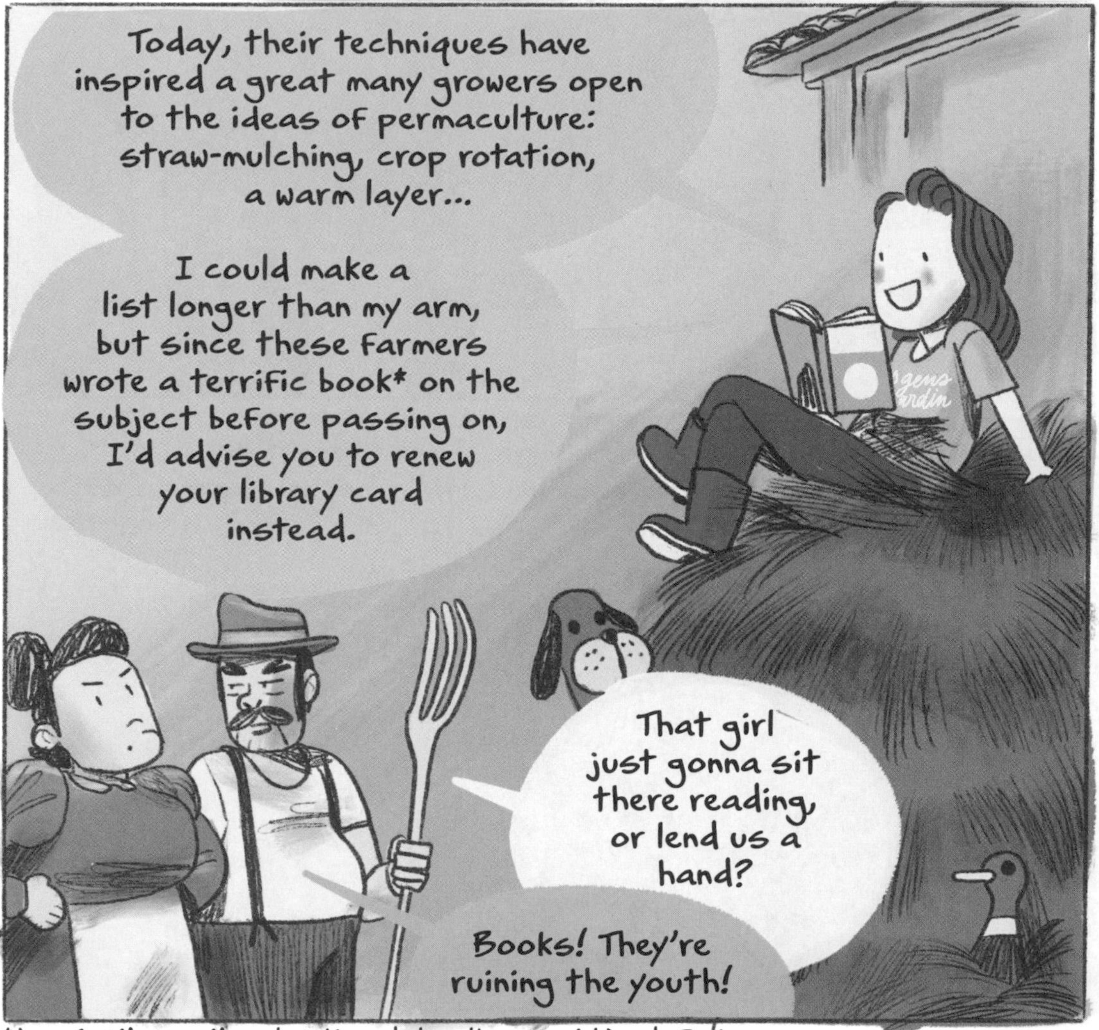
Today, their techniques have inspired a great many growers open to the ideas of permaculture: straw-mulching, crop rotation, a warm layer...
I could make a list longer than my arm, but since these farmers wrote a terrific book* on the subject before passing on, I'd advise you to renew your library card instead.
That girl just gonna sit there reading, or lend us a hand?
Books! They're ruining the youth!

*Jean-Guy Moreau, Manuel pratique de la culture maraîchère de Paris [A Practical Guide to Market Gardening in Paris], 1845

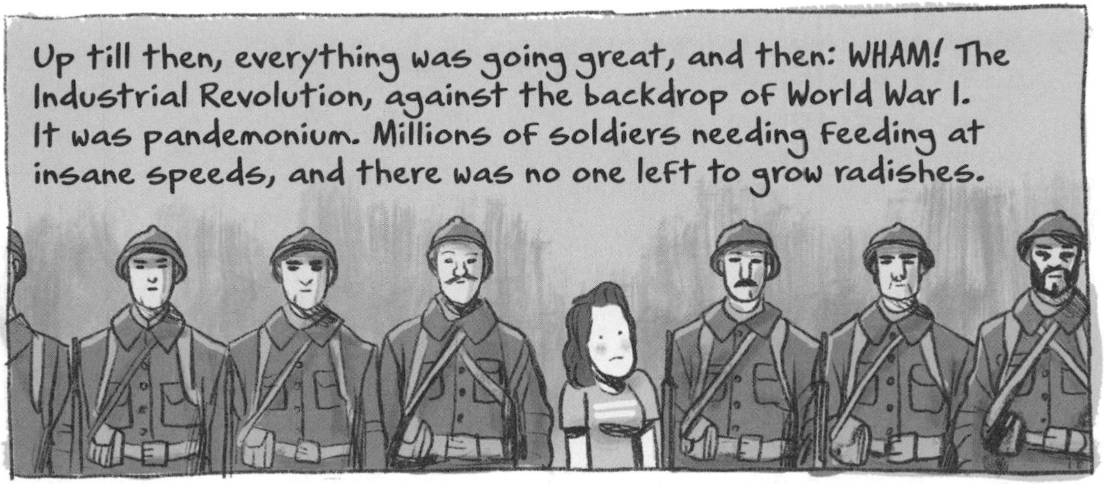
Up till then, everything was going great, and then: WHAM! The Industrial Revolution, against the backdrop of World War I. It was pandemonium. Millions of soldiers needing feeding at insane speeds, and there was no one left to grow radishes.

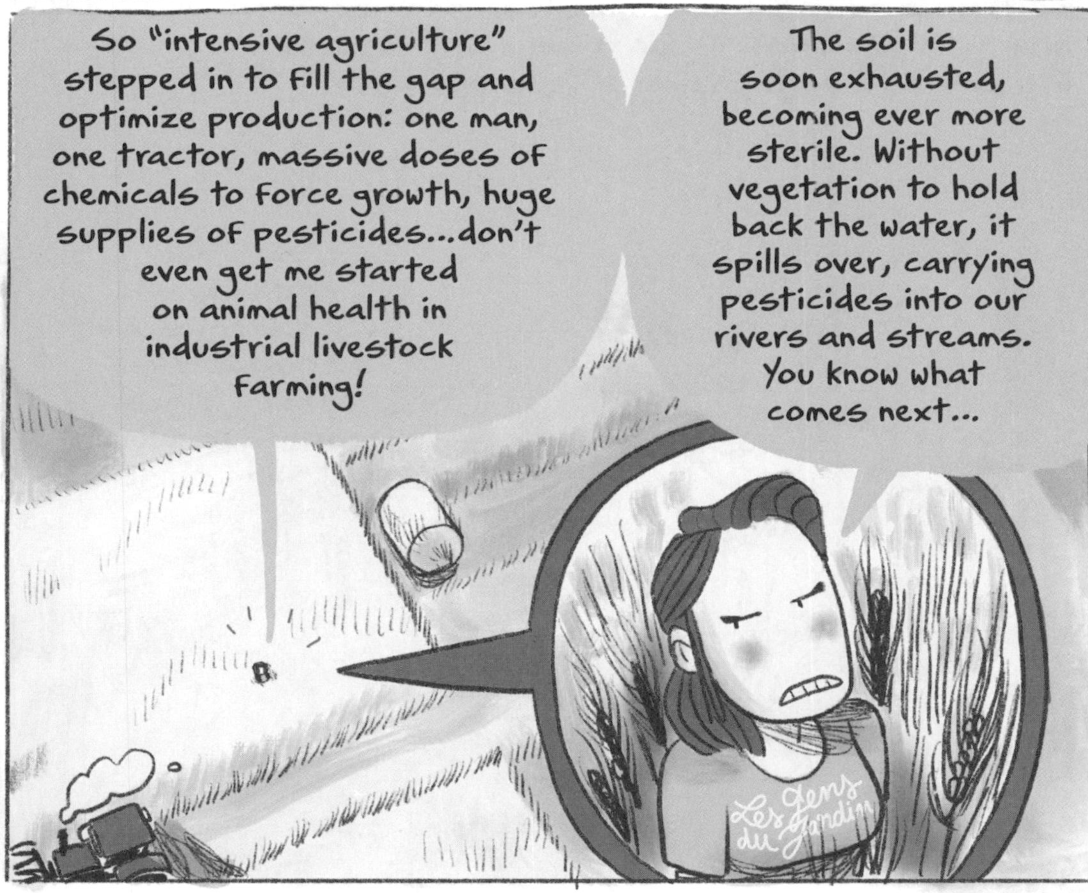
So "intensive agriculture" stepped in to fill the gap and optimize production: one man, one tractor, massive doses of chemicals to force growth, huge supplies of pesticides...don't even get me started on animal health in industrial livestock farming!
The soil is soon exhausted, becoming ever more sterile. Without vegetation to hold back the water, it spills over, carrying pesticides into our rivers and streams. You know what comes next...
Les Gens du Jardin

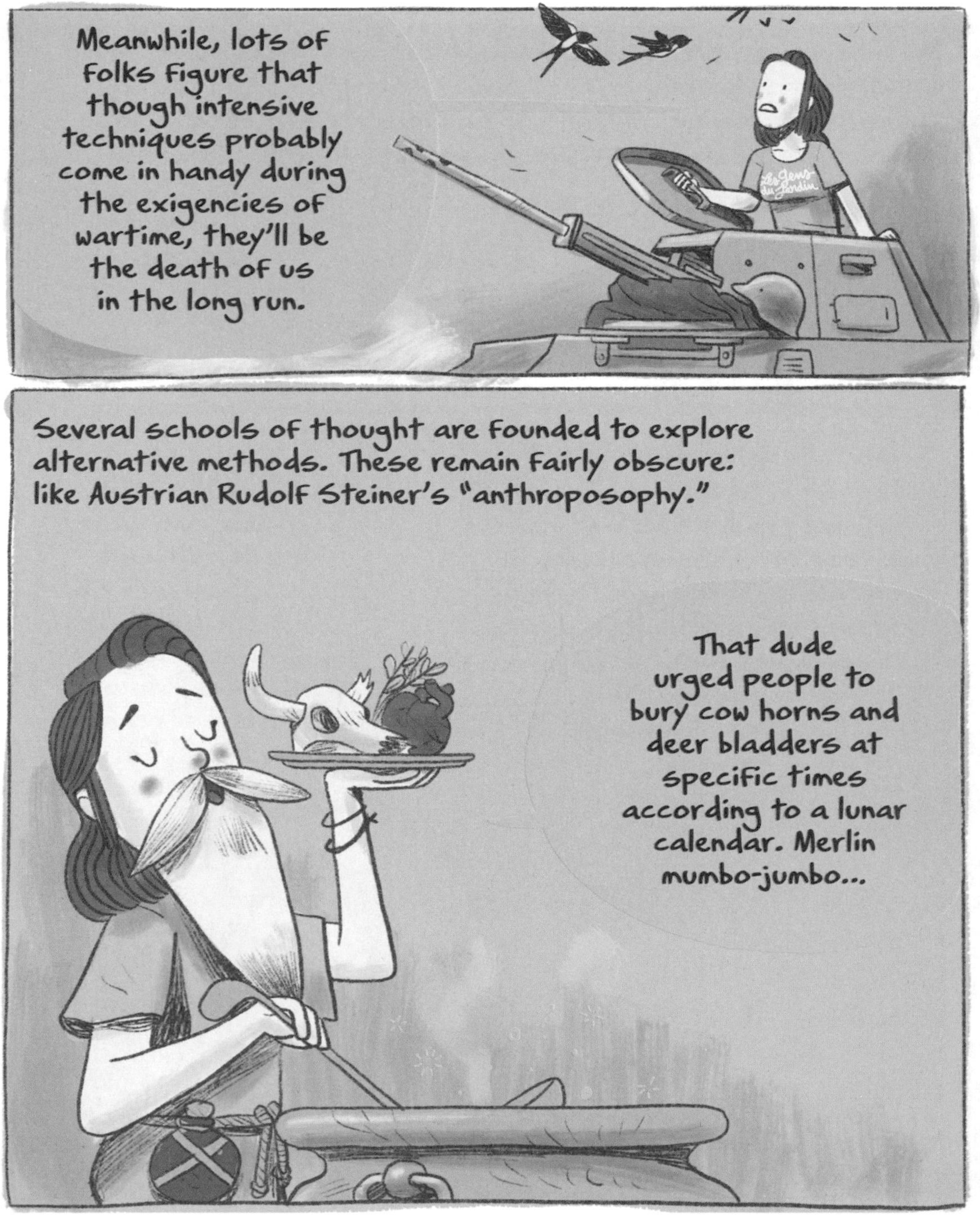
Meanwhile, lots of folks figure that though intensive techniques probably come in handy during the exigencies of wartime, they'll be the death of us in the long run.
Several schools of thought are founded to explore alternative methods. These remain fairly obscure: like Austrian Rudolf Steiner's "anthroposophy."
That dude urged people to bury cow horns and deer bladders at specific times according to a lunar calendar. Merlin mumbo-jumbo...

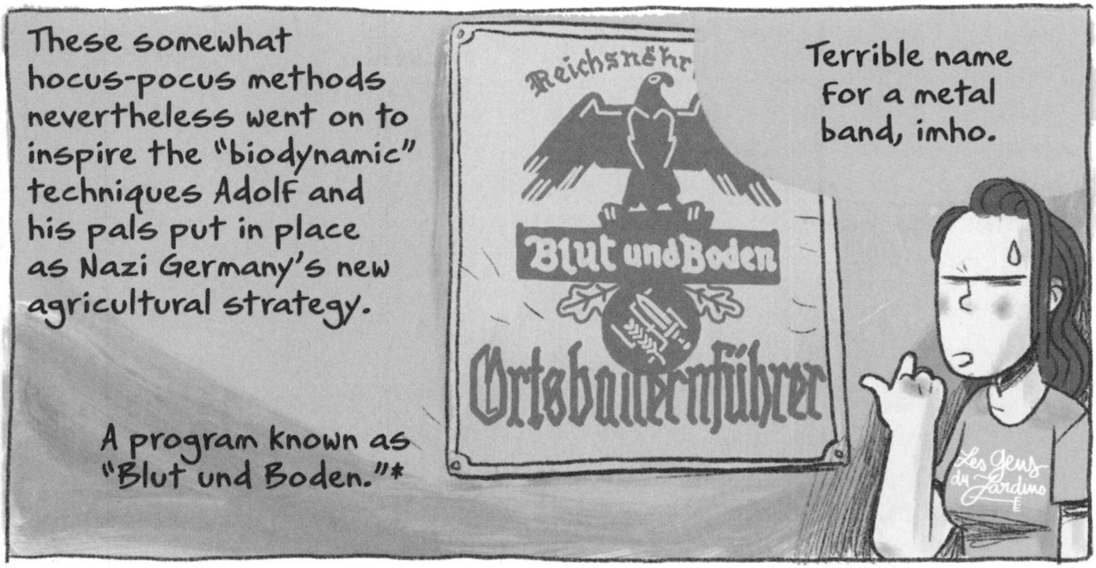
These somewhat hocus-pocus methods nevertheless went on to inspire the "biodynamic" techniques Adolf and his pals put in place as Nazi Germany's new agricultural strategy.
Blut und Boden
Ortsbauernführer
Terrible name for a metal band, imho.
Les Gens du Jardins
A program known as "Blut und Boden."*

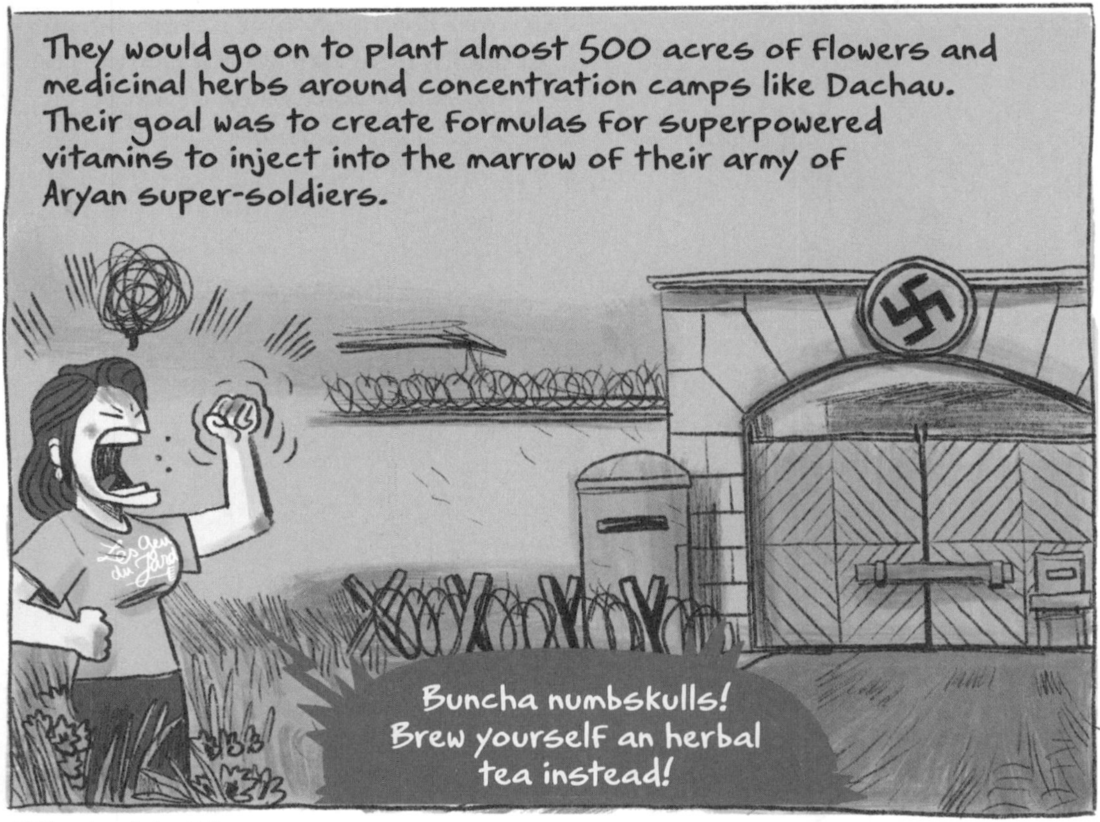
They would go on to plant almost 500 acres of flowers and medicinal herbs around concentration camps like Dachau. Their goal was to create formulas for superpowered vitamins to inject into the marrow of their army of Aryan super-soldiers.
Buncha numbskulls! Brew yourself an herbal tea instead!

*"Blood and Earth"

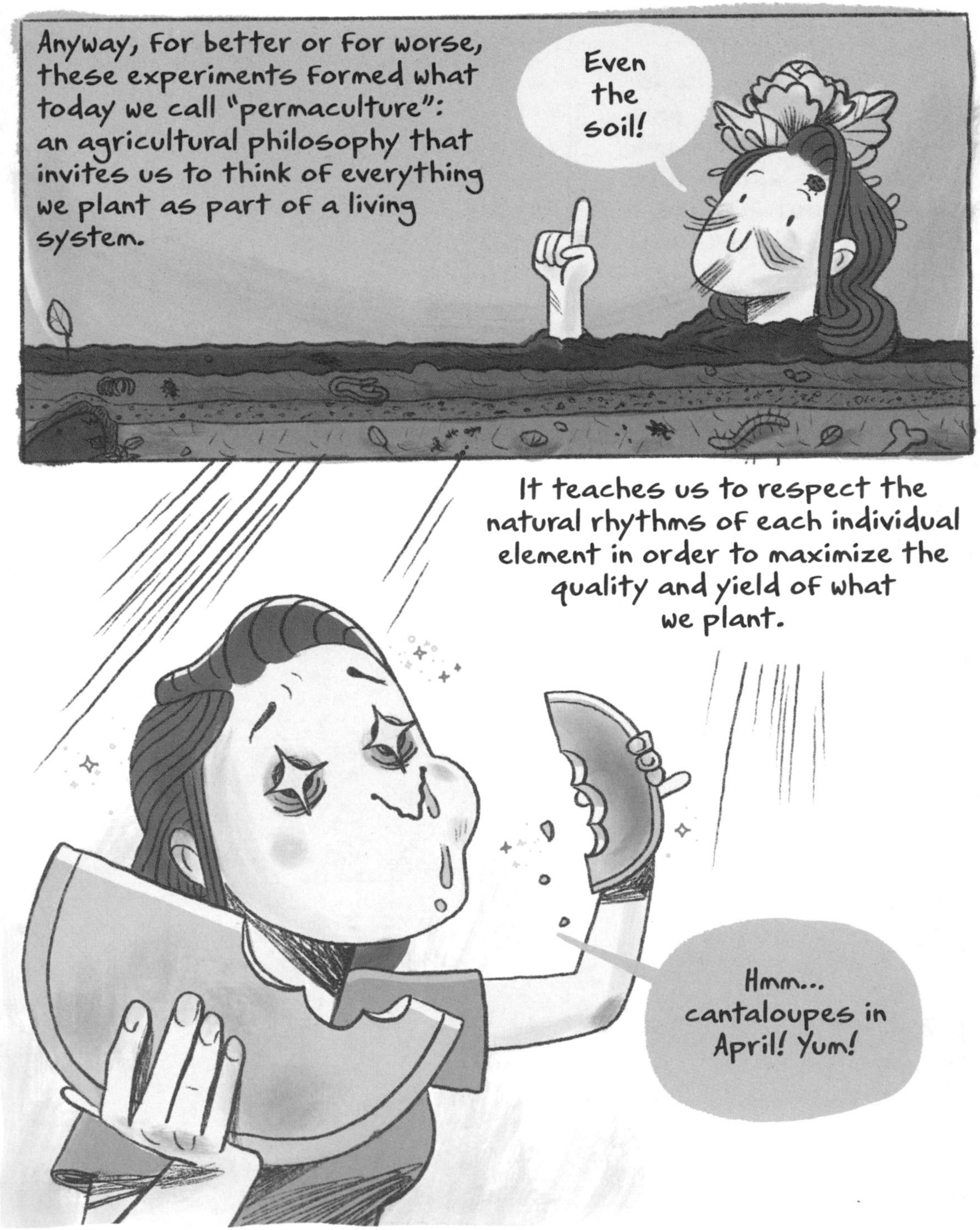
Anyway, for better or for worse, these experiments formed what today we call "permaculture": an agricultural philosophy that invites us to think of everything we plant as part of a living system.
Even the soil!
It teaches us to respect the natural rhythms of each individual element in order to maximize the quality and yield of what we plant.
Hmm... cantaloupes in April! Yum!

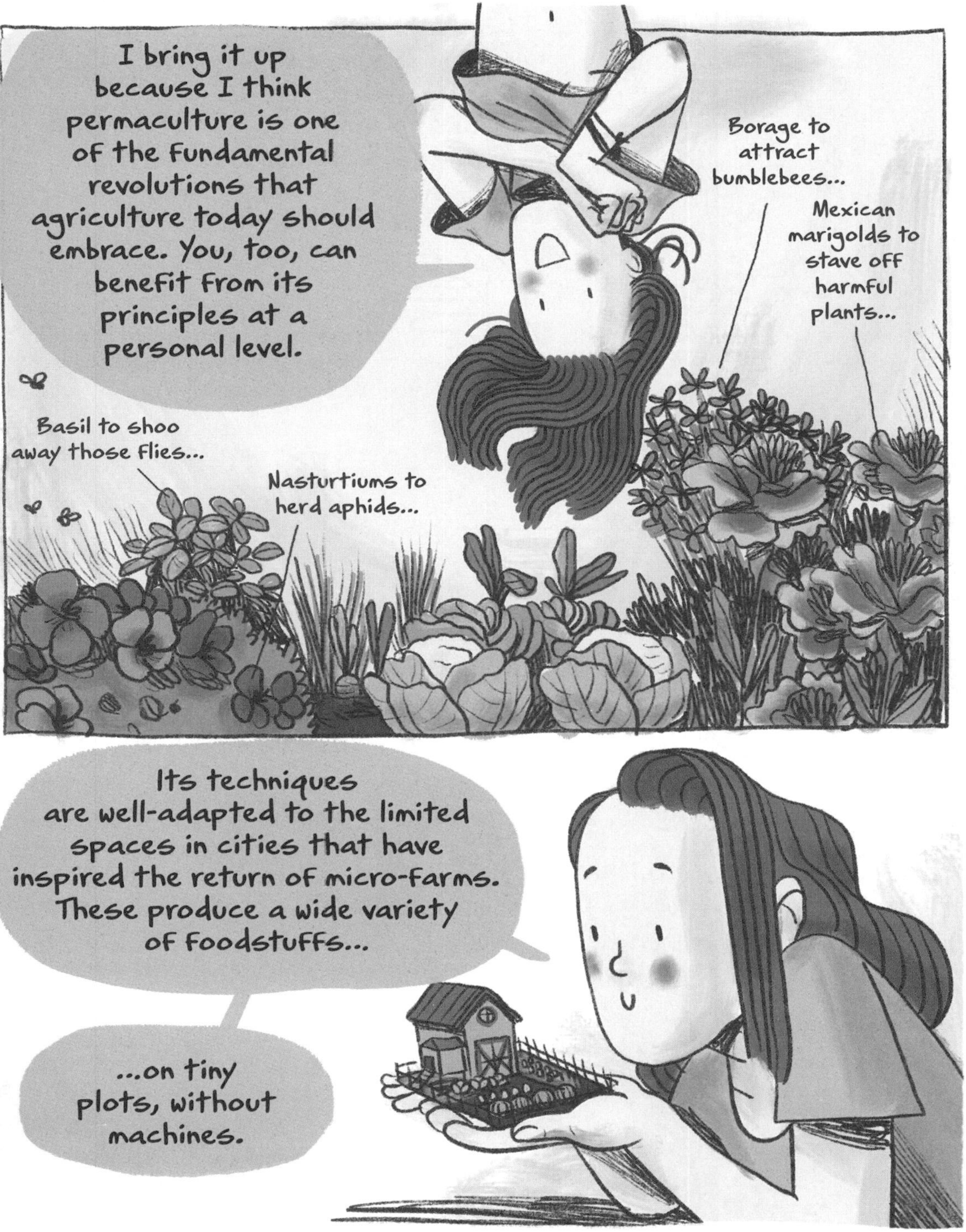
I bring it up because I think permaculture is one of the fundamental revolutions that agriculture today should embrace. You, too, can benefit from its principles at a personal level.
Borage to attract bumblebees...
Mexican marigolds to stave off harmful plants...
Basil to shoo away those flies...
Nasturtiums to herd aphids...
Its techniques are well-adapted to the limited spaces in cities that have inspired the return of micro-farms. These produce a wide variety of foodstuffs...
...on tiny plots, without machines.

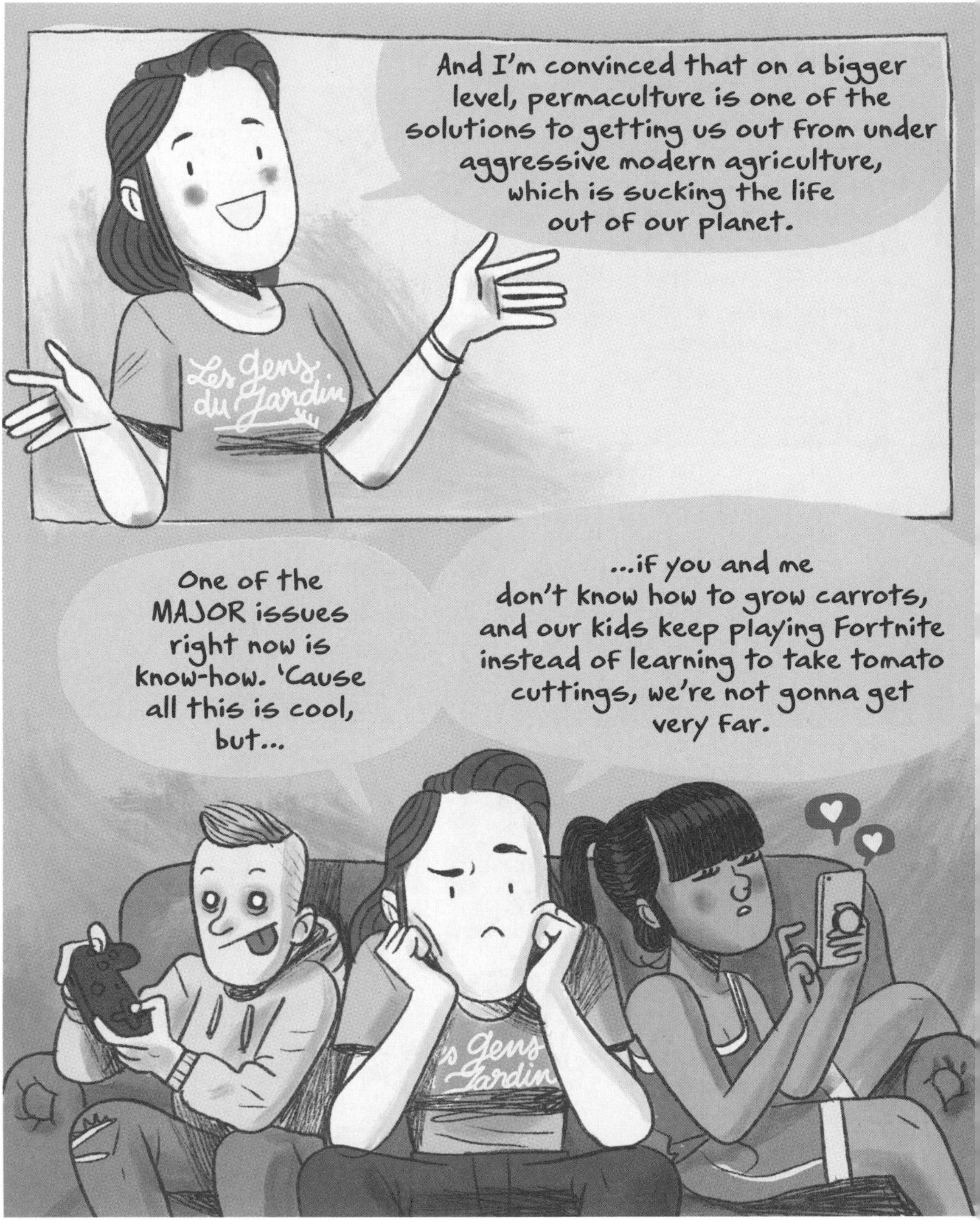
And I'm convinced that on a bigger level, permaculture is one of the solutions to getting us out from under aggressive modern agriculture, which is sucking the life out of our planet.
Les Gens du Jardin
One of the MAJOR issues right now is know-how. 'Cause all this is cool, but...
...if you and me don't know how to grow carrots, and our kids keep playing Fortnite instead of learning to take tomato cuttings, we're not gonna get very far.

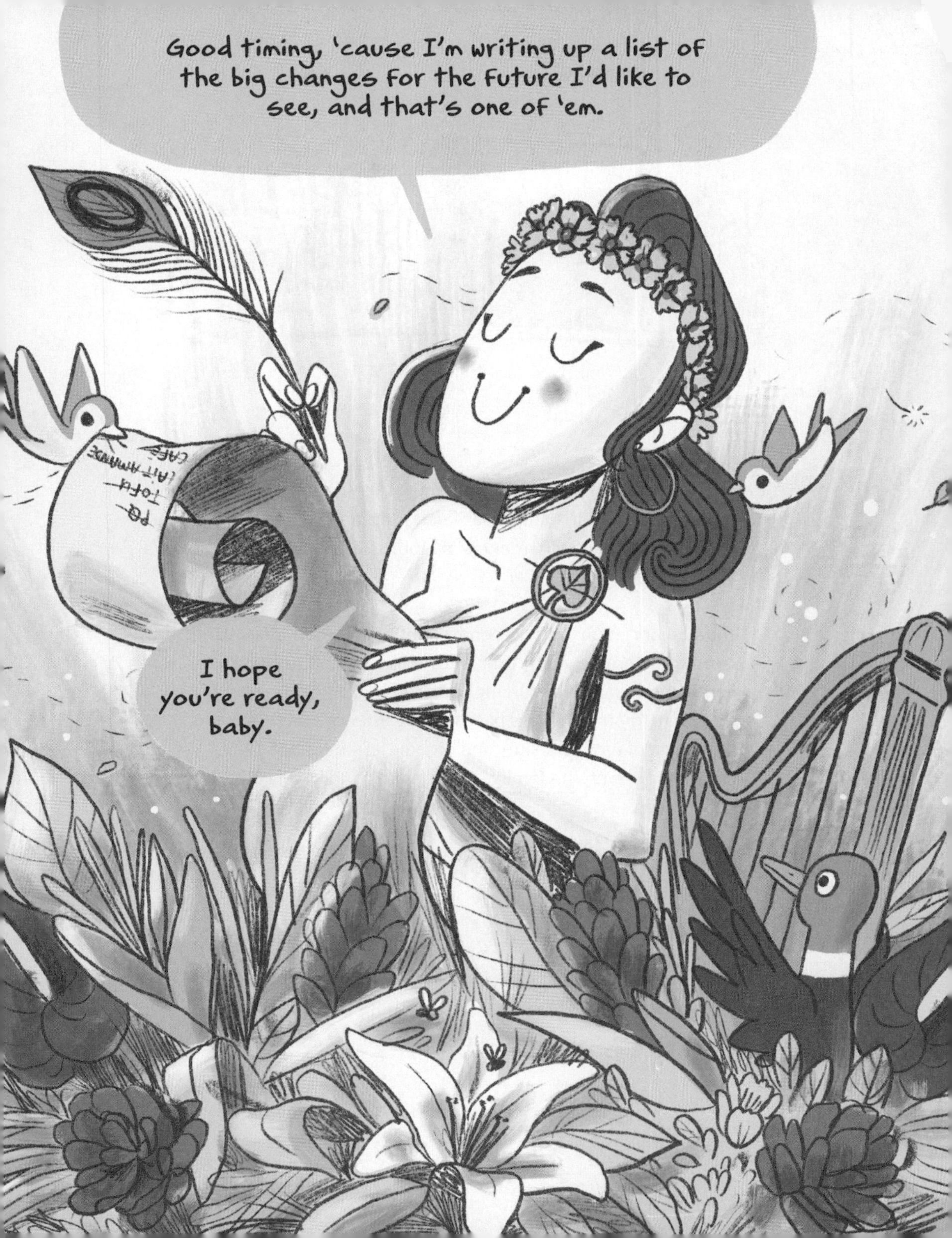
Good timing, 'cause I'm writing up a list of the big changes for the future I'd like to see, and that's one of 'em.
I hope you're ready, baby.

"OPHÉLIE EXPLAINS IT ALL"

A PEACHY IDEA

Espaliered peach trees are among the last vestiges of an era when Paris was self-sufficient as far as fruits and vegetables go. Thanks to the market gardeners of Montreuil, this was as recent as the 19th century.

Today, associations and gardeners fight to protect this farmland, constantly threatened by urban development. In the eastern Paris suburb of Montreuil, I met with Patrick Fontaine, a self-described "grandpa who is part of the resistance." He's been a champion of natural beauty and organic farming since 1973. He invited me into his familial garden, surrounded by walls of peach trees.

PEACH TRELLISES

Walls of peach trees are a frequent sight in the almost 75 acres of gardens hidden on the high Montreuil plateau. The walls are made from cinderblocks, soil, and plaster. They are meant to protect crops from inclement weather and store the

sun's warmth to release it during the night, thus creating a microclimate that allows certain more Mediterranean plants to be grown. In the second half of the 19th century, walls with espaliered peach trees covered over a third of the city: 185 miles of walls over 790 acres!

In 2010, the spot where Patrick started his garden was just an empty lot full of asbestos. Today, he grows fruits and vegetables (peaches, bell peppers, hot peppers, eggplants, tomatoes) there. The branches of his trees intertwine in occasionally incredible ways (like a peach tree shaped like a lyre). He avoids leafy greens (lettuce, chard) and tubers, which absorb too much lead and mercury. The soil in Montreuil is especially polluted with heavy metals, so Patrick plants in aboveground boxes, using soil imported from elsewhere.

When it comes to making his garden grow, Patrick uses ancient Montreuil techniques such as espalier, which consists of using fabric to tie the branches of a tree to a trellis anchored to a roughcast wall; or bagging fruits, which protects apples from codling moths, which are insects that lay eggs inside the fruit. Droppings from his hens have replaced the horse manure of the 19th century!

THREE CHANGES
FOR THE FUTURE

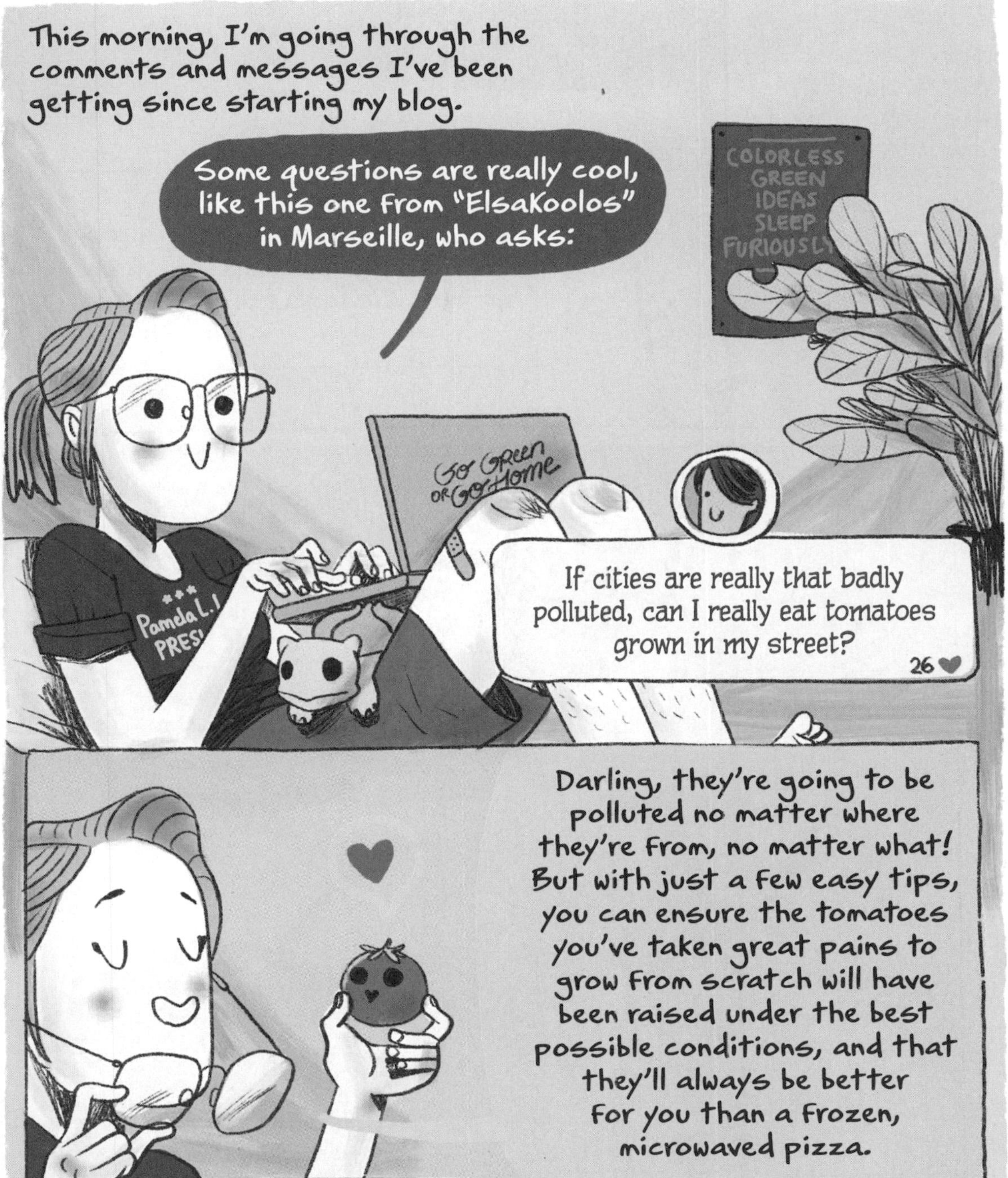
This morning, I'm going through the comments and messages I've been getting since starting my blog.
Some questions are really cool, like this one from "ElsaKoolos" in Marseille, who asks:
COLORLESS GREEN IDEAS SLEEP FURIOUSLY
Go Green or Go Home
If cities are really that badly polluted, can I really eat tomatoes grown in my street?
26
Darling, they're going to be polluted no matter where they're from, no matter what! But with just a few easy tips, you can ensure the tomatoes you've taken great pains to grow from scratch will have been raised under the best possible conditions, and that they'll always be better for you than a frozen, microwaved pizza.

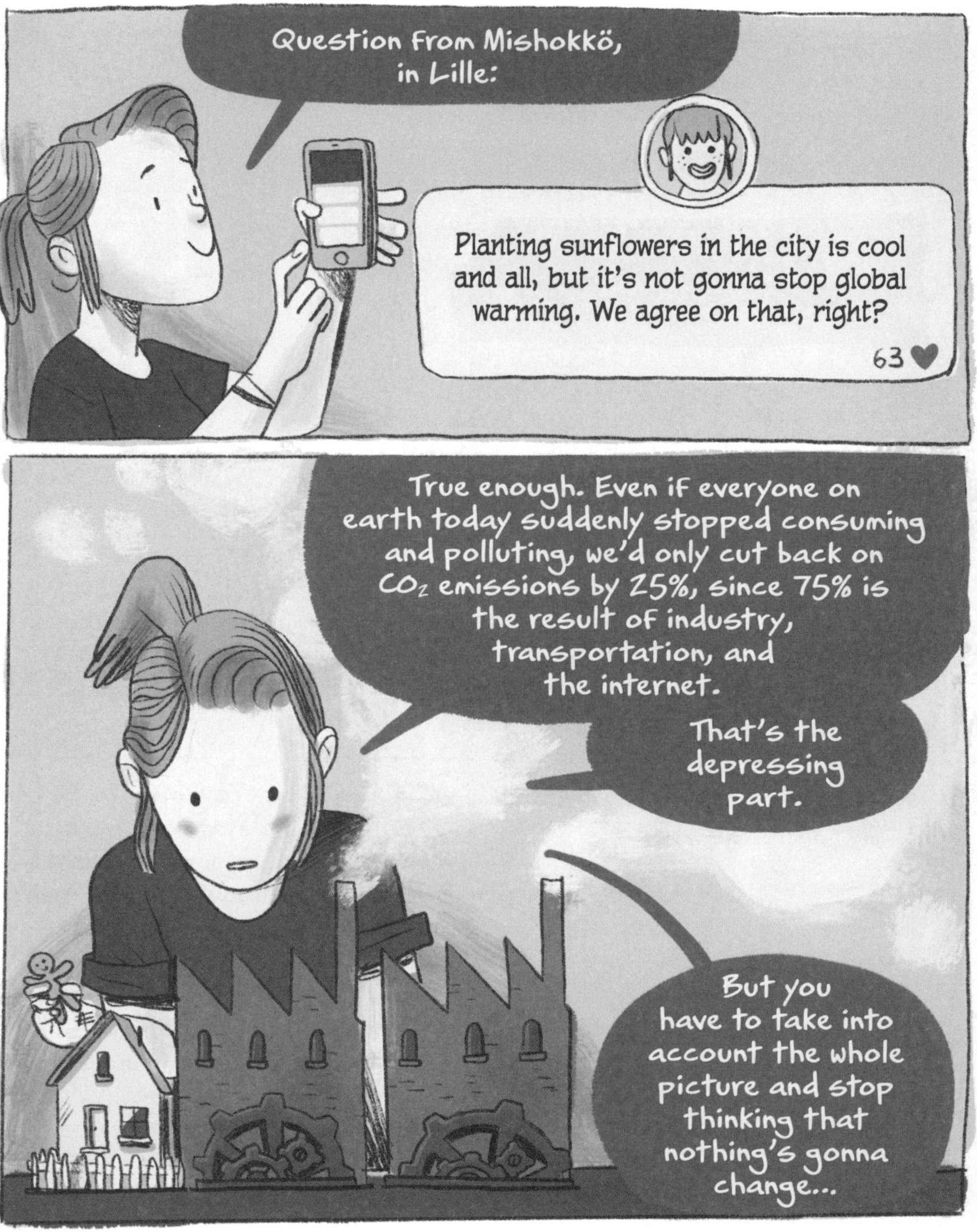
Question from Mishokkö, in Lille:
Planting sunflowers in the city is cool and all, but it's not gonna stop global warming. We agree on that, right?
63
True enough. Even if everyone on earth today suddenly stopped consuming and polluting, we'd only cut back on CO_2 emissions by 25%, since 75% is the result of industry, transportation, and the internet.
That's the depressing part.
But you have to take into account the whole picture and stop thinking that nothing's gonna change...

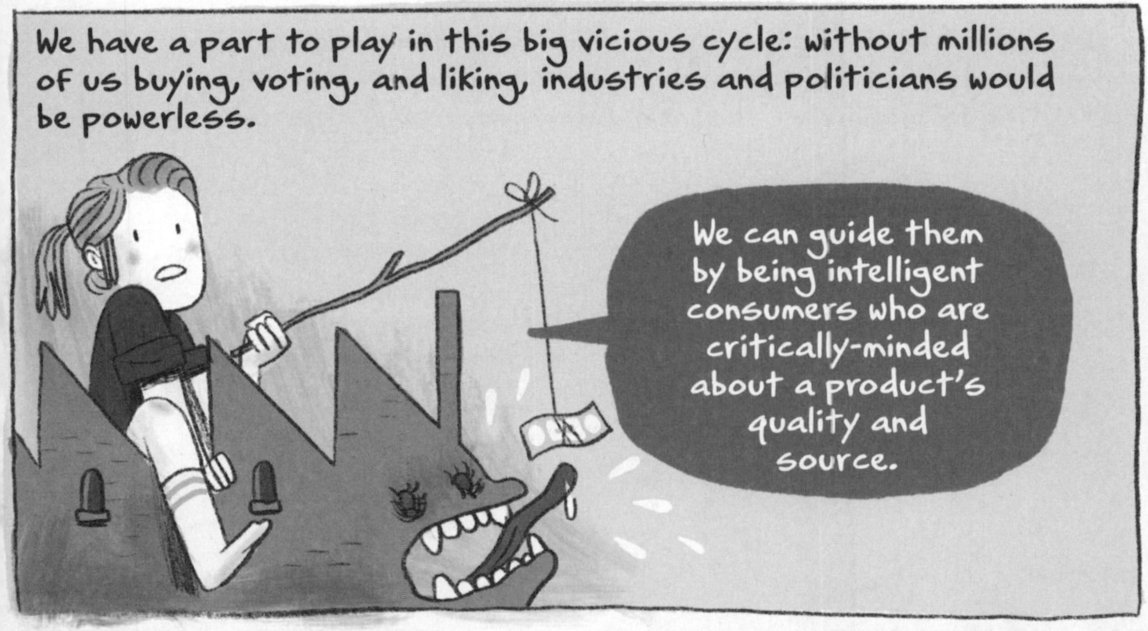
We have a part to play in this big vicious cycle: without millions of us buying, voting, and liking, industries and politicians would be powerless.
We can guide them by being intelligent consumers who are critically-minded about a product's quality and source.

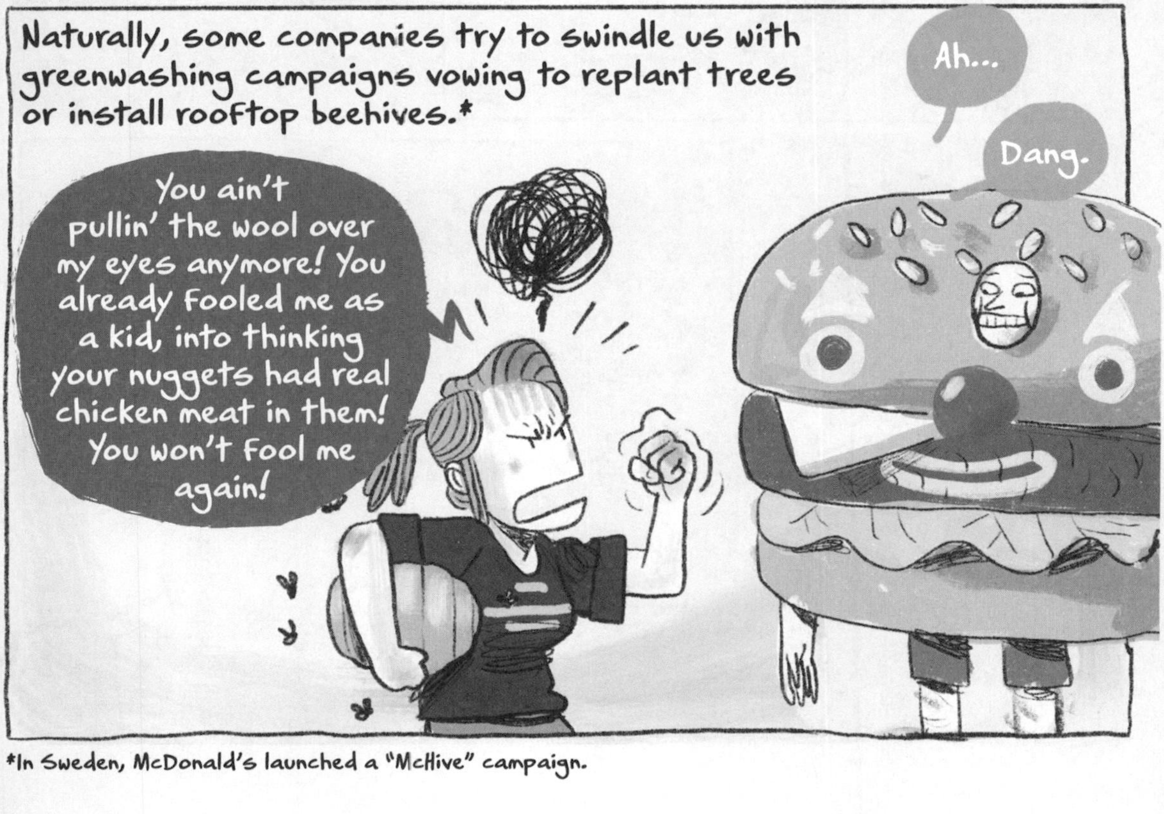
Naturally, some companies try to swindle us with greenwashing campaigns vowing to replant trees or install rooftop beehives.*
You ain't pullin' the wool over my eyes anymore! You already fooled me as a kid, into thinking your nuggets had real chicken meat in them! You won't fool me again!
Ah...
Dang.

*In Sweden, McDonald's launched a "McHive" campaign.

Let us all take inspiration from activist Henry Spira, who succeeded in turning Revlon and L'Oréal around on animal testing by mobilizing the media and proposing alternatives.

He worked WITH them to help them understand how best to change.

Same thing with big tobacco. Politicians and tobacco barons didn't wake up one day and say, "Hey, let's make fewer cigarettes, they're bad for people's health." No, change began with us: millions of individuals worried about their health. The industry had no choice but to follow.

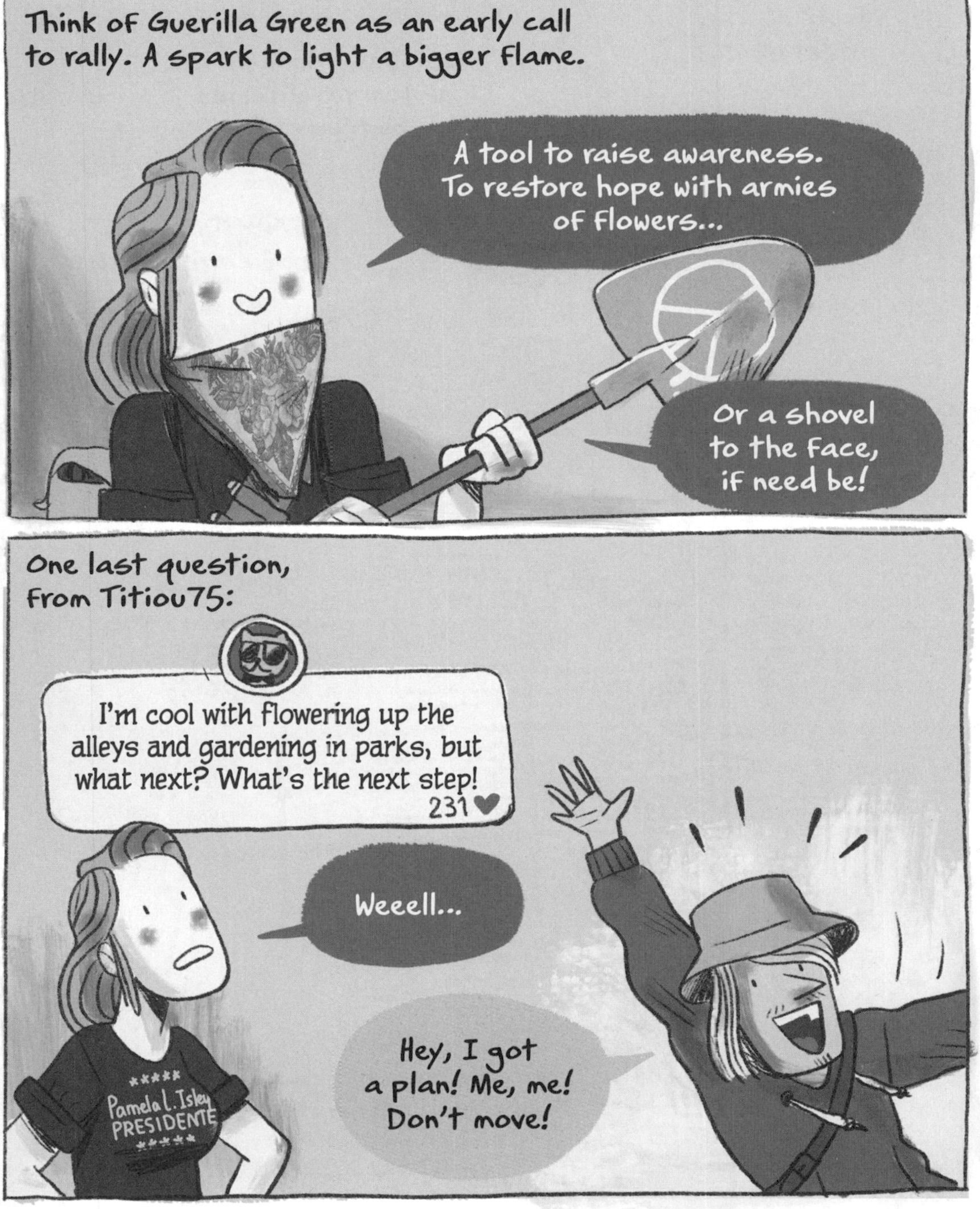

Think of Guerilla Green as an early call to rally. A spark to light a bigger flame.
A tool to raise awareness. To restore hope with armies of flowers...
Or a shovel to the face, if need be!
One last question, from Titiou75:
I'm cool with flowering up the alleys and gardening in parks, but what next? What's the next step!
231
Weeell...
Hey, I got a plan! Me, me! Don't move!
Pamela L. Isley PRESIDENTE

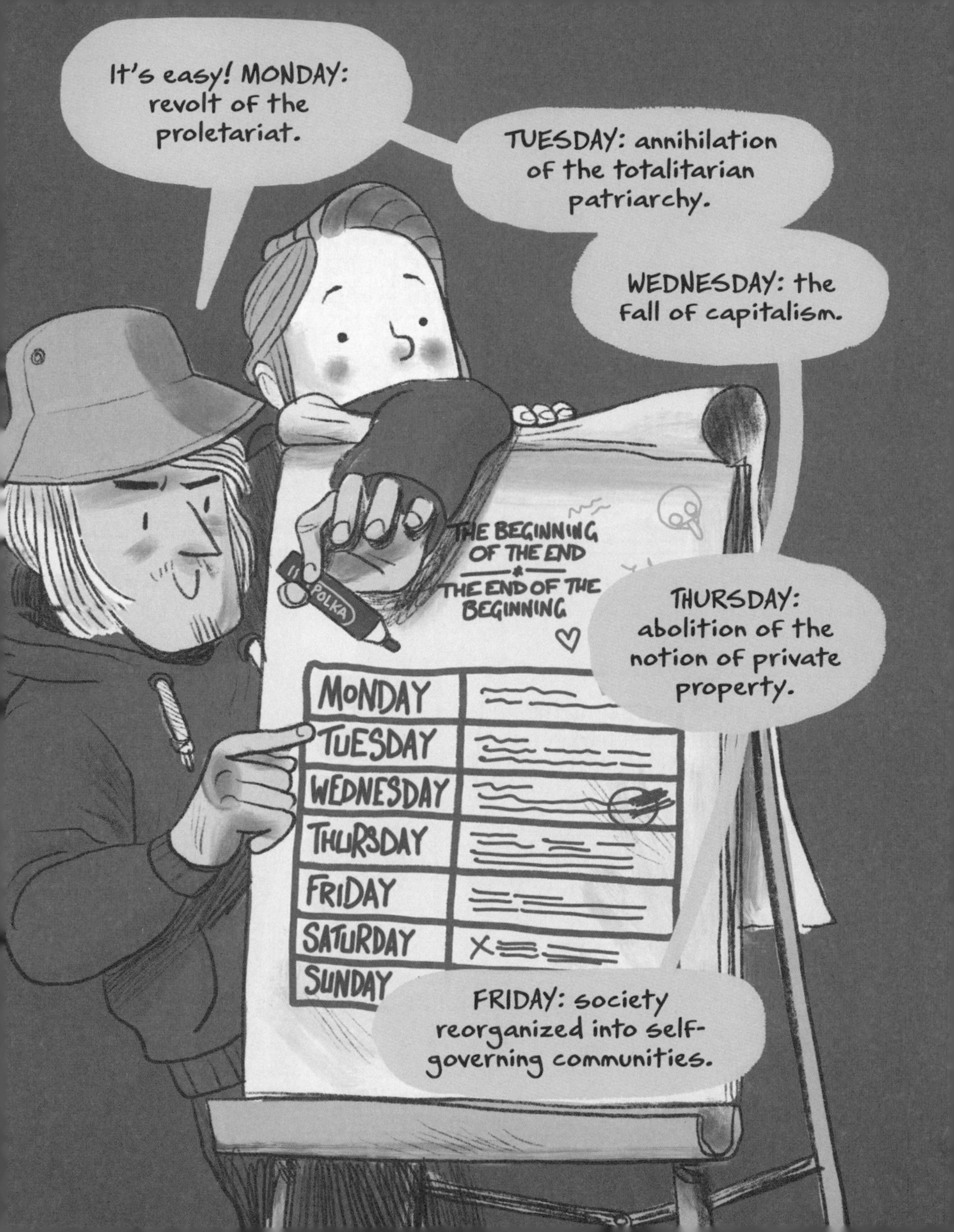
It's easy! MONDAY: revolt of the proletariat.
TUESDAY: annihilation of the totalitarian patriarchy.
WEDNESDAY: the fall of capitalism.
THE BEGINNING OF THE END
THE END OF THE BEGINNING
POLKA
THURSDAY: abolition of the notion of private property.
MONDAY
TUESDAY
WEDNESDAY
THURSDAY
FRIDAY
SATURDAY
SUNDAY
FRIDAY: society reorganized into self-governing communities.

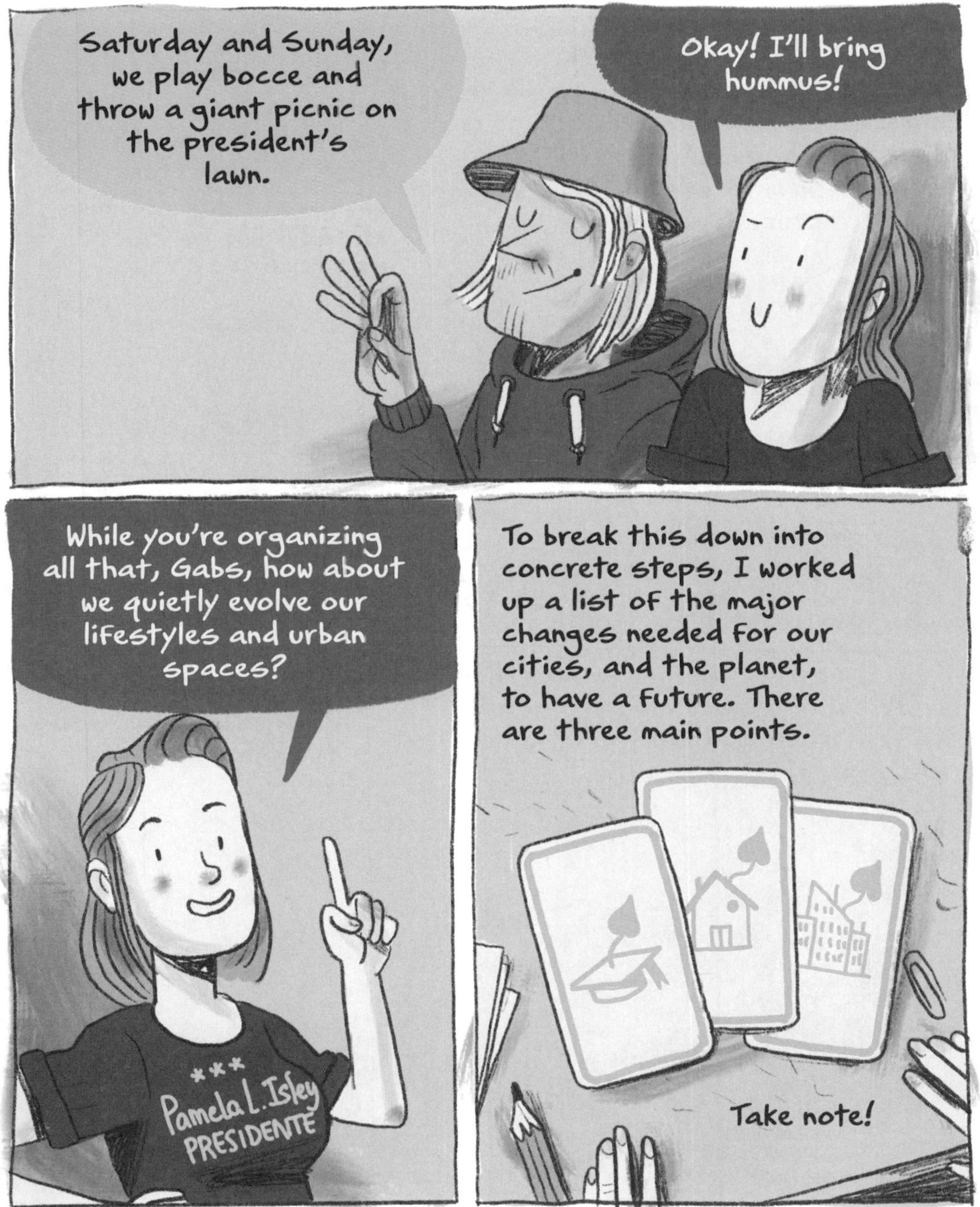
Saturday and Sunday, we play bocce and throw a giant picnic on the president's lawn.
Okay! I'll bring hummus!
While you're organizing all that, Gabs, how about we quietly evolve our lifestyles and urban spaces?
Pamela L. Isley PRESIDENTE
To break this down into concrete steps, I worked up a list of the major changes needed for our cities, and the planet, to have a future. There are three main points.
Take note!

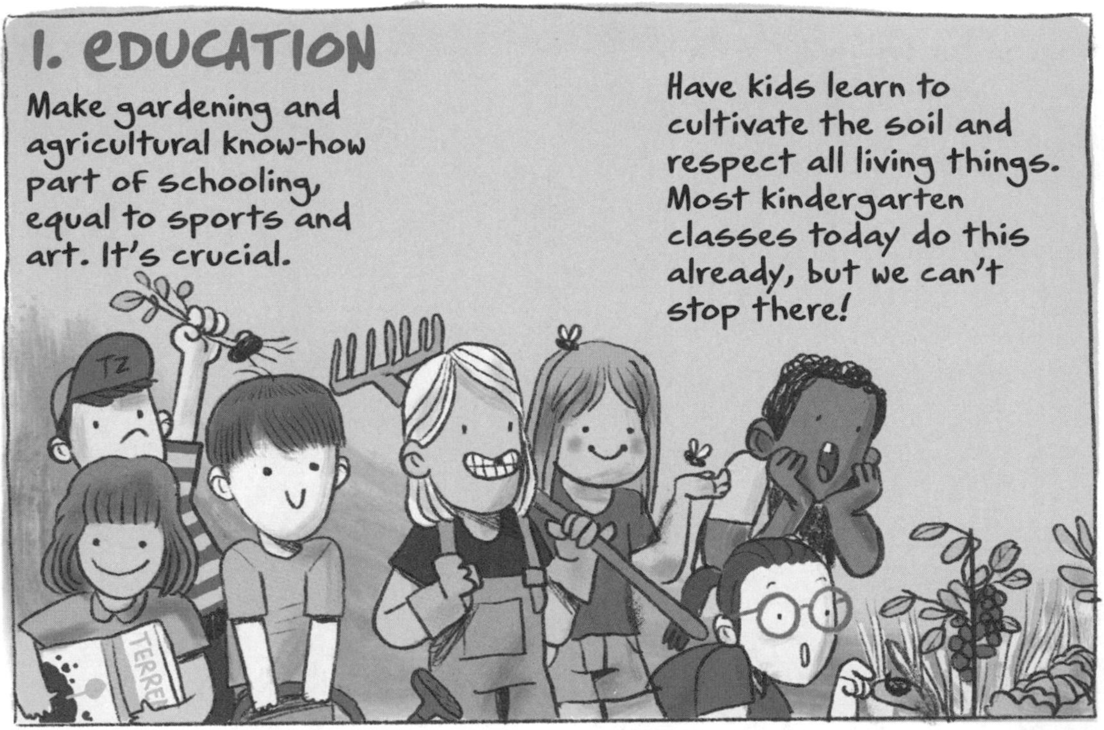
1. EDUCATION
Make gardening and agricultural know-how part of schooling, equal to sports and art. It's crucial.
Have kids learn to cultivate the soil and respect all living things. Most kindergarten classes today do this already, but we can't stop there!
TZ
TERRE

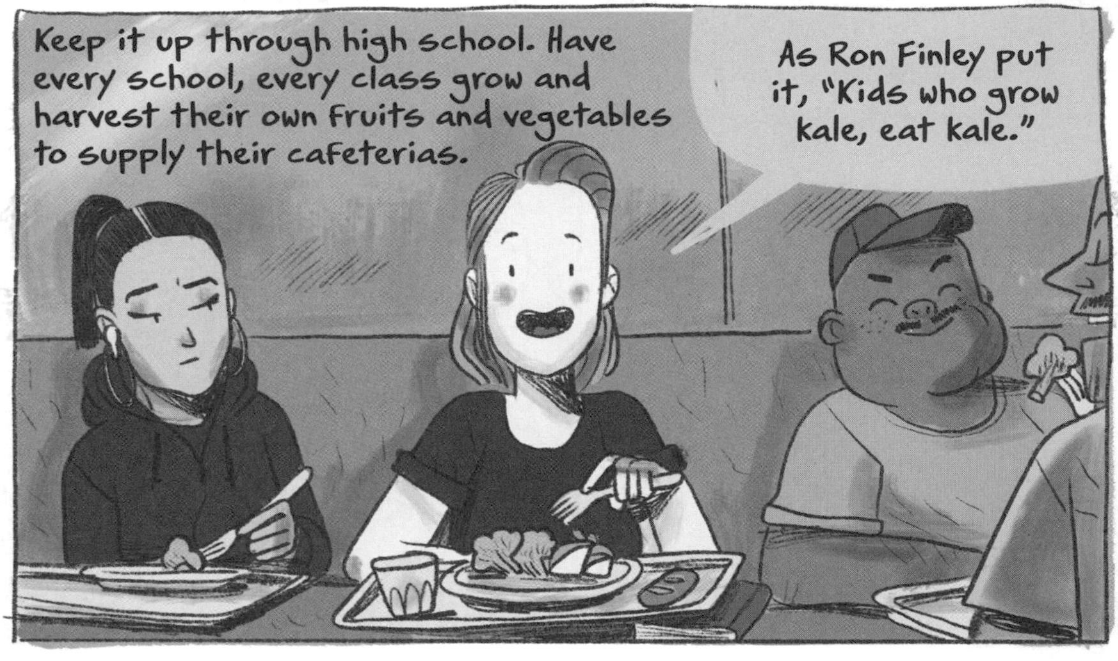
Keep it up through high school. Have every school, every class grow and harvest their own fruits and vegetables to supply their cafeterias.
As Ron Finley put it, "Kids who grow kale, eat kale."

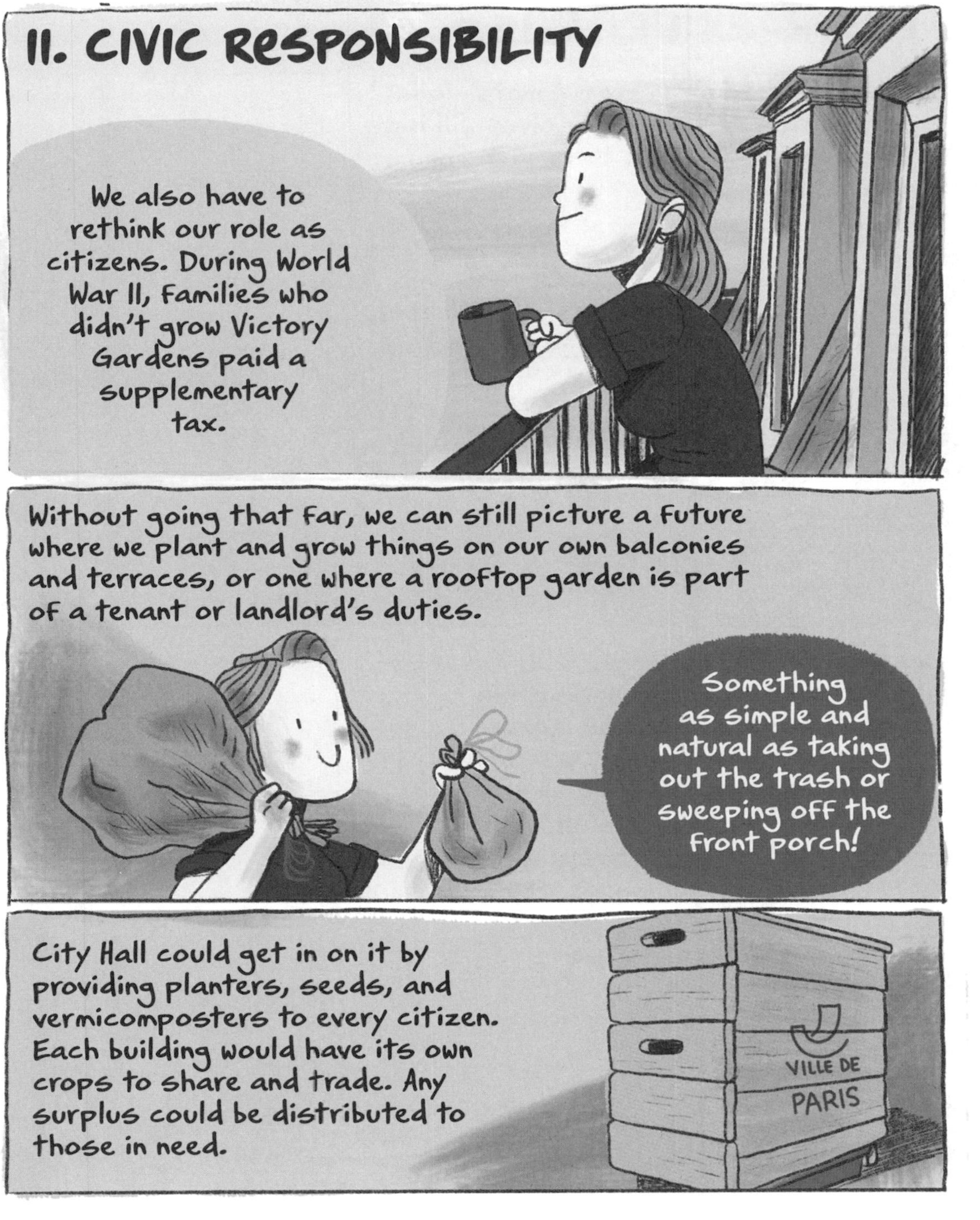
II. CIVIC RESPONSIBILITY
We also have to rethink our role as citizens. During World War II, families who didn't grow Victory Gardens paid a supplementary tax.
Without going that far, we can still picture a future where we plant and grow things on our own balconies and terraces, or one where a rooftop garden is part of a tenant or landlord's duties.
Something as simple and natural as taking out the trash or sweeping off the front porch!
City Hall could get in on it by providing planters, seeds, and vermicomposters to every citizen. Each building would have its own crops to share and trade. Any surplus could be distributed to those in need.
VILLE DE
PARIS

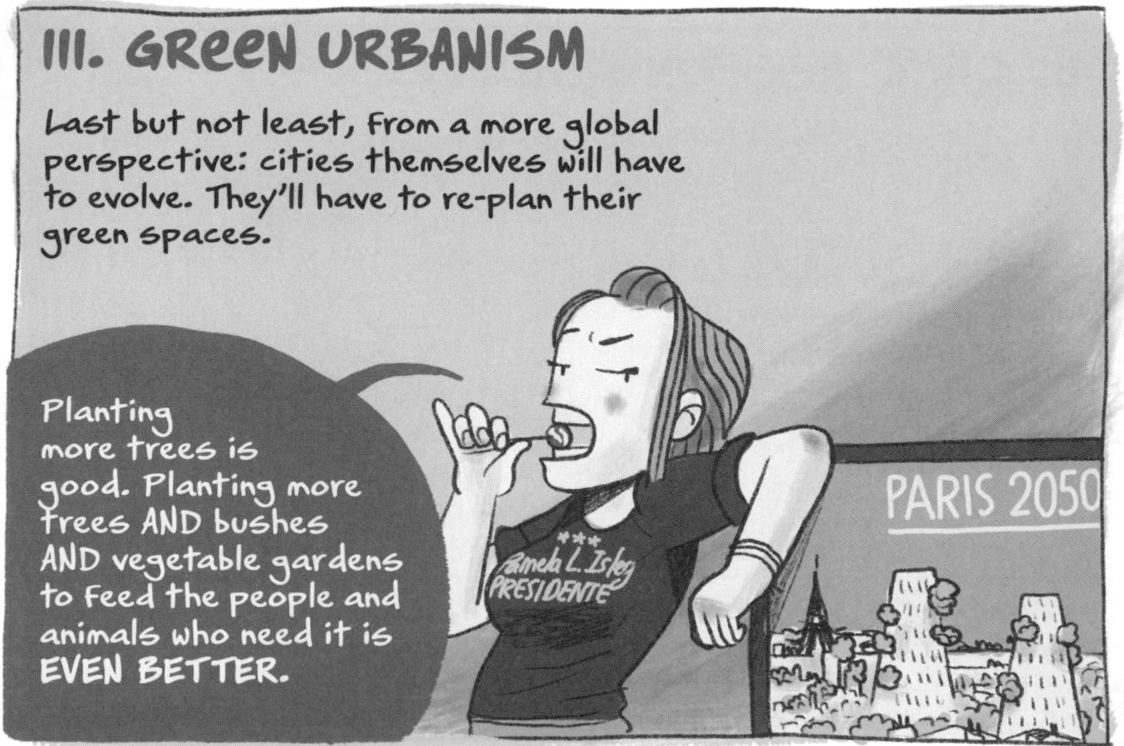
III. GREEN URBANISM
Last but not least, from a more global perspective: cities themselves will have to evolve. They'll have to re-plan their green spaces.
Planting more trees is good. Planting more trees AND bushes AND vegetable gardens to feed the people and animals who need it is EVEN BETTER.
Pamela L. Isley PRESIDENTE
PARIS 2050

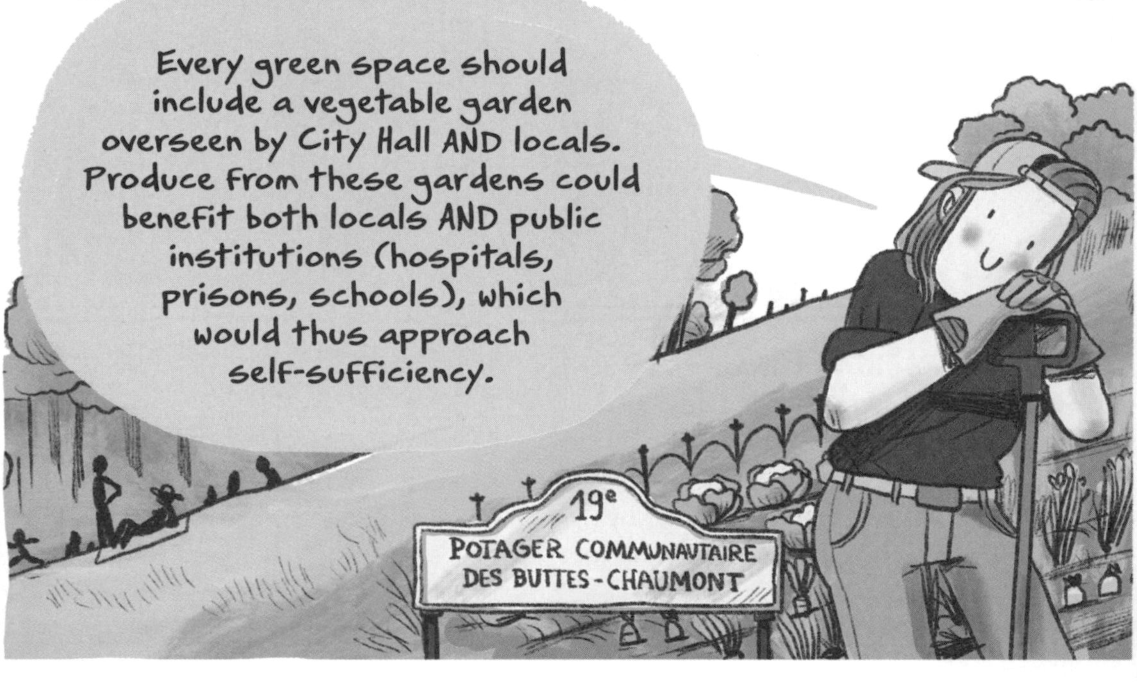
Every green space should include a vegetable garden overseen by City Hall AND locals. Produce from these gardens could benefit both locals AND public institutions (hospitals, prisons, schools), which would thus approach self-sufficiency.
19e
POTAGER COMMUNAUTAIRE DES BUTTES-CHAUMONT

You're probably feeling like this task is too huge; there's too much to do. Well, that's true!

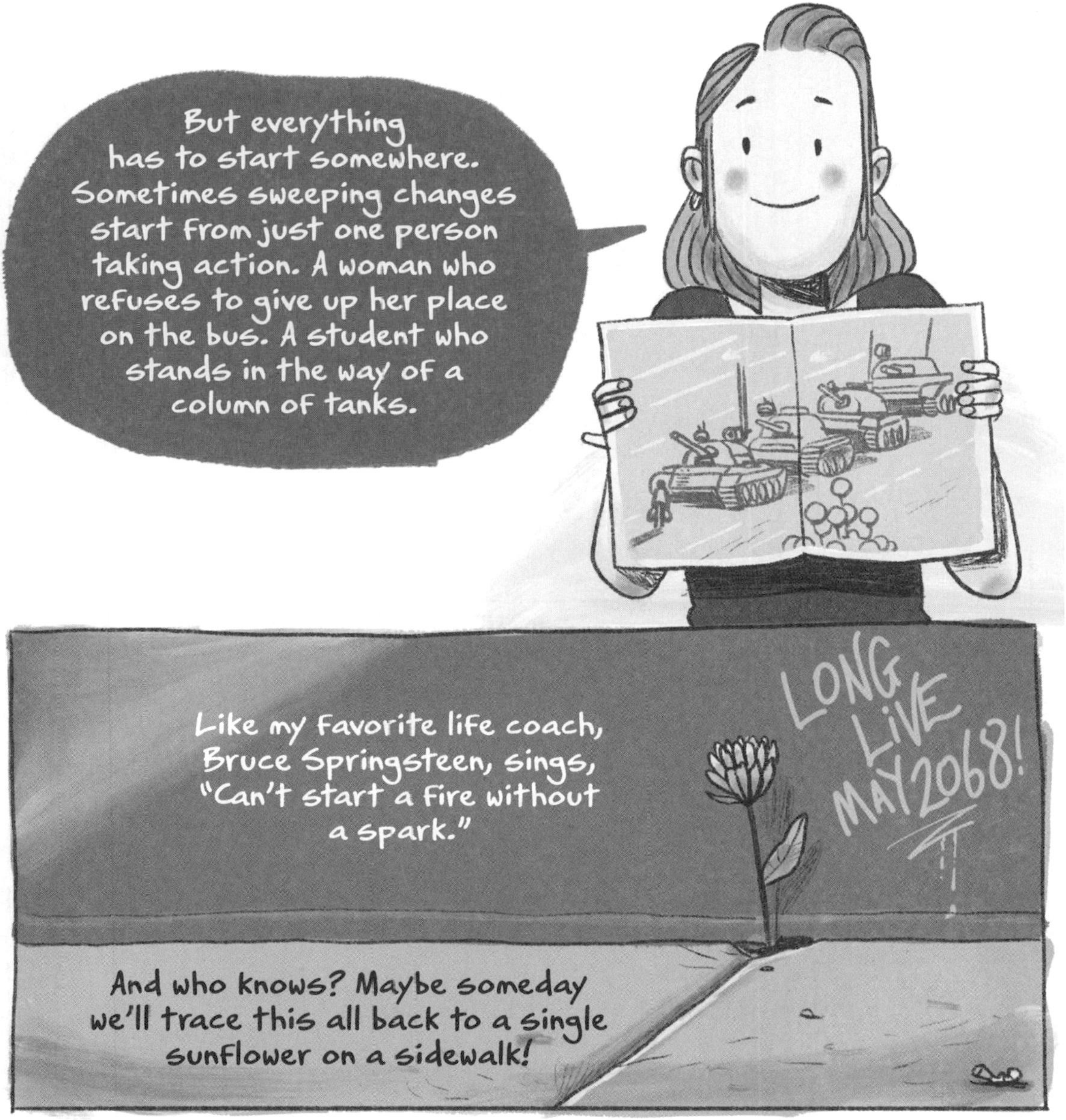
But everything has to start somewhere. Sometimes sweeping changes start from just one person taking action. A woman who refuses to give up her place on the bus. A student who stands in the way of a column of tanks.
Like my favorite life coach, Bruce Springsteen, sings, "Can't start a fire without a spark."
LONG LIVE MAY 2068!
And who knows? Maybe someday we'll trace this all back to a single sunflower on a sidewalk!

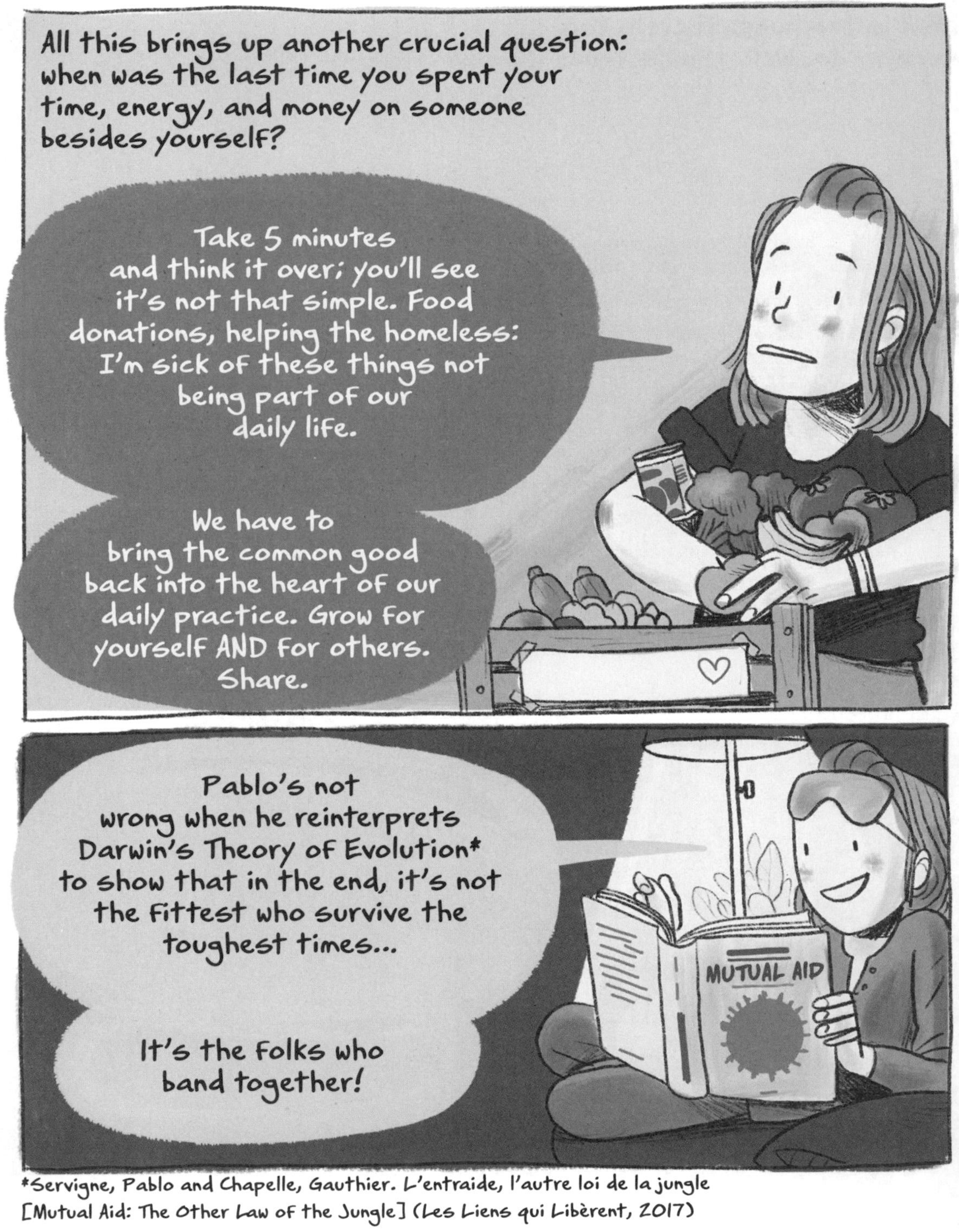
All this brings up another crucial question: when was the last time you spent your time, energy, and money on someone besides yourself?
Take 5 minutes and think it over; you'll see it's not that simple. Food donations, helping the homeless: I'm sick of these things not being part of our daily life.
We have to bring the common good back into the heart of our daily practice. Grow for yourself AND for others. Share.
Pablo's not wrong when he reinterprets Darwin's Theory of Evolution* to show that in the end, it's not the fittest who survive the toughest times...
MUTUAL AID
It's the folks who band together!

*Servigne, Pablo and Chapelle, Gauthier. L'entraide, l'autre loi de la jungle [Mutual Aid: The Other Law of the Jungle] (Les Liens qui Libèrent, 2017)

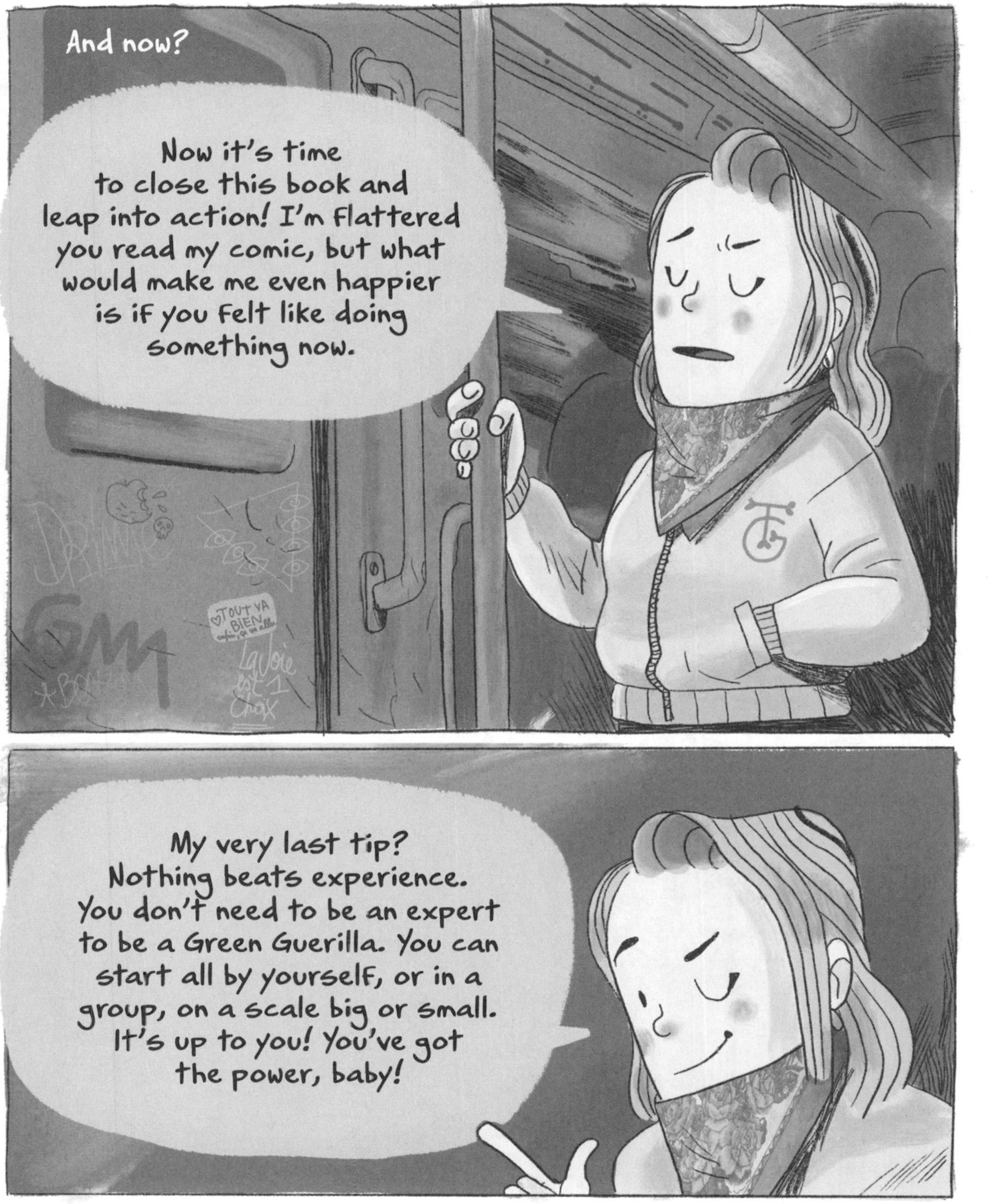
And now?
Now it's time to close this book and leap into action! I'm flattered you read my comic, but what would make me even happier is if you felt like doing something now.
My very last tip? Nothing beats experience. You don't need to be an expert to be a Green Guerilla. You can start all by yourself, or in a group, on a scale big or small. It's up to you! You've got the power, baby!

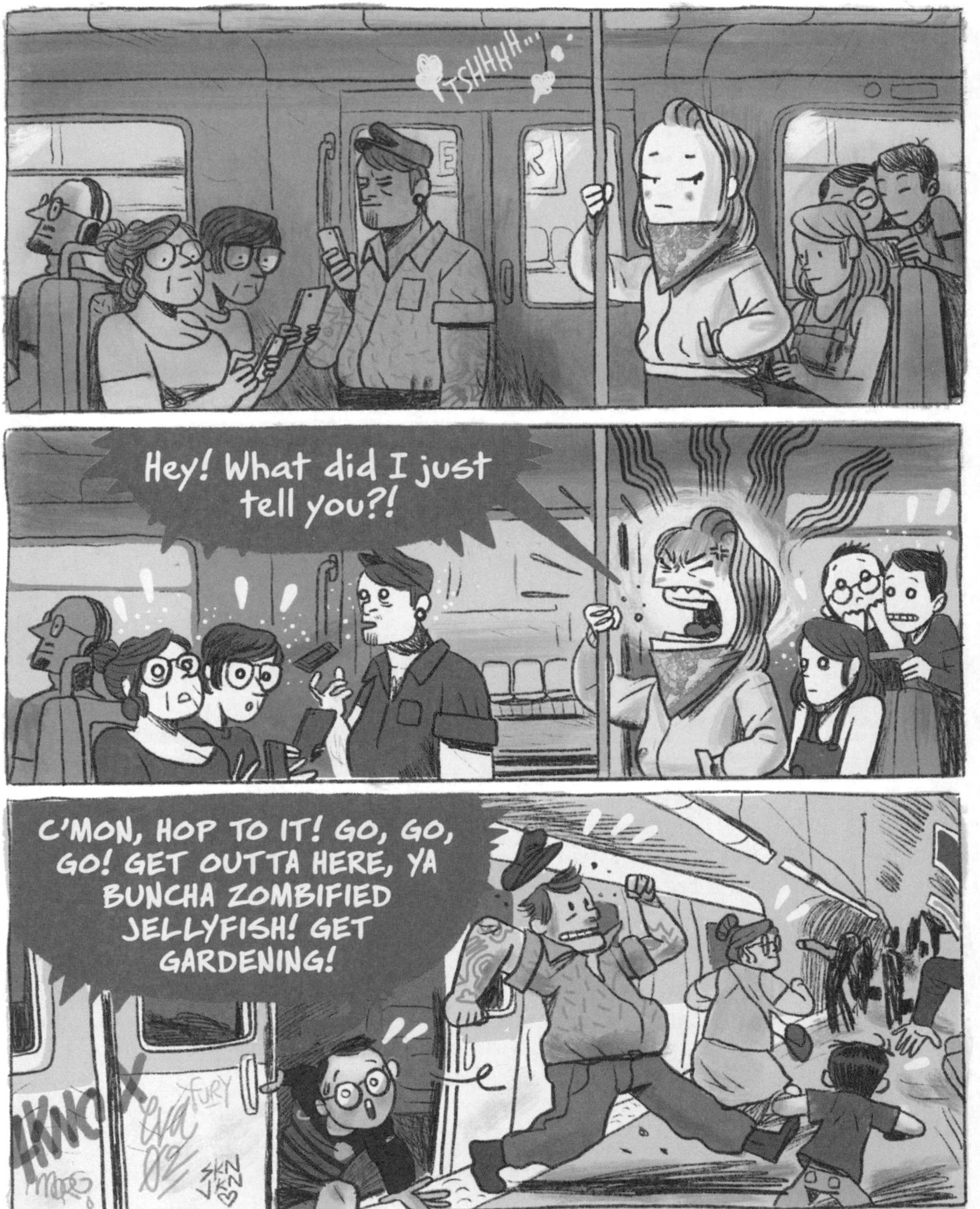
TSHHHH...
Hey! What did I just tell you?!
C'MON, HOP TO IT! GO, GO, GO! GET OUTTA HERE, YA BUNCHA ZOMBIFIED JELLYFISH! GET GARDENING!
FURY
SKN VKN

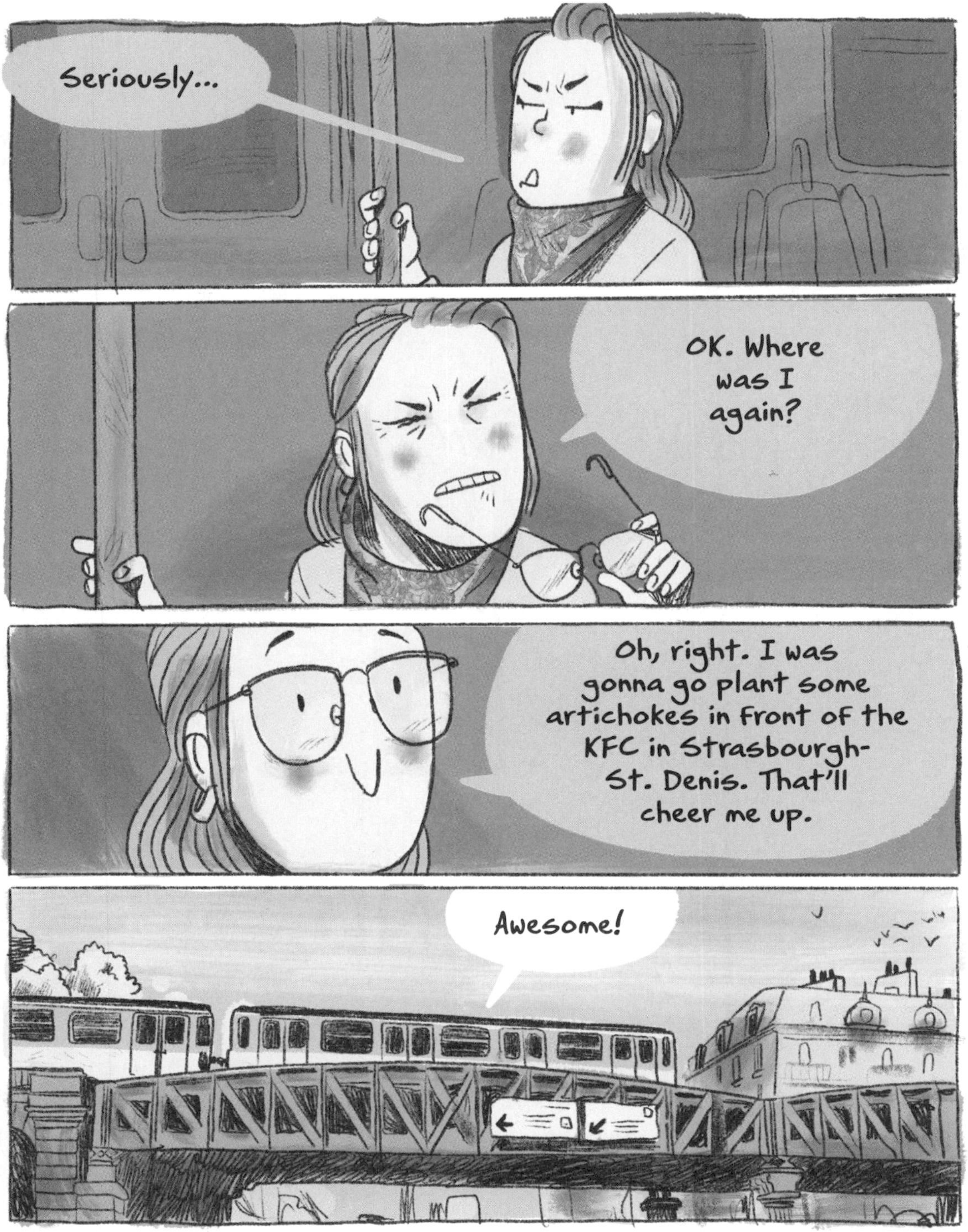
Seriously...
OK. Where was I again?
Oh, right. I was gonna go plant some artichokes in front of the KFC in Strasbourgh-St. Denis. That'll cheer me up.
Awesome!

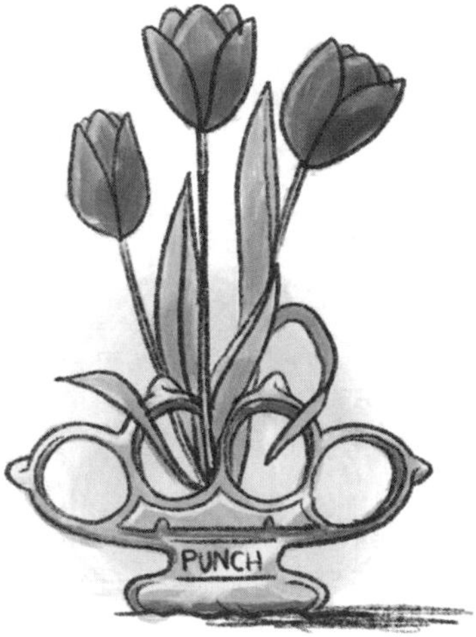
PUNCH

THE END

FURTHER READING (FOR WHEN YOU'RE NOT GARDENING)

IN ENGLISH

Astruc, Lionel. *Vandana Shiva: Creative Civil Disobedience* (Actes Sud, 2018)

Dobson, Johanna and Warhurst, Pam. *Incredible!: Plant Veg, Grow a Revolution* (Matador, 2014)

Fukuoka, Masanobu. *The One-Straw Revolution: An Introduction to Natural Farming*, trans. Larry Korn, preface by Wendell Berry (New York Review Books, 2010)

McKay, George. *Radical Gardening: Politics, Idealism and Rebellion in the Garden* (Frances Lincoln, 2011)

Reynolds, Richard. *On Guerrilla Gardening* (Bloomsbury, 2007)

Singer, Peter. *Ethics into Action: Learning from a Tube of Toothpaste* (Rowman and Littlefield, 2019)

Tracey, David. *Guerilla Gardening: A Manualfesto* (New Society Publishers, 2007)

IN FRENCH

Daverne, Jean-Jacques and Moreau, Jean-Guy. *Manuel pratique de la culture maraîchère de Paris* [A Practical Guide to Market Gardening in Paris] (Éditions du Linteau, 2016)

Denhez, Frédéric. *Le sol. Enquête sur un bien en péril* [Soil: An Investigation into an Endangered Asset] (Flammarion, 2018)

Flohic, Catherine, Les semences en questions de la terre à l'assiette [Seeds at Stake: From Soil to Plate] (Argol, 2018)

Lenoir, Éric. *Petit traité du jardin Punk – Apprendre à désapprendre* [A Short Tract on a Punk Garden: Learning to Unlearn] (Terre vivante, 2018)

Pavé, Alain. *Comprendre la biodiversité – Vrais problèmes et idées fausses* [Understanding Biodiversity : Real Problems and False Notions] (Seuil, 2019).

Servigne, Pablo and Chapelle, Gauthier. *L'entraide, l'autre loi de la jungle* [Mutual Aid: The Other Law of the Jungle] (Les Liens qui Libèrent, 2017)

WEBSITES

www.guerilla-gardening-france.fr

www.les-jardiniers-a-velo.fr

www.lesincroyablescomestibles.fr

www.pepinsproduction.fr

www.lasauge.fr

www.f-f-jardins-nature-sante.org

www.ronfinley.com

www.mursapeches.blog

www.afbiodiversite.fr

www.jagispourlanature.org

www.plante-et-cite.fr

www.vergersurbains.org

Huge thanks to all the Green Guerillas who followed the project #GGGG on Instagram and Youtube: you supported, inspired, enriched, helped, and reassured us. We feel less alone.

A special big thank you to everyone who participated in this book: Anne, Julie, Henri, Gaby, Julie, Nina, Clément, Juliette, Fanny, Stéphanie, Laure, Patrick, Lili, Elliot, Orlane, lil' Léon, and to the organizations who supported the project and helped it see the light of day: Les Internettes, the CNC [National Center for Cinema], and Guerilla Gardening France.

Thank you to Célina, Maud, Manon, Alexandra, Audrey, Lucie, Marie, Flora, and the whole crew at Steinkis for turning millions of pixels into a beautiful book. And finally, thank you to our friends, our families, the earthworms, and the bees for their unstinting support.

Merci, merci, merci!

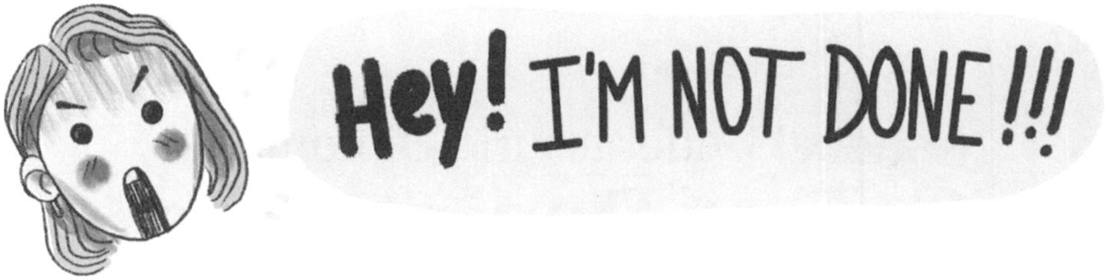
Hey! I'M NOT DONE !!!

WATCH OPHÉLIE'S VIDEOS IN FRENCH ON HER YOUTUBE CHANNEL "YO' MOMMA NATURE"

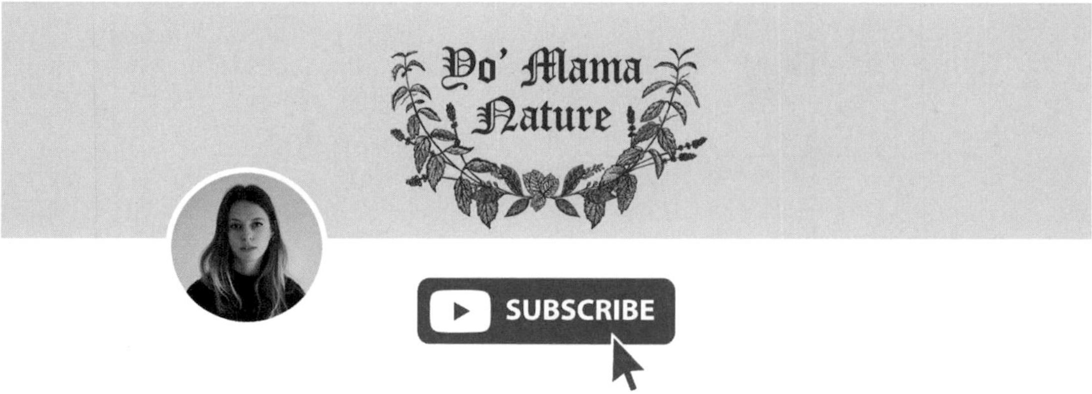
Yo' Mama Nature
SUBSCRIBE

AND COOKIE KALKAIR'S COMICS JOURNALISM ON INSTAGRAM

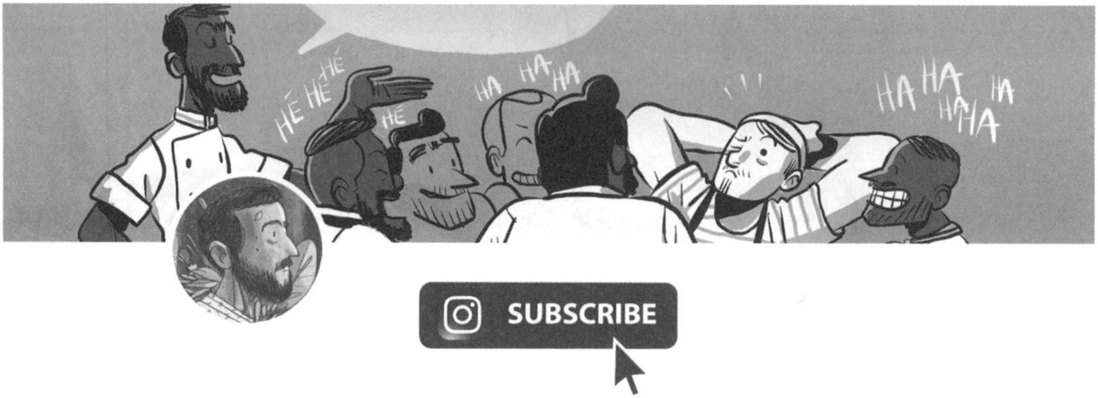
HÉ HÉ HÉ
HÉ
HA HA HA
HA HA HA HA HA
SUBSCRIBE

~~National~~ Underground Diploma for
Green Resistance in an Urban Setting

Name (Last, First): ....

City: ....   Class of: 20.........

Specialization: ....
(seed bomb chucker, covert clipper, etc.)

Student Signature: Dean's Signature:
                            Mlle. Ophélie Damblé

GUERILLA GREEN ACADEMY
MMXIX
PLANTAE AUT MORTEM

Congratulations! Now that you're officially a Green Guerilla, you can fill out and sign this fine "Green Resistance in an Urban Setting" diploma with pride. Don't hesitate to share it on social media with the hashtag #GGGG!

DISCOVER
ALL THE HITS

BOOM! BOX

AVAILABLE AT YOUR LOCAL COMICS SHOP AND BOOKSTORE

To find a comics shop in your area, visit www.comicshoplocator.com

WWW.**BOOM-STUDIOS**.COM

Lumberjanes
Noelle Stevenson, Shannon Watters, Grace Ellis, Brooklyn Allen, and Others
Volume 1: Beware the Kitten Holy
ISBN: 978-1-60886-687-8 | $14.99 US
Volume 2: Friendship to the Max
ISBN: 978-1-60886-737-0 | $14.99 US
Volume 3: A Terrible Plan
ISBN: 978-1-60886-803-2 | $14.99 US
Volume 4: Out of Time
ISBN: 978-1-60886-860-5 | $14.99 US
Volume 5: Band Together
ISBN: 978-1-60886-919-0 | $14.99 US

Giant Days
John Allison, Lissa Treiman, Max Sarin
Volume 1
ISBN: 978-1-60886-789-9 | $9.99 US
Volume 2
ISBN: 978-1-60886-804-9 | $14.99 US
Volume 3
ISBN: 978-1-60886-851-3 | $14.99 US

Jonesy
Sam Humphries, Caitlin Rose Boyle
Volume 1
ISBN: 978-1-60886-883-4 | $9.99 US
Volume 2
ISBN: 978-1-60886-999-2 | $14.99 US

Slam!
Pamela Ribon, Veronica Fish, Brittany Peer
Volume 1
ISBN: 978-1-68415-004-5 | $14.99 US

Goldie Vance
Hope Larson, Brittney Williams
Volume 1
ISBN: 978-1-60886-898-8 | $9.99 US
Volume 2
ISBN: 978-1-60886-974-9 | $14.99 US

The Backstagers
James Tynion IV, Rian Sygh
Volume 1
ISBN: 978-1-60886-993-0 | $14.99 US

Tyson Hesse's Diesel: Ignition
Tyson Hesse
ISBN: 978-1-60886-907-7 | $14.99 US

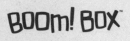